Michael Ashcroft is an international businessman and philan-thropist and is Deputy Chairman of the Conservative Party. He is also the founder and Chairman of the Trustees of Crime-stoppers – the UK crime-fighting charity – and Chancellor of Anglia Ruskin University. He is a major shareholder in Watford FC and over the past twenty years has built up the world's largest collection of Victoria Crosses.

Visit the *Victoria Cross Heroes* website at
www.victoriacrossheroes.com

VICTORIA
CROSS
HEROES

MICHAEL ASHCROFT

FOREWORD BY
HRH THE PRINCE OF WALES

headline
review

First published in 2006
by HEADLINE REVIEW

First published in paperback in 2007
by HEADLINE REVIEW

An imprint of Headline Publishing Group

7

Michael Ashcroft would be happy to hear from readers with their comments
on the book at the following e-mail address: info@lordashcroft.com

ISBN 978 0 7553 1633 5

Text design by Janette Revill
Typeset in GaramondThree by Avon Dataset Ltd, Bidford on Avon, Warwickshire
Printed and bound in Great Britain by Clays Ltd, St Ives plc

Headline's policy is to use papers that are natural, renewable and recyclable
products and made from wood grown in sustainable forests. The logging and
manufacturing processes are expected to conform to the environmental regulations
of the country of origin.

HEADLINE PUBLISHING GROUP
A division of Hachette Livre UK Ltd
338 Euston Road
London NW1 3BH

www.reviewbooks.co.uk
www.hodderheadline.com

CONTENTS

DAVID RATTRAY – A TRIBUTE

Just as I was finishing this paperback version of *Victoria Cross Heroes*, I received some dreadful news. The life of a dear friend David Rattray, the historian, had been cruelly cut short when he was shot by intruders at his home near Rorke's Drift, South Africa.

Only weeks before his death in January 2007, David had been kind enough to read my write-up of the VCs that had been awarded to Lieutenant John Chard and Private Robert Jones for their bravery at Rorke's Drift. As arguably the world's greatest expert on the Zulu War of 1879 (which led to the award of 23 VCs), David had suggested some small factual corrections, which I readily made.

When I heard of David's murder, my thoughts turned to his widow, Nicky. She summed up the tragedy of his death when she said: 'This famous son of South Africa now joins the unacceptable list of citizens who have lost their lives to senseless banditry.' David, a father of three sons, was only 48 when he died. He had been trying to protect his wife from the armed intruders when he was shot.

I had known David for less than a year but during that time we became firm friends and had already planned to meet up twice in 2007. I have nothing but fond memories of our short time together. I first met him in March 2006 when I was in

South Africa and attended some of his lectures on the Zulu War. A few months later, I returned there and David and I spent three days travelling around together so that David could show me the sites of various battles and skirmishes between the Zulus and the British. At the time, I was doing some research for this book and a recce for the Five television series on the VC, which I co-funded. During my trips, I discovered that David was much more than a historian – he was a brilliant storyteller. When he described a battle or an incident, he painted a vivid picture of what it must have been like for those present. It was this unique talent to transport people back in time, and to recreate the sights and sounds of a scene, that earned him the accolade 'the Laurence Olivier of the battlefield'.

As a result of all this, I invited David to come to London in October 2006 to give a lecture on the Battle of Isandhlwana to Crimestoppers, the charity I founded more than twenty years ago to prevent and solve crimes. One unidentified South African commentator summed up his talent perfectly when he was quoted in the *Daily Telegraph*'s obituary of David: 'To listen to David Rattray narrate the story of Isandhlwana was akin to watching the best-scripted, best-directed and best-produced movie Hollywood's finest studios could put on. It was goose-bump stuff.'

I am enormously grateful to David for all the help he has given me, particularly in relation to the Zulu wars. David, a fluent Zulu speaker, was a charming and generous man. He was also a wonderful international ambassador for the Zulu people he loved so much. The world will be a poorer place without him.

ACKNOWLEDGEMENTS

I am grateful to Michael Naxton, my medals consultant, for his expertise and advice in helping me to amass the world's largest collection of VCs. Michael's knowledge of the VC is matched only by his enthusiasm for the medal. He has also provided me with invaluable assistance in writing this book.

I would like to thank Angela Entwistle, my corporate communications director, and her team for helping to get this project off the ground. I am grateful, too, to Iain Dale, who has acted as an astute sounding board throughout the writing and publishing process.

My thanks also go to Emma Tait, Wendy McCance and their colleagues at Headline for their skill in bringing this project to fruition.

As well as the authors of existing books on the VC, I would like to thank a group of unsung heroes. These are the cataloguers who have researched the lives of the recipients of VCs before their medals were auctioned. In some cases, I have relied heavily on their information on individual VC winners for this book. The cataloguers are rarely, if ever, identified but I would like to thank them collectively for their splendid research. I do not know the names of all of them but, as well as being grateful to Michael Naxton for his write-ups while working at Sotheby's, I would also like to acknowledge

Nimrod Dix, David Erskine-Hill, John Hayward, James Morton, Edward Playfair and anyone else who researched the background to VCs owned by the trust that was set up to care for and protect the medals.

My gratitude also goes to Didy Grahame, the secretary of the Victoria Cross and George Cross Association. She was kind enough to help me with information on several recipients who won the VC during and after the Second World War.

I would like to thank my new friends from Empire Media Productions, the television production company, for their help with this book, particularly Mark Souster, Empire's executive producer, who came up with the idea for a series of programmes on the VC. I am also grateful to Peter Georgi, the executive producer of the series, and Steven Clarke, the series producer. I commend their three-part series, made for Five, to anyone who is interested in the VC. It provides a fascinating insight into the courage of the recipients of the award – and also the effect that winning the VC had on them and their families.

Last, but certainly not least, I am extremely grateful to HRH The Prince of Wales for writing the foreword to this book. I know that he and several generations of the Royal Family before him have long had a fondness for the VC and have always been full of admiration for the bravery of its recipients.

FOREWORD

by HRH The Prince of Wales

One hundred and fifty years ago, as the Crimean War was raging, the wider British public became aware, for the first time, of the horrors of war on foreign fields and of the huge courage and fortitude of the British servicemen fighting there. This realisation of what our men were enduring so staunchly, and the reports of the many outstanding individual accounts of courage, led HM Queen Victoria to instruct the striking of a new medal that has since become the most respected and well-known award for military gallantry: the Victoria Cross.

HM wished for an award that did not recognize birth or class, rank or long service. In fact she wanted to honour just one rare and treasured quality – a man's exceptional bravery in the face of the enemy. Under Prince Albert's astute guidance, HM vetoed a suggestion for the medal to be called The Military Order of Victoria and opted instead for the simple Victoria Cross. Similarly when it came to the design, Queen Victoria chose a Maltese cross ensigned with a royal crest and a scroll inscribed 'For Valour'.

Thus, with a royal warrant issued on 29 January 1856, the VC was founded. Since then it has been awarded 1,355 times, the most recent being to Private Beharry for 'saving the lives of his comrades' in Iraq in 2004.

It never ceases to amaze me what our servicemen have done, and continue to do, for their country and their comrades. Their courageous acts in the line of duty are humbling for us all; I and many others are immensely proud of them.

The briefings by the Commanding Officers of the regiments of which I am Colonel-in-Chief on their return from operations, and the stories told to me by 'The Old and Bold' of battles long ago, are wonderfully inspiring; the stoicism and great good humour with which they have dealt with unimaginably awful situations is deeply moving. In troops and platoons, ships and aircraft, and individually, they have carried out acts of immense bravery; yet to a man they are modest and self-effacing.

Over the years, and particularly as President of the Victoria Cross and George Cross Association, in succession to my grandmother, Queen Elizabeth The Queen Mother, I have met many of these remarkable men and women and can understand only too well why they have meant so much to my family over all these years.

The VC is a very special subject for a book. Behind every award is a remarkable story involving all those qualities that we British hold most dear: loyalty, duty, sacrifice, care for others, a great good humour and a deep humility. They are all here amongst the many stories of this most democratic and historic medal.

I commend Lord Ashcroft for his diligence in recording so carefully the 150 years of this most precious brainchild of Queen Victoria and The Prince Consort.

PREFACE

The year 2006 is a special one in the history of the Victoria Cross (VC). It marks a truly significant and memorable anniversary for the medal, as well as a less remarkable, yet more personal, anniversary for me.

It is 150 years ago this year that the VC was created. As the Crimean War drew to a close, it was decided, after considerable thought and debate, to make an award for some quite astonishing acts of bravery during the conflict. And so in 1856, at the behest of Queen Victoria, the world's most prestigious bravery award – in my eyes at least – was born.

It is also exactly twenty years since I bought my first VC, therefore fulfilling a dream that I had retained since being a schoolboy. At the time of purchasing that first medal, I was an energetic and driven forty-year-old businessman who considered himself honoured to be the successful bidder at an auction for a small, yet wonderful, piece of history. It was the VC awarded to Leading Seaman James Magennis at the end of the Second World War.

At the time, I looked upon the purchase as a one-off. Yet today, the trust which was established to care for and protect the medals owns 142 VCs (including three official replacements, an unofficial cross and an unissued, specimen medal). It is a collection which spans every force – Army, Royal Navy and

RAF – and nearly 128 years, from deeds of bravery in 1854 to an astonishing act of courage during the Falklands War in 1982. The range of dates is all the more remarkable because there has been only one VC awarded in the past twenty-four years – to Private Johnson Beharry for bravery in Iraq in 2004.

Today the trust owns just over a tenth of the 1,351 VCs that have been awarded to individuals since 1856 (three men have received 'bars' – the equivalent of a second VC – and there was also an award to the 'Unknown Warrior' in America). The trust's collection is, by some way, the largest and most valuable in the world, and I am proud to have played my part in assembling it.

To mark the 150th anniversary, I can reveal that the trust has decided – with my blessing – to open its collection of VCs to the public for the first time so that the medals and other memorabilia that go with them can be enjoyed by the nation, as well as thousands of visitors who come to Britain each year. The trust is currently looking into exactly when and how this will be done.

This book looks at the history of the VC and how the collection was amassed. It then cites every VC that is in the collection, listing the names of the courageous men who were awarded the decoration and why and when each medal was won. Every VC has a story behind it of one man's courage in the face of the enemy – a tale of how a soldier, sailor or airman showed bravery so far beyond the expectation of 'duty' that his country decided to bestow on him its foremost award for valour.

In the spring of 2006, when I was in the process of writing this book, I was approached by Empire Media Productions, a television production company, which was planning a three-part series on the VC. I decided to co-fund the project with Five and the trust agreed to open the collection to the programme-makers. I am delighted that so many of the trust's VCs feature in the series. This new partnership has had another benefit – to me and readers of this book. As a result of the research for the television series, I have learned more about some of the VCs outside the trust's collection, including some quite extraordinary stories of courage by the recipients. I am therefore including the stories of the VCs that feature prominently in the series in this book, but will make it clear, in each case, that the medals are not part of the trust's collection. In short, these 'extra' VCs are a wonderful bonus for the book. All the write-ups on VCs that are exclusive to the television series – i.e. not in the trust's collection – will be marked with a distinctive dagger symbol (†).

I hope you will enjoy reading about the courage of these exceptional people who have served Britain and the Commonwealth. I hope, too, that once the collection is open to the public it will give visitors as much pleasure as it has given me in the course of bringing the medals together and researching the heroism of the worthy recipients.

1

BUILDING THE COLLECTION

The beginning of a passion

I was twelve years old, give or take a year, when I first developed an interest in bravery. Having been born in 1946, a year after the end of the Second World War, discussions of the momentous events of 1939–45 inevitably filled everyday conversation. I had heard the phrase 'during the war' relentlessly as a youngster, yet I was too young to have experienced any of it. When I was ten, my father, who worked for the Colonial Office, was posted to West Africa. Once my parents learned that they were going to spend several years in Eastern Nigeria, where the schools were of a poor standard, they reluctantly decided that the family would temporarily have to be split up. So as my father, mother and sister, then aged five, headed off for an adventure in Africa, I started boarding school in Britain.

I attended Norwich School in Norfolk, where it had been decided that my maternal grandparents, who lived nearby, could keep an eye on me. My initial years there were not easy, and I had to find new interests and hobbies to fill many lonely hours. I started watching films as well as reading comics and books about wars in general and the Second World War in particular. I was fascinated with the subject of war but, rather than uniforms, weapons or battle plans, my greatest interest was in the concept of bravery. I was in awe of people who had performed heroic acts in the face of terrifying threats. I looked up to those who were prepared to risk sacrificing the greatest gift of all – life itself – for their country and their comrades.

Like most schoolboys, I posed more questions than I had answers. What was it that made some people respond to danger differently from others? Are we all capable of a certain level of bravery, given the right circumstances? What was the crucial factor that made some people more courageous than others? Was it simply in their genes, was it their upbringing or was it their training? Were they motivated by patriotism, religious conviction, a respect for those who fought alongside them or simply an old-fashioned sense of duty? Was most people's bravery premeditated or was it a spur-of-the-moment response to the heat of battle?

During the summer holidays, I used to visit my family in Africa – a tortuous journey from Norwich by road, rail and air that in those days used to take three days, door to door. On the second of these holidays I succeeded in getting my father to sit down and talk in detail about his role in the Second World War for the first time. Like most children of my generation, I had posed the question before: 'What did you do in the war, Dad?' However, like many of the modest men of his generation, Eric Ashcroft did not volunteer any stories of his own courage.

This time, though, I received a full answer from my father, who had been among the first young men to enlist in 1939, joining the South Lancashire Regiment. He had been chosen for officer training and had remained in Britain until the D-Day landings. It was only when he began to describe the scene on 6 June 1944 that I was able to comprehend what real danger meant. Long before they embarked on the D-Day landings, he and other officers had been briefed to expect 75 per cent casualties – dead and wounded – on the beach as they landed in Normandy. At dawn on 6 June, there was no hiding-place as my father found himself on a small, vulnerable landing craft crashing through the waves in the English Channel. He and his men were heading for Sword Beach as part of the British 3rd Infantry Division's assault on German-occupied France.

Many men in the landing craft were, like my father, seeing action for the first time, and it is difficult to imagine that they were anything other than terrified. According to my father, the landing craft were filled with the real smell of vomit and the metaphorical smell of fear. He described how the soldiers could see next to nothing as they approached the beach because they were crouching below the sides of the boat so as not to be shot. Yet when they reached shallow water, the front of the landing craft dropped down and they ran into the unknown as the 'ping' of machine-gun bullets sounded all around them. As they splashed through the sea and reached the beach, they came under relentless enemy fire. There were immediate casualties, including the commanding officer, a colonel, who was shot dead at my father's side. As the battle raged, my father too was hit by shrapnel. Although he had received serious injuries to his back and one of his arms, he fought on shoulder to shoulder with his men. Eventually, wounded and weary, he was ordered from the battlefield to receive medical treatment. Although he eventually made a full recovery and lived until he was eighty-three, the injuries he received at Sword Beach were serious enough to end his front-line service. While he was convalescing from his injuries in Blackpool he met my mother, who was working as a Red Cross nurse. The rest, as they say, is history, and I was born two years later in Chichester, where my father had been stationed after the war ended.

On the journey back to Norwich School from Eastern

Nigeria that autumn, my mind was full of my father's wartime exploits. It had been awesome to hear him talk in such vivid terms about what had happened. At times, I found it almost impossible to imagine that Eric Ashcroft – my father – really had been present at such an extraordinary moment in history and had lived to tell the tale. I felt enormous pride that he had been so courageous and I was puzzled that he had never felt able to recount the story to me before. I began to wonder whether, if I had been in identical circumstances, I would have been equally courageous. Would my mettle ever be tested on the battlefield as my father's had been, and, if so, what would the outcome be? All too often I concluded that, even with the adrenaline flowing, I would never be able to match the bravery of my father and others like him.

It was a year or two later when I first heard of something called the Victoria Cross (VC). I knew that it was a bravery award and that it had first been awarded by Queen Victoria. Other than that, my information about it was sketchy. Indeed, I was initially so naïve that I thought if a man owned a VC, even if he had bought it from someone else, he could put 'VC' after his name. It was only when I put this misconception to one of my teachers that he informed me that only the original recipient was able to have the letters after his name. And so my long fascination with the VC and the heroics of its recipients was born.

At school, I could often be found in my dormitory reading war comics long into the night. Even now, although I have never been a linguist, I can remember the rather rudimentary German attributed to the Luftwaffe pilots in the comic strips. '*Donner und blitzen!*' – in English, 'thunder and lightning' – would be their expression of fear as they caught a glimpse of a British Spitfire pilot in the skies. '*Achtung! Achtung! Der Englischer Schweinhund!*' – 'Danger! Danger! The English pig-dog' – was another phrase that has remained with me for nearly half a century. In today's politically correct age, of course, those producing the comics might be criticised for stereotyping. Eventually, I graduated on to history books in the school library that gave me an understanding of exactly what the VC was, and how and why it came into existence.

The more I read about the VC, the more interested I became in it. In my twenties and thirties I was working flat out as an entrepreneur. Yet even then I found time to read the occasional book on military history in general, and the VC in particular. Little did I know, of course, that I would one day build up the largest collection of VCs in the world, or write a book on the subject.

A short history of the Victoria Cross

The notion of giving a bravery award to low-ranking soldiers and sailors first came under serious consideration in Britain in 1854. Until that point, the government and military leaders had not felt the need to reward 'ordinary' men for their courage. Even great military leaders such as the Duke of Wellington had believed that serving monarch and country was reward enough for any low-ranking soldier and sailor. The Duke believed that patriotism, a modest wage and daily meals were sufficient to buy a man's loyalty and bravery. Others in the War Office and the Admiralty shared his view. This widely held opinion came under scrutiny almost as soon as the Crimean War began. After nearly forty years of peace, Britain was embroiled in a major war against Russia, and from the earliest days of the conflict stories began to circulate of the outstanding bravery of the British Army in the most appalling conditions. Their heroics were performed despite a lack of adequate clothing and other provisions to protect them from the harsh Russian winter. The hospitals tending to wounded men were dire, and there was a general feeling that thousands of men were being ordered to fight in conditions far worse than any army had encountered before. Significantly, too, this was the first conflict to be covered by a corps of war reporters. William Howard Russell, of *The Times*, filed a succession of perceptive and critical articles which highlighted the lack of proper equipment and the ravages of cholera and typhoid, two diseases which claimed 20,000 lives – compared to the 3,400 killed in battle. Newspaper reports meant the suffering, endurance and heroism of 'our boys' in the Crimea caught the British public's imagination as never before. There was a general clamour that something needed to be done to recognise the efforts of rank-and-file British servicemen who were risking their lives thousands of miles from home.

Until the Crimean War, officers – usually majors and above – were given the junior grade of the Order of the Bath for acts of bravery. Yet there was no such equivalent medal for junior officers, non-commissioned officers (NCOs) or ordinary soldiers or sailors. The injustice of the situation was exacerbated because, since the early nineteenth century, the junior grades of the Legion of Honour had been available to officers and regular members of the French forces for gallantry. However, neither the Legion of Honour (instituted by Napoleon in 1803) nor its nearest equivalent in Germany – the Iron Cross (instituted in 1813) – was awarded exclusively for acts of bravery: they could also be earned for long or good service. In Britain, though, there was a growing feeling that a new award was needed to recognise examples of gallantry irrespective of a man's lengthy or meritorious service. Both Queen Victoria and Prince Albert were enthusiastic about addressing the problem, particularly as the enemy, Russia, already had awards for gallantry that ignored rank.

Shortly after the start of the war, the Distinguished Conduct Medal (DCM) was instituted for NCOs and privates, and a campaign medal for the Crimean War was approved, but there was a feeling that more was needed. Pressure mounted for a decoration which was open to all and would reflect the individual courage of men on the front line. It was the Duke of Newcastle, the Secretary of State for War, who seized the initiative on 20 January 1855, writing to Prince Albert: 'It does not seem to me right or politic that such deeds of heroism as the war has produced should go unrewarded by any distinctive outward mark of honour because they are done by privates or by officers below the rank of major . . . The value attached by soldiers to a little bit of ribbon is such as to render any danger insignificant and any privation light, if it can be attained.' The Duke broke the news of a radical new bravery award to the public when he told the House of Lords nine days later that the government had advised the Queen 'to institute a Cross of Merit which would be open to all ranks of the Army in future'. But the Duke conceded that more thought was needed as to the precise nature of the award, and matters were not helped when he lost his job a few days after making the speech.

The civil service, under the guidance of Lord Panmure, the new Secretary of State for War, came up with a plan for the award that was both clumsy and long-winded. Even its name was verbose, and it needed the intervention of Prince Albert to veto the 'Military Order of Victoria' and suggest instead the 'Victoria Cross'. He felt the word 'order' had unwanted aristocratic overtones and noted: 'Treat it as a cross granted for distinguished service, which will make it simple and intelligible.' Victoria herself chose the design, and the inscription: 'For Valour'. The government had wanted the cross inscribed 'For the Brave', but the Queen was concerned that this would imply that non-recipients were not brave.

The VC was founded by a Royal Warrant issued on 29 January 1856 which announced the creation of a single decoration available to the British Army and the Royal Navy. It was intended to reward 'individual instances of merit and valour' and which 'we are desirous should be highly prized and eagerly sought after'. The warrant laid down fifteen 'rules and ordinances' that had to be 'inviolably observed and kept'. 'Firstly. — It is ordained, that the distinction shall be styled and designated the "Victoria Cross", and shall consist of a Maltese Cross of bronze with Our Royal Crest in the centre, and underneath which an escroll bearing this inscription, "For Valour".' The second rule stated that the cross should be suspended from the left breast, by a blue ribbon for the Navy and a red ribbon for the Army. The third decreed that the names of those receiving the decoration should be published in the *London Gazette* and registered in the War Office. The fourth regulation was forward thinking enough to give instructions about what should happen if an individual who had already received a VC were to perform an act of bravery that would entitle him to a second medal. It instructed that any second or further acts of bravery entitled the VC holder to an additional bar, attached to the ribbon suspending the cross. The fifth rule made it clear that the VC was intended only for wartime courage, to be awarded to officers or men who had served Britain 'in the presence of the enemy, and shall have then performed some signal act of valour, or devotion to their country'.

The sixth instruction shows a welcome support for meritocracy in the British armed forces: 'It is ordained, with a view to place all persons on a perfectly equal footing in relation to eligibility for the Decoration, that neither rank, nor long service, nor wounds, nor any other circumstance or condition whatsoever, save the merit of conspicuous bravery shall be held to establish a sufficient claim to the honour.' This clause made the VC, at a stroke, the most democratic decoration in naval and military history.

The seventh regulation enabled a senior commanding officer in the Army or Navy to confer the decoration 'on the spot' if he had witnessed it, 'subject to confirmation by Us [the government]'. The next rule made provision for someone to win a VC even if his bravery had not been witnessed by the commanding officer. In such a case, the 'claimant' had to prove his act of courage to the satisfaction of his commanding officer, 'who shall call for such description and attestation of the act as he may think requisite'. Under the ninth instruction, it was ruled that anyone receiving an 'on-the-spot' award should be decorated in front of his army or navy colleagues. The man's name should appear in a 'General Order, together with the cause of his especial distinction'. Regulation ten, which applied to those receiving an award not witnessed by their commanding officer, indicated that the recipient should simply receive his decoration 'as soon as possible'. Similarly, the man's name should appear in a General Order issued by his commanding officer. Rule eleven made provision for the General Orders relating to the awarding of VCs to be transmitted 'from time to time' to 'our Secretary of State for War, to be laid before Us, and shall be by him registered'.

Instruction twelve tried to be all encompassing, providing for a VC to be awarded in cases 'not falling within the rules above'. It allowed for the Secretary of State for War and the head of the Navy or Army to make a joint award, 'but never without conclusive proof of the performance of the act of bravery for which the claim is made'. Regulation thirteen was longer and more complex and was intended to apply to a situation in which a large number of men – in some cases scores of them – were considered to have been 'equally brave and distinguished'. In this case, for every group of seamen or troop of soldiers, one junior officer and two servicemen should be chosen to receive the medal on behalf of their comrades.

The fourteenth rule made a generous financial provision for the recipient of a VC. Any junior officer, seaman or soldier receiving the medal would also be entitled to a special pension of ten pounds a year. For any additional bar awarded under the fourth rule, he received a further five pounds a year.

The final instruction was intended to ensure that the VC was held only by men of good character. It declared that if any VC holder was later convicted of 'treason, cowardice, felony, or of any infamous crime, or he be accused of any such offence and doth not after a reasonable time surrender himself to be tried for the same', he should have his name erased from the register and lose his special pension. There was, though, a glimmer of hope for anyone forced to forfeit his VC: 'We [the government] shall at all times have power to restore such persons as may at any time have been expelled both to the enjoyment of the Decoration and Pension.'

With this Royal Warrant, the Victoria Cross came into being in the nineteenth year of the Queen's sixty-four-year reign, and with the blessing of the monarch and her consort. Over the previous two years there had been some discussions as to whether the VC should be made from a precious metal – such as gold or silver – to make it even more valuable to the recipient, but it was finally decided that it should be of little intrinsic value. It was intended that the bronze for the medals would be taken from two cannon supposedly captured from the Russians at Sebastopol during the Crimean War. Indeed, until 2005, it was still widely believed that every cross was made in this way – the bronze coming from the cascabels (the ball found at the rear of a cannon's barrel) of the cannon which are now kept at the Royal Arsenal at Woolwich. However, John Glanfield claimed in his book *Bravest of the Brave* that this was a myth. He scoured historical documents and used scientific analysis to show that the cascabels from the pair of Woolwich cannon were not used for this purpose until 1924, sixty-eight years after the first VCs were produced. Furthermore, he says that the precious cascabels disappeared for a time during the Second World War, so a different metal was used for five crosses awarded between 1942 and 1945. 'The truth has been fogged by time, myth and misinformation,' wrote Glanfield, who also claimed there was no evidence that the Chinese-made cannon in Woolwich had even been captured at Sebastopol, the last major battle of the Crimean War. He had good news for anyone hoping to win a VC in the near future, though: there remains enough of the historic cascabels – currently stored by the Royal Logistic Corps at Donnington – for a further eighty-five crosses.

It was more than a year after the Royal Warrant was announced that the first awards of the VC were published in the *London Gazette*, on 24 February 1857. The Queen had told Lord Panmure that she wished to bestow as many of the awards as possible herself. So on 26 June she invested 62 of the 111 Crimean recipients in a ceremony in Hyde Park in front of 4,000 troops and 12,000 spectators. Dressed in a scarlet jacket, black skirt and plumed hat, Victoria remained on horseback throughout the ceremony. Legend has it that, leaning forward from the saddle like a Cossack with a lance, she accidentally 'stabbed' one VC recipient in the chest, leaving him in great pain. One by one, however, she pinned a cross on to each man's jacket, while Prince Albert stood a short distance away, saluting each recipient. The ceremony and the new award were both greeted with great enthusiasm by the public.

Over the years, there have been several significant amendments to the fifteen rules but the basic principle – that the award is for conspicuous bravery – has remained to this day. The first changes to the regulations came little more than a year after the announcement that the VC had been awarded for the first time. A Royal Warrant of 10 August 1858 extended the medal to 'non-military persons'. Under this new clause, four people received the cross for their voluntary service in the Indian Mutiny. The same instructions also allowed the VC to be awarded, subject to the existing rules, for 'acts of conspicuous courage and bravery under circumstances of extreme danger, such as the occurrence of a fire on board ship, or the foundering of a vessel at sea, or under any other circumstances in which, through the courage and devotion displayed, life or public property might be saved'. Just six crosses have been awarded over the years under this provision.

Most of the regulations have been tested at some time or other, and this has occasionally led to the rules being altered. Between 1863 and 1908 eight men had their VCs cancelled for various misdemeanours in accordance with the final rule of the original regulations. This rule never specifically stated that the cross itself should be forfeited, but for the best part of half a century it seems that the regulation was interpreted to mean that the medal must be surrendered, along with the special pension. In 1908 the Treasury Solicitor reversed this practice, saying that holders of the medal should be able to keep it, even if their record of having won it were erased. Several years later, however, George V was evidently still concerned by the prospect of future confusion because in a letter of 26 July 1920 it was declared: 'The King feels so strongly that, no matter the crime committed by anyone on whom the VC has been conferred, the decoration should not be forfeited. Even were a

VC [holder] sentenced to be hanged for murder, he should be allowed to wear his VC on the scaffold.'

A Royal Warrant of 1 January 1867 stated that eligibility for a VC was extended to include members of local forces serving with imperial troops under the command of a 'general or other officer'. The warrant was retrospective and had been drawn up to reward the bravery of those who were dealing with the 'Insurgent native tribes of Our Colony of New Zealand'. This meant that Major Charles Heaphy became the first non-regular serviceman to be awarded a VC. His actions were 'gazetted' – announced in the *London Gazette* – on 8 February 1867 for an act of bravery three years earlier. On 11 February 1864, Heaphy, while serving in the Auckland Militia – part of the New Zealand military forces – went to the aid of a wounded soldier on the banks of the Mangapiko River. While tending to his comrade, Heaphy was fired upon by Maoris, with five musket balls piercing his clothes and cap. Despite being injured in three places, the major stayed with the soldier all day and saved his life.

From 1880 to 1881, there was a rethink over the 1858 Royal Warrant which had extended the decoration to non-operational duties. A further Royal Warrant of 23 April 1881 essentially revoked this order by declaring unequivocally that the VC should be for 'conspicuous bravery or devotion to the country in the presence of the enemy'. Another potentially unfair area was cleared up by a Royal Warrant of 6 August the same year. This extended eligibility to members of the Indian ecclesiastical establishments on the grounds that if they were attached to an army in the field they would be required to perform the same roles as military chaplains, who were eligible for the medal. This Royal Warrant was issued as a direct result of the bravery of the Rev James Adams, who had shown formidable courage in an incident during the Afghan War. At

Killa Kazi, on 11 December 1879, some men of the 9th Lancers had fallen into a deep ditch along with their horses and the enemy was closing in on them. Adams, under heavy enemy fire, jumped off his mount and rushed into the waist-deep water. He dragged the horses off the men so they were free to escape at a moment when the enemy was only a matter of yards away. Under the initial rules, Adams, who managed to escape on foot, would not have been entitled to a VC, but the new Royal Warrant meant that he was 'gazetted' on 26 August 1881, nearly two years after his act of courage.

In July 1898 the government took action to look after recipients of the VC who were struggling financially, even with their annual ten-pound special pension (in 1859, this would be the equivalent of about £600 in today's money). New regulations were enacted which enabled recipients below non-commissioned rank to receive, if need dictated, up to fifty pounds a year (equivalent of about £3,700 in 1898). This figure was later upped to seventy-five pounds, and in 1959 the special pension was increased to a hundred pounds (about £1,500 today) and was paid whatever a man's rank.

The original Royal Warrant of 1856 made no mention of whether the award could be won posthumously. However, the government and the military authorities decided from the beginning that a cross would not be given to a potential recipient if he had been killed in action or had died shortly afterwards. Instead, in cases of outstanding bravery, an announcement was made in the *London Gazette* which indicated that, had the man survived, he would have been recommended for the VC.

During the Boer War, fought in Africa between 1899 and 1902, an exception was made to this practice which caused great controversy and later prompted the rules to be rewritten. The Hon Frederick Roberts was the son of Field Marshal Earl

Roberts, who had himself won a VC for an act of bravery in 1858 during the Indian Mutiny. Frederick was twenty-seven when he was seriously wounded on 15 December 1899, at the Battle of Colenso, when heroically trying to rescue the guns of the 14th and 66th Batteries of the Royal Field Artillery. He died from his wounds the next day. It was therefore a surprise to everybody when he was gazetted on 2 February 1900, and given a posthumous VC. Although nobody doubted his courage, there was some anger that he had been treated as a special case apparently because of the seniority and influence of his father. The families of other potential recipients of posthumous VCs began to ask why their relatives had not been similarly rewarded. As a result of this, there was much discussion and considerable research into the backgrounds of potential recipients. Nearly two years later, in the *London Gazette* of 8 August 1902, Edward VII approved the award of six post-humous VCs, all relating to incidents during the Boer War. Although the families of these recipients were satisfied with this outcome, those of six other men who had been gazetted between 1859 and 1897 were still unhappy that their relatives had not been awarded the medal. The King twice resisted attempts by the War Office to award the VC to the six soldiers, but eventually a war widow succeeded where the government had failed. Sarah Melvill, whose husband Lieutenant Teignmouth Melvill was killed in Zululand in 1879, made a direct appeal to the King and, in 1906, he reversed his earlier decision. Since Melvill's case could hardly be considered apart from the other five, the following year all six crosses were gazetted and were thought to have been delivered to the families of the dead men (although see Ensign Phillipps' entry in Chapter 3). So the controversy surrounding Frederick Roberts' decoration ultimately meant that the precedent for a posthumous award of the VC was established once and for all.

In the run-up to the First World War, new regulations relating to the VC were introduced. A Royal Warrant of 21 October 1911 extended eligibility to native officers and men of the Indian Army and new guidelines were introduced relating to their special pensions. Furthermore, in the event of the recipient's death, these pensions were to be continued until his widow either died or remarried.

After the First World War, further changes were made to the rules. It was decided in 1918 that the crimson ribbon used by the Army should be adopted by all services, including the newly formed Royal Air Force (RAF). A committee was also formed in 1918 to consider the whole question of the VC. The following year its recommendations formed the basis of a new Royal Warrant which was eventually signed on 20 May 1920. This was the first wholesale shake-up of the initial 1856 regulations. The Royal Warrant used simpler language and – according to P.E. Abbott and J.M.A. Tamplin, the authors of *British Gallantry Awards* – it 'consolidated, varied and extended the previous provisions'. There were some significant alterations, and the 1856 rules were renumbered to incorporate amendments made in previous Royal Warrants. The list of those eligible for a VC – both men and women – was widened and the regulations regarding the award of a VC to groups for bravery were tweaked. Perhaps the most significant change came in the enlarged conditions under which an award could be made: for 'most conspicuous bravery or some daring or pre-eminent act of valour or self-sacrifice or extreme devotion to duty in the presence of the enemy'. Specific provision was made for posthumous awards, while erasures and restorations of the VC would be published in the *London Gazette.*

Since 1920, only relatively minor changes to the regulations have been made. A Royal Warrant of 5 February 1931 gave permission for a half-sized replica of the decoration to be worn 'on certain occasions'. It also provided that forfeiture of a VC and restoration of it should be entirely discretionary. This rule followed a recommendation from the inter-departmental Rewards Committee that gallantry awards should be considered irrevocable, except in cases of extreme infamy. There has been no erasure of a VC since 1908 – and hopefully there never will be another. Whatever crime a man commits in life, one cannot and should not erase a past act of bravery.

As the make-up of the British armed forces, international borders and the Commonwealth changed in the twentieth century, a few further tweaks to the regulations were deemed necessary. A Royal Warrant of 9 May 1938 enabled members of the Burmese military to be entitled to a VC. This was needed because Burma had stopped being part of India the previous year. A Royal Warrant of 24 January 1941 made all ranks of the newly formed Indian Air Force eligible, while another issued on 31 December 1942 extended eligibility to the Home Guard, the Women's Auxiliary Services and the paramilitary forces of India and Burma. To allow for inflation, the size of the special pensions gradually rose in the UK and other countries in the Commonwealth.

Constitutional changes in the Commonwealth led to a Royal Warrant of 30 September 1961 which made servicemen and women eligible, provided the government of each country was prepared to agree to take on the terms of the warrant. A further Royal Warrant was needed on 24 March 1964 to transfer responsibilities relating to the VC from the Secretary of State for War to the newly named Secretary of State for Defence.

Since its institution, the VC has been made and supplied by Messrs Hancocks (now Hancocks & Co.), the London jewellers, who were originally based in Bruton Street in Mayfair but are now situated a couple of hundred yards away in Burlington Arcade. There have been many attempts to produce fakes and copies, but most forgers have been unable to get everything exactly right: the size, the thickness, the weight, the colour and the engraving. Hancocks pride themselves on being able to tell a genuine VC from a fake under close examination, including testing the metal. In addition, since 1906 the company has made a minuscule, secret mark of authenticity on each cross to deter forgers further. On rare occasions, replacement VCs have been issued, provided the recipient has been able to prove, beyond reasonable doubt, that the original cross has been destroyed or stolen. Most gallantry medals in the world are unidentified and unmarked, so each VC, with its clear record of the name and rank of the recipient, is a unique record of the man and his achievement.

The cross is 1.375 inches wide and weighs 0.87 ounces troy, together with the suspender bar and V-shaped link. The face of the bar is embossed with laurel leaves, while the recipient's details are engraved on the reverse. The date of the act of bravery is engraved in the centre of the circle on the reverse of the cross. The details given on the suspender bar may vary but the norm is to provide the rank, name and unit of the recipient. In most cases only the recipient's initials are given, but there have been occasions when his first name has appeared on the cross. The medal is worn on the left breast, suspended from a crimson ribbon which is 1½ inches wide.

The first award went to the formidable bearded figure of Charles Lucas, then a mate but later a rear admiral in the Royal Navy. On 21 June 1854, during the Crimean War, HMS *Hecla* and two other British ships were bombarding an enemy fort in the Baltic. The fire was returned from the shore and a live shell landed on *Hecla*'s upper deck with its fuse hissing. All hands were ordered to fling themselves flat on the deck but Lucas ran forward, picked up the shell and hurled it into the sea. It exploded before it reached the water but his actions ensured that nobody was killed or seriously wounded. His VC was one of the sixty-two invested by Queen Victoria on 26 June 1857. Unfortunately, his bravery in winning the cross was not matched by his care of it afterwards – he left it on a train and it was never recovered.

At the time of writing, the most recent award was to Private Johnson Beharry, who received it in March 2005, aged twenty-five. Beharry, of the Princess of Wales's Royal Regiment, became the first person to receive a VC for twenty-three years, and the first British recipient not to be killed in the process of winning it since 1965. His medal was awarded for outstanding gallantry while based in Al Amarah, Iraq. As the driver of a Warrior armoured vehicle, Beharry saved the lives of thirty comrades in two separate incidents in May and June 2004. In the second incident, he received serious head injuries after his vehicle was hit by a rocket-propelled grenade. I was moved when I saw a photograph of Beharry meeting Lieutenant Colonel Eric Wilson, by then ninety-three, who won a VC while serving as a captain during the Second World War. They are, despite the near seventy-year age difference, the only two living holders of the VC from their regiment. (Wilson was commissioned into the East Surrey Regiment which is now part of the Princess of Wales's Royal Regiment.)

The youngest recipient of the VC was Andrew Fitzgibbon, who was fifteen and working as a hospital apprentice when he earned it for storming the North Taku Fort in China in 1860. He tended two wounded men under heavy fire, and while doing so was seriously wounded himself. However, he survived and lived for a further twenty-three years. Today, even fighting for your country at fifteen seems amazing, but winning a VC at such an age is astonishing.

The oldest recipient was Lieutenant William Raynor, who

was two months short of his sixty-second birthday when he was one of nine men who held out at their post for more than five hours against scores of rebels during the Indian Mutiny of 1857. Five of the defenders were killed during the battle and another died shortly afterwards. Raynor and the other two survivors won the VC in the days before it could be awarded posthumously.

Five civilians have won the VC, four during the Indian Mutiny and one in Afghanistan in 1879, while fourteen foreign nationals have been awarded it, in addition to the American Unknown Soldier: five Americans, three Danes, two Germans, a Belgian, a Swede, a Swiss and a Ukrainian.

The largest number of VCs awarded in any conflict was for the First World War, when 633 were given, 188 of them posthumously. This considerably outnumbered the figure for the Second World War, when there were 182 awards, 87 of which were posthumous. The largest number of VCs earned in a single action was at Rorke's Drift during the Zulu War, when eleven were awarded for acts of outstanding bravery on 22 January 1879. Of the 1,351 awarded in total over the past 150 years, 295 have been given posthumously.

Three men have won the VC twice, therefore qualifying for a 'bar' to be added to their original medals. The truly remarkable Arthur Martin-Leake won his VC for bravery during the Boer War in 1902 while serving as a surgeon captain: he was shot and seriously injured when tending to a wounded officer. He earned his bar in 1914 during the First World War for rescuing, while under fire, wounded men from a trench close to enemy lines. Captain Noel Chavasse was awarded his VC for rescuing twenty wounded men in France with a group of volunteers in 1916. A year later, he saved more wounded men in Belgium in appalling weather. However, he died from wounds received during the second rescue operation and received his bar posthumously. Charles Upham, of the New Zealand military forces, was a second lieutenant when he won his VC in Crete in 1941 during the Second World War. He was seriously wounded in that incident but recovered sufficiently to earn his bar just a year later when, now as a captain, he led his men in fierce fighting in the Western Desert. Once again he was badly injured in the action.

The medal can be won by a woman, but to date this has never happened. However, a gold replica of the VC, but without any wording in the scroll, was presented to Mrs Webber Harris, the wife of the commanding officer of the 104th Bengal Fusiliers. She received the award from officers for her 'indomitable pluck' during the Indian Mutiny. In September 1859, she had nursed the regiment during an outbreak of cholera that was so severe that twenty-seven men died during a single night.

There have been some quite remarkable acts of bravery within families. Four pairs of brothers have won VCs, along with three fathers and sons, four uncles and nephews, three pairs of cousins, three pairs of brothers-in-law, a father-in-law and son-in-law and a great-uncle and his great-nephew. If ever there had been an award for the 'bravest family', it surely must have gone to the Goughs. Major Charles Gough (later Sir Charles) won a VC for saving the life of his brother Lieutenant Hugh Gough (later Sir Hugh) during the Indian Mutiny in August 1857. Hugh then won a VC of his own in November of the same year when he was wounded charging enemy guns. More was to come: Battalion Major John Gough, the son of Charles, won the family's third VC in Somaliland in 1903.

Amassing the world's largest collection of VCs

It is hardly surprising, given the rich history of the VC and all the decoration stands for, that so many people should want to own one. My desire for one of the medals was fostered by my boyhood dreams, my fascination with bravery, my admiration for my own father's courage and my growing interest in military history. One of the finest qualities of the VC is the egalitarian cornerstone on which it was founded. It is wonderful that Britain and the Commonwealth's most prestigious bravery award can be won by any man or woman (or even child – as Andrew Fitzgibbon proved), regardless of class, colour, religion, creed or rank, provided they exhibit truly exceptional courage in the face of the enemy.

I was in my twenties when I became aware that VCs occasionally come up for sale at auctions. I started ordering the relevant catalogues but the guide prices were prohibitive for someone of my limited means at the time. Nevertheless, I continued to ask for the catalogues to be sent to me by Sotheby's, Christie's and the other major auction houses so that I could learn more about the medals and gauge how much I would have to pay. Every time I read of another daring exploit which had earned a soldier, sailor or airman a VC, I became even keener to fulfil my boyhood ambition of eventually owning one.

By the time I had reached my thirties, I was more financially secure, thanks to the success of various business ventures. Unfortunately, though, while I could now afford one, it was years before a suitable VC turned up for sale. The opportunity I had been waiting for finally came round in 1986, three months after I had turned forty. There had been some publicity in the newspapers that the VC won by Leading Seaman James Magennis was going to be sold at auction. I was sent the Sotheby's catalogue and was won over by the courage of Magennis, a tough, hard-drinking Ulsterman from Belfast. This colourful, formidable character had performed heroics while working as a diver on a mini-submarine at the end of the Second World War. His brave deed, which led to the crippling of a Japanese warship, had taken place on 31 July 1945.

I rang Sotheby's and arranged to view the cross privately at the auctioneer's London offices. Despite the heightening anticipation over the years, there was no sense of anticlimax when I saw and handled the cross. Far from it: I felt that I was in the presence of a unique and exhilarating piece of history. I discussed the VC with Michael Naxton, then the head of Sotheby's medals and coins department, during a short, businesslike meeting. Having returned the medal to his care, I told myself that I would be back five days later with a single purpose: to buy the Magennis VC.

On a warm summer's day – 3 July 1986 – I arrived at Sotheby's a few minutes before the last and most prestigious item was put up for sale. Apparently most bidders like to spend plenty of time in an auction room to become accustomed to its peculiarities, but time was precious to me, and I had no interest in anything else that was up for sale. Michael Naxton, the auctioneer that day, still laughs when he tells the story of how I bid for the Magennis VC. He claims that I arrived looking 'smart but anonymous' at the entrance, directly opposite his position on the rostrum, and caught his eye as I stepped into the room. The bidding started at £10,000 and the price quickly escalated, until it looked as though one of the seated bidders had secured the cross. It was only then, after all the other prospective purchasers had dropped out, that I, with a gentle nod of my head, bid for the first time. Less than a minute later I had secured the VC for a hammer price of £29,000 (plus a buyers' premium and VAT on that premium). Michael recalls that there was huge interest among dealers, private collectors and the press over the identity of the successful bidder. However, he says that by the time they all looked towards the door, I had already turned on my heels and left. The identity of the new owner of the Magennis VC remained a mystery, for a time at least.

I was not a regular customer at Sotheby's, so it took a few days for my cheque to clear. Eventually, though, my driver picked up the VC and brought it to my office in Hanover Square. I put the medal on my desk and looked at it. I felt an overwhelming sense of awe. 'Wow! I really own a VC,' I said to myself. Until that point, I had never intended to own more than one VC, but there and then I knew that my fascination with this subject was not going to end with ownership of James Magennis's medal. I decided quite spontaneously that collecting VCs would be a hobby that I would pursue and enjoy for the rest of my life.

Every few seconds throughout the day that I took possession of my first VC I looked at the medal – loose on the desk – and felt a surge of passion and pride. It was humbling to be so close to the story of one man's bravery. I even felt I appreciated the true extent of his courage all the more for being in possession of his cross. I – and I suspect many other collectors – treasure medals because they are the tangible mementoes of an individual's service and bravery.

Although I decided almost immediately that I wanted to own more VCs, I never had an objective or target about how many. I was told at the time that one collector owned twenty and that it would be impossible to top that figure. I took on board what the expert had said and came to the conclusion that twenty VCs was an incredible number of medals to be in the hands of one person. Contrary to what some people might think, I have not simply thrown money at my hobby and gone after every VC in existence with an open chequebook. Instead, the collection has been built up honourably, sensitively and patiently over twenty years. It has also been amassed with a firm sense of commercial reality as to what the medals are worth.

A trust was established many years ago to look after and protect the medals. In 2005, for example, five VCs became available at auction. The trust bought three but pulled out of the bidding for the other two because the price went too high. I and later the trust have embarked on the task of collecting VCs within precise rules. There is no 'ambulance chasing' or going in pursuit of medals that are not on the market. The only medals in the collection are those which either the recipients or their families wanted to sell. They have been bought at public auctions or, in fewer circumstances, as the result of someone wanting to sell them privately and discreetly. The trust, however, has never hidden its desire that the medals would one day be put on public display so that the acts of courage and self-sacrifice could be remembered and cherished by a wider audience. I know that if we had not bought the medals, many would now be in the hands of foreign private collectors and institutions, and would therefore have been lost to Britain for ever.

Occasionally people I meet think it is sad that VCs do not remain with the recipient's families – unfortunately this is not always possible. Some families part with their VCs because the medal means little to the remote descendants; some families cannot agree which member should have the medal; some hit hard times and need to sell it. It is only such medals that I am interested in buying for the trust. Certainly, the price paid for some medals has changed the lifestyles of the individual or family that has sold them, particularly those living in some of the poorer Commonwealth countries. The simple truth is that possessions – whether they are homes, vintage cars or VCs – rarely stay in the same family indefinitely. When a VC does come on to the market, it is perfectly legitimate for anyone with the inclination and the means to bid for it.

I still get a feeling of elation whenever the trust takes possession of a VC because every medal is unique. Each comes with its own story of bravery. Similarly, if the trust has been the under-bidder for a medal, I am always disappointed that it has been unable to add to the collection. That disappointment is tempered, though, by the fact that someone out there has a greater love for that specific medal than the trust did, so it must mean an awful lot to whoever was able to purchase it. When any VC comes up for sale – whether at auction or privately – Michael Naxton, the trust's medals consultant, informs me and lets me know a little about its history. Through his great knowledge, he often helps me appreciate the particular value of a certain medal. If it is being auctioned, we discuss what it might go for and agree a maximum bid.

I am naturally drawn to some VCs more than others. I have a special interest in the fighter aces who won their medals for their exploits in the First World War. These were men of extraordinary courage who took to the skies time and time again in single-engine biplanes, often with only a single machine-gun for protection. The planes were relatively cumbersome and slow – obvious targets from both the ground and the skies. These men knew that, even if they were experienced and skilled fliers, they had a short life expectancy, yet many of them flew missions not just every day but many times a day. Whenever they went up they knew there was no guarantee that they would return. The trust owns three of the six VCs awarded to fighter aces during the Great War.

I have also always been interested in the Falklands War. This is particularly because it took place in my lifetime and because I felt Britain was right to defend the islands. During the war, two Britons won the medal posthumously for their heroics on East Falkland in 1982: Colonel Herbert Jones, known to his men only as 'H', for resolutely charging an enemy position at Darwin; and Sergeant Ian McKay, for single-handedly charging an enemy position on Mount Longdon, enabling his comrades to extricate themselves from a perilous situation. Today the trust is fortunate enough to own the second of these medals.

On one occasion, I have even been rather self-indulgent. Towards the end of 1998, Michael Naxton was approached by the agent of a private collector who was selling most of his medals. He offered for sale an unissued, but completely authentic, VC. Genuine, unissued VCs are almost as rare as hens' teeth. Hancocks, the makers of the medal, go to enormous lengths to ensure that the only VCs in existence are those awarded to recipients. It is not known how this medal – definitely twentieth century and probably from the First World War – came into the public domain. It is possible that it was stolen by someone working for Hancocks, but that is highly unlikely. It may have been used as an emergency stand-in VC at a Buckingham Palace investiture, perhaps because there was not enough time to engrave the issued one for a recipient. However, that is similarly unlikely. The most probable scenario is that it was made up because a member of the Royal Family, a government minister or a senior official at the War Office wanted to see and handle a genuine VC. Perhaps it was then mislaid, eventually forgotten about, and never returned to Hancocks, as it surely should have been.

The specimen VC was for sale at a modest price because it had never been issued. Initially, I was reluctant to buy it because it was not linked to a worthy recipient. However,

Michael persuaded me that it was still of great interest and I bought it in December 1998 – as a Christmas present to myself. I had it framed and it now sits on a desk in my home in Belize. It gives me a great deal of pleasure to see it constantly. Indeed, it somehow cements my fifty-year fascination with this wonderful bravery award.

Sometimes I like to visit the location where a VC has been won so that I can put the story into context. In January 1995, for example, I visited the Falklands and chartered a plane so I could see from the air where McKay had displayed his great bravery and where he had fallen. I have also visited the battlegrounds of the Crimean War, including the scene of the Charge of the Light Brigade. In addition, I made a trip to the beaches made famous by the Gallipoli campaign of the First World War. There I saw where another VC now owned by the trust was won: the award to Sergeant Alfred Richards for his heroics in helping to secure the cliffs at Cape Helles in 1915 despite coming under fierce enemy fire. In June 2006 I visited Rorke's Drift for the second time, on this occasion chartering a helicopter to see the battlefields. The trust owns two VCs that were won there in 1879 during the Zulu War, belonging to Lieutenant John Chard, the commander of the post that was under ferocious attack, and Private Robert Jones, who defended a hospital ward in order to save the lives of patients. Visiting such a scene gives me a greater understanding of the circumstances in which a medal was won. Sometimes a VC citation might say, for example, that the soldier fought his way up a steep hill, but it is only when you see the incline for yourself that you can fully appreciate the true scale of the task that he and his comrades faced.

It is difficult for me to pick out other 'favourites', for want of a better word, because each VC in the trust's collection has a special place in my heart. However, I deeply treasure the VC won by Sergeant Norman Jackson during the Second World War. He was returning from a bombing raid over Germany when his Lancaster was hit by an enemy fighter plane on 26 April 1944. When a fire broke out, Jackson clipped on his parachute, climbed out of the plane, and crawled along the fuselage in a bid to extinguish the blaze. He did all this while the Lancaster was travelling at 200 m.p.h. at 20,000 feet. As he tried to put out the fire, his parachute partially opened and he slipped on to the wing. He was engulfed by flames, badly burned, and fell off the wing with his partly inflated, smouldering parachute trailing behind him. A heavy landing broke his ankle and he was taken prisoner. Because of this astonishing story, which is told in more detail in Chapter 9, the trust was determined to buy Jackson's VC when it was auctioned by Spink in London in 2004. It is a matter of public record that the medal fetched a hammer price of £200,000, then the highest auction price ever paid for a VC. In July 2006 that record was well and truly topped: a VC was sold at public auction to an anonymous bidder who paid AU$1,214,500 (£491,567) for the VC and other medals, including a Military Cross, belonging to Captain Alfred Shout. He had won his VC at Gallipoli on 9 August 1915 and died from wounds he received two days later. Of the nine Australians to win the VC at Gallipoli, Shout was the most decorated soldier. I did not bid for the VC on behalf of the trust when it was offered at Bonhams and Goodmans in Sydney as I realised that the Australian authorities would never allow it to leave their country: indeed the medal seems destined to join the eight other Australian VCs from Gallipoli at the Australian War Memorial in Canberra.

The collection does not represent my only contribution to preserving VCs for the nation. I have been a benefactor for well over a decade of the Victoria Cross and George Cross

Association. Indeed, when I celebrated my fiftieth birthday in 1996, I asked each of my guests that, instead of buying me a present, they make a donation that would be divided between three charities. The association was one of those charities, and as a result received a substantial gift shortly after the party.

The trustees of the medals know that I wish to see the collection preserved long after my death, and I am glad that the trust's rules prevent it from selling any of the medals. The trustees are currently looking for a site in the UK to display all the VCs. It will probably be within an existing museum where there can be a permanent display. I want others to be able to share the joy that the whole collection has given me, so I am determined that it should not be broken up but displayed in its entirety. In return, the trust is willing to make a long-term financial commitment to the museum or institution that agrees to display it.

Nobody has ever been able to accumulate such a large collection of VCs before, and I doubt that anyone will ever match it in future. There are many VCs in museums in the UK and abroad which will, quite rightly, never be sold. Similarly, the families of many recipients will never sell the medals that their relatives won. This means that only a limited number – what some call the 'free float' – will ever be available on the open market. Because the trust's collection has grown to a size that I never thought possible, it is only right that it goes on public display and that historians know of the medals' whereabouts. It is also appropriate that citizens of the UK and those visiting this country should be able to treasure the world's largest VC collection. I hope that the trust's display will become a place of pilgrimage for everyone interested in military history; a destination where people can pay tribute to one of mankind's greatest qualities.

The bulk of this book is devoted to the 142 VCs in the

trust's collection: who they were awarded to and how they were won. The entries very much vary in length: in some cases, the information on the recipient and the incident in which he was involved is sketchy with only a short citation from the *London Gazette* available. In others, a substantial amount of information is known about both the man and why the medal was given to him, with a wordy citation and many other various accounts on record. It has been calculated by the great and the good from the military world that the chance of surviving an act that would earn a Victoria Cross is one in ten. How many people today could put their hand on their heart and say they were brave enough to embark on any single act knowing that nine times out of ten they will be killed while doing it?

No system of rewarding bravery is infallible. For every VC awarded, there were no doubt several others that ought to have been given but slipped through the net. Nobody will ever know how many men over the past 150 years have missed out on the decoration because their daring actions went unnoticed, or the witnesses to it were killed. Other worthy recipients have no doubt died lonely deaths, some of them destined to remain for ever in unmarked graves. The fact that so much bravery inevitably goes unrecorded is the reason why the tomb of any nation's unknown warrior usually has the highest gallantry decoration bestowed upon it. Yet make no mistake: every VC recipient featured in this book deserves his place in history for being in that special category – the bravest of the brave.

2

THE CRIMEAN WAR

The Crimean War lasted from 1854 to 1856 and was a conflict between Imperial Russia, on one side, and the Ottoman Empire, Britain, France and Sardinia, on the other. The majority of the fighting took place on the Crimean peninsula in the Black Sea. The war was won by the Ottoman Empire (later Turkey) and its Western allies. There were an estimated 140,000 casualties – including those killed or wounded in battle and those who died from disease.

In the 1840s, Lord Palmerston and other British leaders had become concerned that Russia would encroach into India and Afghanistan. Tensions grew in the 1850s, and when Tsar Nicholas I sent troops into Moldavia and Walachia, Britain dispatched a fleet to the Dardanelles, the entrance to the Black Sea. By 1853 Russia and the Ottoman Empire were at war, and when the former ignored an Anglo-French ultimatum to withdraw from Moldavia and Walachia, Britain and France declared war too on 28 March 1854.

The Crimean War saw some fierce battles and several grim sieges. It also marked the introduction into warfare of railways and the telegraph, as well as trenches and blind artillery fire (whereby gunners rely on 'spotters' rather than being on the field of battle themselves). This has led to it being labelled the first 'modern war'. The poor treatment of wounded soldiers in the harsh conditions prompted the work of Florence Nightingale and the development of modern nursing methods. Basic ambulances were also used for the first time during the conflict.

The first major confrontation between the two sides came at the Battle of the Alma on 20 September 1854. On 25 October, the Russians were driven back at the Battle of Balaclava, noteworthy for the foolhardy Charge of the Light Brigade. Eleven days later, the two sides fought the Battle of Inkermann, again with heavy casualties. On 11 September 1855, the British and French forced the fall of Sebastapol. Peace was eventually concluded in Paris the next year.

The Crimean War led directly to the creation of the Victoria Cross. In 1856, 111 men were awarded the medal for their contribution to the war. The trust has eight of these medals in its collection.

MIDSHIPMAN (LATER LIEUTENANT) EDWARD ST JOHN DANIEL

Royal Navy (Naval Brigade)

DATE OF BRAVERY: 18 OCTOBER 1854–18 JUNE 1855

GAZETTED: 24 FEBRUARY 1857

†CAPTAIN (LATER SIR) WILLIAM PEEL

Royal Navy (Naval Brigade)

DATE OF BRAVERY: 18 OCTOBER 1854–18 JUNE 1855

GAZETTED: 24 FEBRUARY 1857

Edward Daniel, the first person to forfeit his VC for bad behaviour, was born in Clifton, Bristol, on 17 January 1837. He joined the Royal Navy at the age of thirteen and, by the time the Crimean War began, had already served during the Second Burma War. He went to the Crimea on the frigate HMS *Diamond*, serving under Captain William Peel.

Peel, the third son of Sir Robert Peel, the former Prime Minister and founder of the Metropolitan Police, was born in London on 2 November 1824. He was a handsome and poised sailor who prided himself on his statesmanlike appearance. Sir Evelyn Wood, who as a seventeen-year-old midshipman became one of two aides-de-camp to Peel in May 1855 (the other was Daniel), later wrote: 'I was evidently much struck with Captain Peel's appearance and manners, for I recorded in boyish language, "Captain Peel, very intelligent, sharp as a needle; I never saw a more perfect gentleman." His looks and bearing were greatly in his favour, for both in face and figure there was an appearance of what sporting men, in describing well-bred horses, call "quality".' (For more on Wood, see his individual entry below.)

The two ADCs, Daniel and Wood, were devoted to Peel and rarely left his side, which was dangerous because their captain had a reputation for courage bordering on recklessness. In turn, though, he was fond of his two men and therefore tried to keep them from danger, even when it occasionally cramped his own style. Indeed, he later complained to his brother: 'I really sometimes thought it rather inconvenient having two such spirits with me as Messrs Daniel and Wood.'

Daniel and Peel were awarded their VCs for three acts of bravery during the Crimean War. On 18 October 1854, as the British and French forces prepared for the siege of Sebastopol, Daniel was one of the volunteers from HMS *Diamond* who, under Peel's command, brought powder to the battery from a wagon. He was under heavy fire throughout, and the horses that were meant to be pulling the wagon had already been shot and disabled. The zinc-lined cases each weighed 112 pounds but Daniel made several journeys to ensure he and his comrades had the necessary ammunition to tackle the enemy. On the same day, Peel excelled himself when a Russian shell landed among some powder kegs. With the fuse still burning, the shell was likely to explode at any second, yet Peel, calmly but purposefully, picked it up and quickly threw it over the nearest parapet. The shell exploded almost immediately, but harmlessly.

Daniel and Peel's second acts of bravery came at the Battle of Inkermann on 5 November 1854. As ADC to Peel, Daniel stayed by his captain's side during a long and dangerous day. Mounted on a pony, he helped Peel to defend the colours of the Grenadier Guards at the Sandbag Battery, and remained close as Peel led no fewer than seven attacks on the Russian forces. Peel identified that the group protecting the colours was in danger of being cut off by the Russians during a period of sustained pressure, and planned and executed a successful retreat from danger.

The duo's final VC-worthy actions took place at Sebastopol, where the captain, ably supported by his ADC, led the first scaling party in the assault on the Redan fortress on 18 June 1855. Furthermore, Daniel and Wood followed their captain's orders that they should 'always walk slowly and with their heads erect when under fire as an example to the rest'. Wood later recalled: 'We had fully made up our minds that our chief would be killed in the assault, and had agreed to stand by him or bring in his body.' In fact, Peel was merely wounded in the battle. Daniel attended to him and bound up his injured arm when he was forced to leave the battlefield. Daniel's own pistol case had been shot in two places and his clothes were shredded, but he escaped injury.

Peel and Daniel were awarded their VCs after the conclusion of the Crimean War. A little later, Admiral Lord Lyons declared in a speech at the Mansion House: 'I doubt whether there is anything in the annals of chivalry that surpasses the conduct of Captain Peel's aides-de-camp, Messrs Daniel and Wood.'

However, Peel and Daniel would soon both meet sad ends.

The former contracted smallpox while on his way home to England from India and died in Cawnpore on 27 April 1858, at the age of thirty-three. With his former captain's death, Daniel lost a much-loved boss and a significant patron. He was promoted to lieutenant in September 1859, but from that moment onwards his life took a distinct downward turn: one officer remarked that he became a 'drunkard that none of us could mess with'. In 1860, he was placed on half pay for twice being absent without leave from HMS *Wasp*. Then matters turned from bad to worse: he was court-martialled for drunkenness and dismissed from the *Wasp*. However, in January 1861, he found a position on HMS *Victor Emmanuel*. He served in the Mediterranean but jumped ship at Corfu on 27 June of that year, shortly after being placed under arrest for 'taking indecent liberties with junior officers' (a euphemism for sodomy). His slide from 'hero to zero' was complete when he was removed from the VC register. He was the first person, and the only officer, to suffer such an indignity. (Seven other men have since been obliged to relinquish the award.) Queen Victoria issued the warrant of forfeiture on 4 September 1861 on the grounds that he 'has been accused of a disgraceful offence, and . . . evaded enquiry by desertion from Our Service'.

Daniel, all too aware of his public humiliation, fled to Australia, and later volunteered to fight the Maoris in New Zealand: he was one of the Taranaki Military Settlers who landed in North Island in February 1864. Yet, six months later, and still clearly afflicted by alcoholism, he was sentenced to 'intensive labour' for 'excessive drunkenness'. Despite his criminal record, he later became a constable in the New Zealand Armed Constabulary Field Force and helped to quell the Fenian disturbances among Irish gold miners in Hokitika. Shortly afterwards, though, he fell ill and died, on 20 May 1868, aged just thirty-one.

ABLE SEAMAN THOMAS REEVES
Royal Navy (Naval Brigade)
DATE OF BRAVERY: 5 NOVEMBER 1854
GAZETTED: 24 FEBRUARY 1857

SEAMAN (LATER QUARTERMASTER AND PETTY OFFICER) MARK SCHOLEFIELD
Royal Navy (Naval Brigade)
DATE OF BRAVERY: 5 NOVEMBER 1854
GAZETTED: 24 FEBRUARY 1857

Thomas Reeves was born in Portsmouth in 1828; his date of birth is not known. Mark Scholefield was born in Middlesex on 16 April 1828. They were two of three men (the other was James Gorman) to win the VC as a result of an act of bravery during the Battle of Inkermann. This was known as the 'Soldiers' Battle' because of the ferocity of the fighting and the fact that many men had to use their own initiative as they became separated from the main force because of dense fog.

The Russians had decided to make the most of the conditions by launching a sustained attack on the British forces, their aim being to drive the Allies into the sea once and for all. Part of the plan was a surprise attack on the weakly defended British flank at Home Ridge, later to become known as Mount Inkermann. After the British had come under a heavy bombardment, there was ferocious hand-to-hand fighting in the glens and valleys close to the village of Inkermann. One pocket of resistance from the Right Lancaster Battery fought desperately for their lives but suffered many casualties. Five sailors from the Navy Brigade were also in the battery and they became worried that the Russians would overrun their position and kill the wounded servicemen. One of the five was reported as saying at the time: 'I wouldn't trust any Ivan getting within bayonet range of the British wounded.'

Reeves, Scholefield, Gorman and their two comrades went on the offensive. They mounted the defence-work *banquette* and kept up 'a rapid repulsing fire'. Amid desperate scenes, the wounded British soldiers lying in the trench below them reloaded the sailors' rifles and passed them up. Eventually, the Russians retreated and 'gave no more trouble'.

Two of the sailors were killed in the battle (and thus were ineligible for the VC under the rules in place at the time), but the three surviving seamen from HMS *Albion* were gazetted twenty-seven months after their act of bravery. Reeves was one of those presented with his VC by Queen Victoria at the inauguration of the new decoration at a military parade in Hyde Park, London, on 26 June that year. He died in Portsea, Hampshire, five years later.

After the Crimean War, Scholefield continued his service at sea and went to fight in the China War aboard the sloop *Acorn*. However, he contracted a disease and died at sea on 15 February 1858, two months short of his thirtieth birthday. He and his two comrades were among twelve men to win VCs at Inkermann.

BOATSWAIN HENRY COOPER

Royal Navy

DATE OF BRAVERY: 3 JUNE 1855
GAZETTED: 24 FEBRUARY 1857

Henry Cooper, who was born in Devon in 1825, joined the Royal Navy when he was fifteen. Even before he saw action in the Crimean War, he had enjoyed an action-packed and colourful life. He was undoubtedly the sort of man that any serviceman would want at his side in the heat of battle. Yet, he was also a committed family man – when he was not at sea he lived in his home town of Torpoint, Cornwall, where he and his wife Margery had seven children.

In 1848, while he was serving on HMS *Philomel* off the west coast of Africa, there was a serious confrontation with a pirate-slaver in which the *Philomel* was riddled with shot, leaving one man dead and nineteen injured. Cooper was among the boarding party which subsequently overran the slaver and imprisoned its crew of sixty. Some years later, while he was serving on HMS *Miranda*, there was an explosion as the ship was leaving Plymouth for the Black Sea. The blast ripped off the hands of one of the seamen and sent him overboard. Cooper immediately leapt into the sea and kept the seriously injured man afloat until they were both rescued.

When he arrived in the Crimea, Cooper, who sported a wonderfully bushy beard and moustache, saw fast and furious action once again. He was dispatched on *Miranda* to serve in the White Sea in 1854 and was present at the capture of the town and forts of Kola, the capital of Russian Finland. A year later, a large British force was sent across the Black Sea to seize the Straits of Kertsch and to operate beyond them in the Sea of Azov. The Russians refused to challenge the British fleet at sea, so the Azov operation involved a series of commando-style raids on enemy positions on shore. On 29 May, Cooper was part of a supporting crew for three volunteers who landed at a beach near the heavily fortified town of Genitchi. Despite encountering a volley of enemy fire, the volunteers torched corn stores, ammunition dumps and other Russian equipment. As they retreated, they encountered a party of Cossacks, but they still managed to return to their waiting boat and escape to safety. All three men won the VC for their actions.

Just five days later, Lieutenant Cecil Buckley, one of the three volunteers, was at it again. This time he landed with

Cooper at the town of Taganrog in the north-east corner of the Sea of Azov. As they came ashore, the town – defended by some 3,000 Russian troops – was under heavy bombardment from the Allied forces. Time and time again, the daring pair landed their small boat – a four-oared gig manned by other volunteers – whenever they saw a likely target. They destroyed government buildings and stores, as well as arms and other equipment, before escaping back out to sea, often under fire from the shore. Today military experts see this phase of the war as a turning point. The effectiveness of the hit-and-run raids had a devastating effect on the enemy. The Russians, who could not match the power of the Allied fleet and so preferred land battles, learned there was sometimes no substitute for the speed and flexibility provided by sea power.

It was for his bravery at Taganrog on 3 June 1855 – rather than any of his many other acts of courage – that Cooper won his VC. Unsurprisingly, though, his days of heroism were not yet over. Two weeks later, *Miranda* was hit by heavy fire from the fort of Sebastopol and Captain Lyons was mortally wounded. He was picked up and carried below deck by Cooper but died from his injuries the following week. In a final act of bravery, Cooper later took charge of the ship's boats during an attack on the fortress of Kertsch: he was the first man to take the British flag ashore and set it flying.

Cooper was present at the initial VC investiture in Hyde Park in June 1857 to receive his decoration from Queen Victoria. Such was his exceptional record that he was also one of the few men of junior rank to receive a Legion of Honour from the French for his bravery during the Crimean War. When he retired from the Royal Navy, he settled in his home town, where he died on 15 July 1893.

LIEUTENANT (LATER MAJOR GENERAL AND SIR) HOWARD CRAUFURD ELPHINSTONE

Army: Corps of Royal Engineers

DATE OF BRAVERY: 18 JUNE 1855
GAZETTED: 2 JUNE 1858

Howard Elphinstone, whose bravery on the battlefield was matched by his charm as a courtier, was born in Sunzel, northern Russia, on 12 December 1829. He was the fourth son of Captain Alexander Elphinstone, a count of Livonia who had served in the Royal Navy. The young Elphinstone had carried out survey work in Scotland before he was ordered to the Crimea in 1854, aged twenty-four. Even en route to the war zone, between Galata and Scutari, he was involved in a risky rescue of four drunken sailors from the sea. He landed at Balaclava on 20 September and was given command of a company of sappers and miners. He and another officer, Lieutenant Charles Gordon, who was to become a close friend, set to constructing some of the siege works before Sebastopol and came under sustained fire for days on end. He was twice mentioned in dispatches for courageous actions during 1854, but it was for his bravery during the assault on Sebastopol that Elphinstone won his VC.

During daylight on 18 June 1855, the Anglo-French forces had conducted a sustained assault on the Redan but the Russian defences had stood firm. That night, under cover of darkness, Elphinstone commanded a group of volunteers who searched for the scaling ladders and other equipment left behind after the abortive attack. It was a hugely dangerous assignment into no man's land and was made all the more difficult because of his decision to prolong the search to look for wounded Allied soldiers. Eventually, Elphinstone's party recovered much of the equipment and brought twenty injured and vulnerable soldiers back to the trenches so their wounds could be treated.

Later, in the final assault on Sebastopol, Elphinstone was 'killed'. His seemingly lifeless body was taken from the battlefield and placed in a mound of corpses awaiting burial. His servant, who had been searching for his master, recognised Elphinstone's boots and dragged his body from the pile. It was then discovered that he was unconscious rather than dead and he was given urgent medical treatment. Elphinstone had been struck in the head by a shell splinter and his injuries were so severe that he never regained the sight in his right eye.

In 1858, after he had returned to Scotland to resume his survey work, he began his service for the Royal Family. He was appointed by the Queen and the Prince Consort to look after and guide their third son, Prince Arthur (later to become Field Marshal the Duke of Connaught), who was then only eight years old and Victoria's favourite. Elpinstone stayed in Arthur's service for the rest of his life, while at the same time continuing a military career and rising to the rank of major general. In this time Queen Victoria wrote more than 600 letters to him and turned to him for advice on many issues, particularly after the death of Prince Albert in 1861. Her admiration for him was summed up in a personal tribute written in 1865: 'Since God deprived our poor children of their beloved father, it is impossible to overrate the value of such an excellent and devoted young man as Major Elphinstone.' Later, she wrote equally affectionately of him: 'Few if any gentlemen ever were on such confidential terms with me as dear excellent Sir Howard.'

Once Arthur came of age, Elphinstone worked as his treasurer and comptroller. He was even entrusted by Victoria with the task of finding the young prince a suitable bride in Prussia, and fulfilled this match-making duty so discreetly and effectively that Prussia awarded him the Red Eagle. This was one of Elphinstone's twelve medals and decorations, including two Orders of the Bath (highly unusually from both the military and the civil divisions) and the French Legion of Honour, which are all now in the trust's possession. The trust also possesses a wonderful journal written in Elphinstone's own hand.

His remarkable life ended tragically on 8 March 1890. Now sixty and suffering from poor health, he took his young wife and their children on holiday to Tenerife. After dinner on the first night of the voyage, he and another passenger took a stroll on the upper deck before going to bed. Elphinstone lost his footing and plunged overboard. A lengthy search failed to find him and his body was never recovered. The Queen, who had knighted him thirteen years earlier, wrote in her journal: 'Dear Sir Howard is an awful loss, he was such a confidential devoted friend, and has been quite a father to Arthur, with whom he has been since 1859, having been chosen by beloved Albert. I am quite in despair, the whole thing haunts me.'

BOATSWAIN'S MATE HENRY CURTIS

Royal Navy (Naval Brigade)

DATE OF BRAVERY: 18 JUNE 1855
GAZETTED: 24 FEBRUARY 1857

Henry Curtis, a carpenter's son, was born in Romsey, Hampshire, on 21 December 1822. He joined the Royal Navy in June 1841. After completing ten years' service, he became a coastguard in August 1851 and did that job for four years until he was conscripted – he preferred to use the term 'picked up' – into HMS *Rodney*. As a member of *Rodney*'s crew, he served in the naval brigade in the Crimea.

Curtis and his comrades participated in the ill-fated attack on the Redan at Sebastopol on 18 June 1855. The British and French forces had underestimated the strength of the Russian defences, and a 'surprise' attack by the French on Waterloo Day 1855 was anticipated and dealt with by the Russians. Lord Raglan, the British commander-in-chief, reluctantly decided that he should encourage the battered French Army by ordering British troops to join the assault. His men were hit by a volley of shots from guns which were meant to have been put out of action the previous day and chaotic scenes ensued. However, a few men succeeded in crossing the 400 yards of open ground to the abattis – a field fortification – at the front of the Redan. Here, they sheltered in craters and folds in the ground but the heavy fire from the Russians meant it was too dangerous to move. Eventually, they were forced to retreat and had to climb over dead and wounded men to return to their initial positions.

One soldier from the 57th (Middlesex) Regiment could be seen from the British trenches, sitting up and calling for help. Lieutenant Henry Raby, of HMS *Wasp*, and three men, including Curtis, left the safety of their battery. They ran across seventy yards of no man's land in order to help the wounded man, who had been shot in both legs. Despite coming under intense fire, the four sailors then carried the soldier to safety. Miraculously, they all escaped uninjured, one bullet even passing between Curtis's legs as he ran for cover. However, one of the heroes, Lieutenant Henry D'Aeth, died a week later from cholera. The other three were 'mentioned' by Captain Lushington and gazetted for the VC in early 1857.

Curtis remained on the *Rodney* until January 1856. He then married a brewer's daughter, but the sea continued to give him his living, as he served on more ships, as a coastguard and on a cross-Channel ferry. He died in Portsmouth on 23 November 1896, a month short of his seventy-fourth birthday.

COMMANDER (LATER ADMIRAL OF THE FLEET AND SIR) JOHN EDMUND COMMERELL

Royal Navy

DATE OF BRAVERY: 11 OCTOBER 1855
GAZETTED: 24 FEBRUARY 1857

QUARTERMASTER (LATER CHIEF OFFICER OF COASTGUARDS) WILLIAM THOMAS RICKARD

Royal Navy

DATE OF BRAVERY: 11 OCTOBER 1855
GAZETTED: 24 FEBRUARY 1857

John Commerell, who enjoyed a long and distinguished naval career which ended with him becoming Admiral of the Fleet, was born in London on 13 January 1829. Educated at Clifton and the Royal Naval School, he entered the Royal Navy in 1842. William Rickard was born in Stoke Damerel, Devon, on 10 February 1828. He joined the Royal Navy as a Boy 2nd Class in 1845, aged seventeen, and first saw active service on board HMS *Britomart* in West African waters, but he was invalided home with a foot injury in 1847. Nevertheless, he later served in the Crimean War.

Commerell began that war as a lieutenant but within a year had been promoted to commander. At the same time, in February 1855, he was ordered to sail to the Black Sea, accompanied by a gunboat, in the six-gun paddle sloop HMS *Weser*. Initially, he was beset by problems – the ship caught fire, struck a rock and ran aground entering the Dardanelles in April 1855. Despite having nineteen holes in her hull, though, the *Weser* was refloated and repaired. Within a month a force of

56 ships and 15,000 men was sent to seize the Straits of Kertsch and operate in the Sea of Azov. The Russians were overwhelmed at sea: their warships retreated, enabling the Allied forces to destroy two hundred Russian supply ships in seven days. British military operations now took the form of commando-style hit-and-run raids aimed at enemy stores and supply lines on the Spit of Arabat and the mainland.

One of the most daring of these raids was carried out by Commerell, Rickard and George Milestone, while two other men waited and kept guard on the rowing boat that they had launched from the *Weser*. After landing at 4.30 a.m. on 11 October, the three men made their way under cover of darkness to their target two and a half miles away: a large fodder store containing 400 tons of corn. Commerell used a hand-held compass to guide them to their destination and they had to wade, neck high, through two canals to reach it. As they set fire to the store, the twenty or thirty Cossack guards nearby were alerted and gave chase on horseback. The three commandos made it across the first canal but Milestone was so exhausted that he urged the other two to go on without him. They refused to abandon him and helped him to the next canal, where they swam alongside him. Milestone had to be half carried, half dragged towards the boat, and by now the Cossacks were close behind, firing on them. Milestone faltered again as he got stuck in the mud, but Rickard went back and dragged him to safety as the Cossacks drew ever closer. As they reached the boat, Commerell turned and shot dead the closest Cossack with his revolver at a distance of some sixty yards. After reaching the *Weser*, they were told the fodder store had burned to the ground.

Commerell and Rickard were each awarded the VC. They were to be among the first group of recipients but were both unable to attend the presentation in Hyde Park in June 1857.

At the time, Commerell was distinguishing himself again – this time in China. He went on to have a brilliant naval career in which honours were showered upon him. Later, he was MP for Southampton from 1885 to 1888, using his position to champion the need to maintain a formidable Navy. In 1889, he was made commander-in-chief at Portsmouth, and in this role he hosted a visit from the Kaiser. His rewards from the German emperor were a magnificent jewelled sword and the Prussian Order of the Red Eagle. He became a groom-in-waiting to the Queen in 1891 and Admiral of the Fleet the next year. He finally retired in 1899 and died two years later at his home in London, aged seventy-two. When his impressive collection of medals, including the Order of the Bath (civil division), was sold in 1994, it was accompanied by the sword given to him by the Kaiser.

Because he was on active service, Rickard probably received his VC some time in 1857 from his commanding officer. A formidable, bearded man, Rickard may have celebrated too vigorously for he was reduced to the rank of able seaman at the end of 1857 with the loss of a good-conduct badge. However, the following July, he was restored to the rank of quartermaster. His final appointment was aboard HMS *Impregnable* and afterwards he was employed with the Coastguard. Ending up as Chief Officer of Coastguards, he settled on the Isle of Wight with his wife. He died at the Royal Infirmary at Ryde on 21 February 1905, aged seventy-seven. Rickard has been one of the few recipients of a VC also to be awarded the Conspicuous Gallantry Medal. Furthermore, he received the French Legion of Honour.

3

THE INDIAN SUBCONTINENT

The Indian Mutiny

The Indian Mutiny broke out in 1857 and comprised a prolonged period of armed uprisings in northern and central India. The sepoys – native Indian soldiers from the Bengal Army serving under British officers – were protesting against British occupation of that part of the subcontinent. Small pockets of simmering discontent had begun in January 1857, but in May a large-scale rebellion broke out that turned into a fully fledged war in the affected regions. The mutiny lasted for thirteen months: from the rising at Meerut on 10 May 1857 to the fall of Gwalior on 20 June 1858. The mutineers were eventually suppressed by the British – with the help of soldiers from other Indian armies – but not before a considerable loss of life on both sides.

Even the phrase 'Indian Mutiny' is controversial. Many Indians, along with some historians, prefer to refer to it as the 'First War of Independence' or the 'War of Independence of 1857'. The British East India Company had expanded substantially in India over the previous hundred years. This had inevitably caused tensions among local inhabitants and an army was needed to secure the Company's commercial interests.

The trigger for the rebellion was the introduction of a new gun which, like the old musket, required soldiers to bite open a cartridge and pour the gunpowder it contained into the muzzle. According to local rumour, the cartridge had been greased – to make it waterproof – with lard (pork fat) or tallow (beef fat). This was offensive to Muslim and Hindu soldiers alike, who were forbidden by their religions to eat pork or beef, respectively. There were large uprisings in Cawnpore, Lucknow (where the British residency was besieged for ninety days), and Jhansi, which became the heart of the rebellion. The principal outcome of the conflict was the end of the East India Company's hegemony in the subcontinent and the onset of almost a century of direct rule of India by Britain.

Of 182 VCs awarded for acts of bravery in the Mutiny, the trust owns 15.

†JOHN BUCKLEY

Deputy Assistant Commissary of Ordnance, Commissariat Department

DATE OF BRAVERY: 11 MAY 1857
GAZETTED: 18 JUNE 1858

John Buckley was born in Stalybridge, Cheshire, on 24 May 1813 and enlisted in the East India Company's artillery on 28 January 1832, arriving in India on 1 November the same year. He was based first in Calcutta, but in 1857 he and his family moved to Delhi so that Buckley could take up his new role as deputy assistant commissary of ordnance at the Delhi Magazine, a storehouse for guns and ammunition. In May of that year, the Indian Mutiny broke out and the rebels soon reached Delhi. Obviously, one of their principal objectives was to break into the magazine and seize the weapons.

Buckley and eight soldiers – the so-called 'Devoted Nine' – were horrendously outnumbered by hundreds, if not thousands, of mutineers. Yet for five hours they courageously defended the magazine, killing many of their attackers. Finally, as the walls were being scaled and realising they had no hope of support, they decided to blow up the building – and themselves – rather than let the guns and ammunition fall into enemy hands. Of course, the explosion was massive, but Buckley and three of his fellow-defenders survived (although one of them died shortly afterwards). Buckley, who was badly injured and captured by the enemy, soon learned that his wife and three children had been massacred by the rebels. He was a broken man and begged his captors to kill him to put him out of his misery. However, because of his incredible bravery, they refused.

Buckley subsequently escaped from his captors and joined the British Army. He repeatedly volunteered for dangerous missions, as if taunting death, but he also relished exacting revenge: one day he oversaw the execution of 150 rebels who were strapped to the muzzles of cannon and blown apart. He was promoted to lieutenant in 1858 but fell ill and returned to Britain, where he received his VC from Queen Victoria. The two other surviving members of the 'Devoted Nine' – Lieutenant George Forrest and Lieutenant William Raynor – collected theirs, too. However, as this was in the days before posthumous VCs were awarded, the bravery of the remaining six went largely unrecognised. For a time, Buckley tried to resettle in Stalybridge, but he returned to India in October 1861 with the rank of major. His final years were spent in London, where he died on 14 July 1876.

MICHAEL ASHCROFT

ENSIGN EVERARD ALOYSIUS LISLE PHILLIPPS

Army: King's Royal Rifle Corps (1st/60th Rifles)

DATE OF BRAVERY: 30 MAY–17 SEPTEMBER 1857
GAZETTED: 21 OCTOBER 1859 AND
    15 JANUARY 1907

Everard Phillipps was born in Coleorton, Lancashire, on 28 May 1835. His VC is controversial for two reasons: it was one of the six awarded posthumously by Edward VII in 1906; and its authenticity was later questioned by none other than Hancocks, the makers of the cross throughout its history. This latter query makes it the only 'unofficial' VC in the trust's collection.

Phillipps was a keen sportsman and a devout Roman Catholic who spent time in Paris as part of the circle of Count de Montalembert, the writer and politician. He was commissioned ensign in the Bengal Army in 1854, arriving in India later the same year. On the evening of 10 May 1857, Indian servicemen rioted. Colonel John Finnis, who was in command, went to ensure that his own regiment stayed loyal. However, he was shot at Phillipps' side as he prepared to deliver an address in Hindustani at Meerut. This was the signal for the wholesale mutiny of regiments, but Phillipps managed to flee from Meerut. Shortly afterwards, Delhi fell to the rebels, and for the next four months the recapture of the city was the main aim of the British forces.

Between late May and mid-September, there were many battles and Phillipps was at the forefront of several of them, being wounded in action on three occasions. At 4 p.m. on 30 May, a force of several thousand mutineers set off from Delhi to prevent the British forces from advancing on the city. Phillipps was heavily involved in two actions which saw

Mirza Abu Bakr, the rebel leader and his followers, repulsed. In early June, he served exclusively with the 60th Rifles under the command of Lieutenant Colonel John Jones, 'taking part in almost every operation in which the Corps was engaged, and being wounded twice'. His first injury came when acting as galloper to his colonel on 12 June, and the second seven days later in another critical battle. As a reward for his gallantry, he was recommended for a commission in the regiment by Jones.

During the long-awaited assault on Delhi on 14 September, Phillipps was moving with Lieutenant Hare's D Company when he came under 'showers of grape and volleys of musketry'. He was uninjured and crossed a steep ditch before racing on, with a small party of riflemen, to the enemy ramparts. His group were among the first to mount the walls of the city and their caps were waved in the air as a token of their 'victory'. The Rev Rotton, who watched the battle, wrote: 'a little incident deserves notice; and the more so, as it affects the reputation of a very young and . . . very valuable Officer . . . Ensign Everard Aloysans [sic] Lisle Phillipps . . . In co-operation with some Riflemen placed under his command, he most gallantly carried the Water Bastion, and turned the guns which he found therein, with all possible speed and dexterity, against the retreating rebels.'

Over the next few days, the British forces consolidated their gains, but on 17 September, during street fighting, the twenty-two-year-old Phillipps was shot and killed. Once again the Rev Rotton recorded what happened: 'During the afternoon he was busily engaged in front of the enemy's guns, superintending the erection of breastworks, and while thus employed, he was marked out and slain by the rebels. His death was almost instantaneous, and elicited many an unfeigned expression of deep sorrow from his brother Officers and the soldiers of the Regiment. I was present at his burial, which took place at sunset on the same day as his death.'

At the time, it was impossible for a man to win the VC post-humously. Phillipps' courage was, however, noted in the *London Gazette* in 1859: 'Ensign Everard Aloysius Lisle Phillipps . . . would have been recommended to Her Majesty for the decoration of the Victoria Cross, had he survived, for many gallant deeds which he performed during the Siege of Delhi.' That would have been the end of the matter were it not for the controversy over the award of a posthumous VC to Frederick Roberts more than forty years later (see Chapter 1). As a direct consequence of that, Phillipps and the other five pre-Boer War heroes were gazetted in 1907, and until recently it was believed that their families were all sent their VCs at roughly the same time.

However, in 1998 the Phillipps VC was due to be auctioned by Spink in London, but there was concern among collectors that its box was different from those containing other VCs and it was withdrawn from the sale. Subsequent research revealed that the Phillipps family had a connection to Queen Victoria, and it now appears that his VC was specially made up on the Queen's instructions and presented to the family not in 1907 but almost certainly in the 1870s. It seems it was given to Phillipps' mother, perhaps because the Queen felt guilty that his bravery had not been properly recognised.

I kept in touch with the owner of the unofficial medal and bought it privately, with the blessing and co-operation of Spink, in 1999. The whereabouts of his 'official', posthumous VC, which should have been sent to his family in 1907, is not known.

LIEUTENANT (LATER CAPTAIN) WILLIAM ALEXANDER KERR

Indian Army: 24th Bombay Native Infantry

DATE OF BRAVERY: 10 JULY 1857
GAZETTED: 27 APRIL 1858

William Kerr was born in Melrose, Scotland, on 18 July 1831. He was twenty-five when he became involved in putting down the Indian Mutiny. On 8 July 1857, the news came through that 140 men of the 27th Bombay Native Infantry had mutinied and killed three young officers before embarking on a looting spree. The mutineers then took up a position in a stronghold close to the town of Kolapore. Kerr, who was seventy-five miles away at the time, volunteered to take a group of fifty men from the 24th – all that could be spared – to quell the uprising. He and his men were on the move within half an hour of hearing about the unrest.

It was the height of the monsoon and there were no fewer than five swollen rivers and seven water-filled ravines to cross. Yet within twenty-seven hours, the small group arrived at its destination exhausted, wet and caked in mud. The task facing them was formidable: the mutineers had possession of the fort and Kerr had no big guns at his disposal. As dusk fell, he selected seventeen men to storm the stronghold, which was occupied by thirty-four sepoys.

A ferocious battle ensued in which Kerr set fire to one side of the building to gain entrance. Crowbars were also used to break down some of the teak doors. In the mêlée, a bullet cut through the chain of Kerr's helmet, while another struck his sword. A musket discharged close to his face temporarily blinded him but, when he regained his sight, Kerr killed his assailant with his sword. However, when trying to withdraw the blade, Kerr was hit on the head with the butt-end of a musket. He staggered and was about to be bayoneted when his most trusted follower, Gumpunt Rao Deo Kur, sprang to his defence. Kur snatched another musket and shot dead Kerr's attacker. As the man fell, Kerr cut down another sepoy.

Eventually, Kerr and his men killed, wounded or captured all of the mutineers in the fort. The outbreak of violence – apparently an attempt to restore the House of Sivaji to power in Satara – was therefore suppressed. Kerr's group had itself paid a heavy price, though: eight were killed in the fighting and four more died later of their injuries. The 27th Bombay Native Infantry was subsequently disarmed: 63 sepoys were executed, 66 transported, 18 imprisoned and 14 acquitted. When his bravery was gazetted in April 1858, Kerr was commended for his 'dashing and devoted bravery'.

In the following year, he again acquitted himself with distinction. He played an important and courageous role in the pursuit of Tantia Topi, a rebel commander who was trying to enter the former Mahratta state of Nagpur and make a last-ditch attempt to rekindle the failing rebellion. Kerr's efforts received the high commendations of the Bombay government.

He resigned in 1860 as captain and second-in-command of the Southern Mahratta Horse on learning the regiment was going to be disbanded, and married the same year in England. He died in Folkestone on 19 May 1919, aged eighty-seven.

WILLIAM FRASER McDONELL

Civilian: Bengal Civil Service

DATE OF BRAVERY: 30 JULY 1857
GAZETTED: 17 FEBRUARY 1860

William McDonell, one of very few civilians to receive the VC, was born in Cheltenham on 17 December 1829. He joined the Bengal Civil Service in 1849 and became involved in trying to quell the Indian Mutiny as the rebellion spread in the summer of 1857. By the end of July that year, the British were determined that Arrah should not fall to the rebels because the whole of the Bihar region might then be seized. An initial force sent by steamer to defend the city had run aground but a second was dispatched and McDonell, a keen sportsman, was asked to join it. He acted as the force's guide because he knew the country well. On 29 July, the second force met up with the first and marched on Arrah House with 410 men. When they were a mile from their destination, the troops were ambushed by sepoys. After some fierce fighting the British had to retreat to the River Sone.

Sir John Kaye, who assessed the fighting later, wrote of McDonell: 'Always in the front, always in the thick of battle, he did excellent service . . . on the march. Many a Mutineer sank beneath the fire of his rifle. He was beside [Captain] Dunbar when he fell, and was sprinkled with the blood of the luckless leader. Wounded himself, he still fought on gallantly during the retreat and reached the nullah [on the Sone] with a stiffened limb, but with no abatement of vigorous courage.'

When they reached the river, McDonell and others helped members of the retreating force into boats so they could reach the safety of the steamer. McDonell and his comrades then got into the final boat only to discover the rebels had removed the oars and tied the rudder to the side. Under incessant fire from the enemy, McDonell urged one of the thirty-five men sheltering in the large boat to cut the ropes that were restraining the rudder but they did not respond. So he clambered out of the boat himself, perched on the rudder and used a knife to cut the lashings in a storm of bullets from the bank. In the words of Sir John Kaye: 'It was a truly providential deliverance that he escaped instant death. Coolly and steadily he went about his perilous work, and though some [musket] balls passed through his hat not one did him any harm. Thus the rudder was loosened, the boat answered to the helm, and by McDonell's gallant act the crew was saved from certain destruction.'

Captain Medhurst, one of those saved, said: 'I may safely assert that it was owing to Mr McDonell's presence of mind and at his personal risk that our boat got across that day.' McDonell was subsequently recommended for the VC by the Government of India and with the support of Lord Clyde, the commander-in-chief in India.

A Royal Warrant of 1858 extended VC eligibility to all civilians who bore arms while under the orders of an officer who was in command of troops, and there was no question of McDonnell's bravery, but there were initially some doubts about whether he, as a civilian, had been under the orders of an officer. This potential problem was eventually settled, though, and he was gazetted in February 1860, more than two years after his courageous act, and praised for his 'great coolness and bravery'.

McDonell stayed on in India well after the Mutiny had been suppressed. He served as a judge in Patna and in 1874 was appointed to the High Court in Calcutta, where he also became a steward of the Turf Club. After resigning from the civil service and judiciary in 1886, he returned to Britain. He died in his home town on 31 July 1894 aged sixty-four. His original VC was stolen during his time in India, so a replacement was issued through the War Office in 1878. In theory, this should have cost McDonell £1 4s, but the fee was waived. It is the replacement VC that is in the trust's possession.

MAJOR (LATER GENERAL AND SIR)
CHARLES JOHN STANLEY GOUGH

Indian Army: 5th Bengal European Cavalry

DATE OF BRAVERY: 15 AUGUST 1857–23
    FEBRUARY 1858
GAZETTED: 21 OCTOBER 1859

Charles Gough, a member of Britain's 'bravest family', was born in Chittagong, India, on 28 January 1832. He and his brother Hugh are one of only four pairs of siblings to have won the VC; and he and his son John are one of only three fathers and sons who have done so. As a family, they are unique because no other family has won three VCs.

Charles Gough, a dashing cavalry officer who won his VC for four separate incidents, was brought up in County Tipperary, but returned to India at the age of sixteen. He was commissioned cornet in the Punjab Campaign of 1848–9. After the Indian Mutiny broke out in 1857, the Indian Corps was instructed to join the main army to prepare for the advance upon Delhi. Gough, who by this point was a captain, took part in operations with his regiment around the rebel stronghold from 17 July to 1 August.

On 15 August 1857 at Khurkowdah, near Rohtuck, Charles saved the life of his younger brother, Hugh, after the latter had been injured. He also killed two of the enemy. Three days later, he led a troop of the Guide Cavalry in a charge and cut down two of the enemy's sowars (Indian cavalrymen), one of them after prolonged hand-to-hand combat. In a further act of bravery at Shumshabad on 27 January 1858, he attacked one of the enemy's leaders and pierced him with his sword, which he then lost in the heat of battle. Forced to defend himself with his revolver, he shot two of the enemy. His fourth and final act of valour took place at Meangunge on 23 February. He came to the assistance of Brevet Major O.H. St George Anson and killed his opponent before 'immediately afterwards cutting down another of the enemy in the same gallant manner'.

Long after the Mutiny, Gough continued to see action, including the Afghanistan Campaign of 1878–9. He was twice mentioned in dispatches in the *London Gazette* and was knighted in 1881 for his service in Afghanistan. He was promoted to general in 1891 and retired four years later. He died in Clonmel, County Tipperary, on 6 September 1912, aged eighty.

LIEUTENANT (LATER COLONEL) JOHN CHARLES CAMPBELL DAUNT

Indian Army: 11th and 70th Bengal Native Infantry

DATE OF BRAVERY: 2 OCTOBER AND
   2 NOVEMBER 1857
GAZETTED: 25 FEBRUARY 1862

CORPORAL (LATER SERGEANT) DENIS DYNON

Army: 53rd Regiment (later the King's Shropshire Light Infantry)

DATE OF BRAVERY: 2 OCTOBER 1857
GAZETTED: 25 FEBRUARY 1862

John Daunt was born in Normandy on 8 November 1832. He was first commissioned as ensign in the 70th Bengal Native Infantry in July 1852. Five years later, as the Mutiny was breaking out, he was promoted to lieutenant. During the Mutiny, he served under two senior officers, initially as baggage-master to the column commanded by Lieutenant Colonel Fisher, 27th Madras Native Infantry, then as interpreter to the column commanded by Lieutenant Colonel

English, HM's 53rd Foot. Daunt received his VC for two acts of bravery in successive months.

Denis Dynon was born in Kilmannon, Queen's County, Ireland, in September 1822 and enlisted nineteen years later in the 44th Regiment of Foot, in which he served for nearly three years. In 1844, he volunteered for the 53rd Regiment, which needed men to serve in India. When the Mutiny began, Dynon was with his regiment at Fort William, Calcutta. He was promoted to corporal on 1 July 1857 and became a sergeant in July 1858, after the act of bravery for which he earned his VC.

Daunt and Dynon were present at the attack and defeat of the Ramghur Light Infantry Battalion at Chuttra, Chota Nagpore, on 2 October 1857. The rebels outnumbered the British force of 350 men by nearly ten to one, yet for an hour there was fierce fighting. Daunt and Dynon acted with 'conspicuous gallantry' in the capture of two guns, in the second instance rushing the position and shooting the gunners who were mowing down their detachment, a third of whom were unarmed at the time.

Exactly a month later, Daunt was again in the thick of the action. He chased mutineers across a plain into a richly cultivated area accompanied by a handful of Rattray's Sikhs (named after Captain Thomas Rattray, who raised the force). The *London Gazette* noted: 'He was dangerously wounded in the attempt to drive out a large body of these mutineers from an inclosure [*sic*], the preservation of many of his party on the occasion being attributed to his gallantry.' Eventually Daunt, a splendid specimen with his puffed-out chest and bushy beard, made a full recovery from his injuries. After rejoining the 70th Native Infantry in April 1858, he served in China, where he again saw action. He became a civilian in 1862 and worked as a district superintendent in the Bengal Police Department. He died in Bristol on 15 April 1886, aged fifty-three.

After the end of the Indian Mutiny, Dynon and his regiment came home. He was discharged in February 1861 at Raglan Barracks, Devonport, after nineteen years' service. However, he was suffering from a lung complaint and liver disease and died two years later in Dublin, aged just forty.

PRIVATE JOHN FREEMAN

Army: 9th (the Queen's Royal) Lancers

DATE OF BRAVERY: 10 OCTOBER 1857
GAZETTED: 24 DECEMBER 1858

John Freeman was born in Sittingbourne, Kent, in 1832 but his exact date of birth is not known and little has been recorded about his long life. On 10 October 1857, he went to the assistance of a lieutenant who had been shot, killed the leader of the enemy's cavalry, and defended his officer against several assailants. He was mentioned in a dispatch from Major General Sir John Hope Grant on 8 April 1858 and his VC was gazetted eight months later. He died in Hackney, London, on 1 July 1913.

†THOMAS HENRY KAVANAGH

Civilian: Bengal Civil Service

DATE OF BRAVERY: 9 NOVEMBER 1857
GAZETTED: 6 JULY 1859

Henry Kavanagh, the first civilian to receive the VC, was born in Mullingar, West Meath, Ireland, on 15 July 1821. During the siege of Lucknow, while working for the Bengal Civil Service, he learned that a British spy had entered the city and was planning to return to nearby Alum Bagh, where Sir Colin Campbell, the British commander-in-chief, was based with his relief force of 6,000 men.

Kavanagh himself wrote an account of what happened after he located the spy in Lucknow. 'I found him intelligent, and imparted to him my desire to venture in disguise to Alum Bagh in his company. He hesitated a great deal at acting as my guide, but made no attempt to exaggerate the danger of the road.' Kavanagh had seen some of the plans being drawn up by Sir James Outram to assist Campbell in his relief of the city, and resolved to sneak this information through enemy lines disguised as a rebel, irregular soldier. He wrote: 'I secretly arranged for a disguise so that my departure might not be known to my wife, as she was not well enough to bear the prospect of an external separation.' He blackened his face, holstered his double-barrelled pistol and set off out of the city with the spy, codenamed Kunoujee Lall.

They forded a deep river before talking their way past some rebel soldiers, and skirting silently past others. 'I was in great spirits when we reached the green fields, into which I had not been for five months. Everything around me smelt sweet, and a carrot I took from the roadside was the most delicious I had ever tasted,' Kavanagh wrote. They continued on through the night, narrowly avoiding capture after startling a farmer who raised the alarm. When they encountered more rebel soldiers, Kunoujee Lall grew so frightened that he discarded the letter he was carrying addressed to Campbell. After tramping through a swamp (which washed off Kavanagh's black face paint) and losing their way, they eventually reached a British cavalry outpost. Kavanagh was taken by an officer to his tent,

> where I got dry stockings and trousers, and – what I much needed – a glass of brandy, a liquor I had not tasted for nearly two months. I thanked God for having safely delivered me through this dangerous enterprise; and Kunoujee Lall for the courage and intelligence with which

he had conducted himself during this trying night . . . My reception by Sir Colin Campbell and his Staff was cordial and kind to the utmost degree, and if I never have more than the remembrance of their condescension and of their heartfelt congratulations of Sir James Outram and of all officers of his garrison on my safe return to them, I should not repine; though – to be sure – having the Victoria Cross would make me a prouder and happier man.

The information Kavanagh provided proved vital to the advancing British forces, who were able to relieve Lucknow after a fierce fight. Kavanagh got his wish to be a 'prouder and happier man' when he received his VC two years later. He died in Gibraltar on 13 November 1882.

LIEUTENANT (LATER GENERAL AND SIR) JOHN WATSON

Indian Army: 1st Punjab Cavalry
DATE OF BRAVERY: 14 NOVEMBER 1857
GAZETTED: 16 JUNE 1859

John Watson was born in the Rectory, Chigwell, Essex, on 6 September 1829. Aged nineteen, he came to London in the hope of serving in the East India Company's private army and was offered a position in Madras – then a sleepy backwater – but held out for Bombay. He kept a detailed diary of all his campaigns and battles which he collated in 1886–7. This work, *Extracts from My Diaries and Echoes from My Memory*, has been of great value to historians, but Watson's writing was as colourful as his life, and his diaries should never be considered an unbiased account of events.

He describes how he first 'smelt powder' with his regiment, the 1st Bombay European Fusiliers, on 27 December 1848, when he saw action at the siege of Mooltan. Less than two months later he was present at the Battle of Gujerat. By 1857, at the onset of the Mutiny, he was serving as second-in-command at Asnee, which he calls 'the hottest and most desolate hole in India'.

With a growing crisis in Bengal and the raising of the rebel standard at Delhi, Watson was ordered to form a squadron made up of Sikhs and Afghans. He arrived to join the British force on Delhi Ridge in early July and for the next two months participated in the siege of the great city. On 11 September, three days before the British assault on the city, he was wounded as he played an important role in repulsing an enemy cavalry attack. He and a small force charged at the enemy, who fled, but Watson and his fellow-horsemen gave chase:

> We were soon in among them. I dispatched two easily but a third checked his horse as I came alongside of him my thrust did not seem to hurt him much for he laid his sword right heavily on my helmet beating down my guard and the point laid open my cheek and upper lip. I passed on and the men behind me finished him. We went on cutting and thrusting, and I had another small wound on my right shoulder which cut my braces in two . . . Probyn with his men now came up on my left and we drove the sheep over the broken aqueduct into Delhi, but we could not follow far across the cut as it was thick cover. However they left about 40 on the ground while our loss was trifling.

Following the capture of Delhi, the British force continued to fight effectively against the mutineers for the next two months. On 15 October, the British force's Flying Column continued the march to Lucknow via Cawnpore. The column reached Cawnpore on 26 October and preparations began for the relief and evacuation of the Lucknow garrison. On 14 November, Watson distinguished himself by single-handedly attacking a group of rebel cavalrymen. It was for this brave act that he won his VC, so unsurprisingly he vividly records the events of that day:

> I saw a long column of Cavalry galloping up six abreast between the jungle and the river and their leader evidently an enterprising Cavalry soldier not twenty yards from me. Now if I had turned and galloped back to bring up my line this man and his troops would have been close at my tail & the effect might have been bad for my men & he would have been able to bring all his men into the open & formed a line to meet us, whereas by stopping him where he was he could not form more than a very small front. I do not say that these considerations passed through my mind at the time, quick as thought is, there was hardly time for it; but what I did was to ride straight at him and thrust my sword into him. He was carrying a pistol which he fired off within a yard of my body but no bullet struck me.
>
> My thrust was not a very efficient one [due to a wound received at Kanouje] . . . however he fell from his horse & I was surrounded instantly by his men who began hammering away at me & I guarding their blows as best I might . . . I don't know how long this lasted, not more than a minute or two I suppose for Probyn who had seen what happened brought up the line at full speed and my foes were soon in full flight leaving about a dozen on the ground. To my great astonishment I had not lost one drop of blood though I had several severe blows . . . helmet, coat, boots and everything I had almost had sword cuts on them . . . It was rather a nasty time.

Eventually, the enemy cavalry was routed.

After the evacuation of Lucknow, Watson took part in the Third Battle of Cawnpore and, later, in the fall of Lucknow. This ended his active service in India and he returned to Europe to collect his VC and regain his health. However, he went on to have a distinguished military career, including serving in Afghanistan and was advanced to full general in 1891. He died in Finchampstead, Berkshire, on 23 January 1919, eight months short of his ninetieth birthday.

†ABLE SEAMAN (LATER QUARTERMASTER) WILLIAM HALL
Royal Navy (Naval Brigade)
DATE OF BRAVERY: 16 NOVEMBER 1857
GAZETTED: 1 FEBRUARY 1859

William Hall, the first black man, first Nova Scotian and first Canadian sailor to win the VC, was born in 1827 in Horton's Bluff, Nova Scotia, and was the son of African-American former slaves. As a young man, he worked in the shipyards of Hantsport, building wooden ships for the merchant marine. He then joined the crew of a trading vessel and, by eighteen, had visited many of the world's most important ports. His search for adventure led him to enlist in the Royal Navy in Liverpool in 1852. During his first service as an able seaman in HMS *Rodney*, he spent two years in the Crimean War.

He won his VC while serving on HMS *Shannon* as 'captain of the foretop' under Captain William Peel during attempts to lift the siege at Lucknow. The *Shannon* brigade had dragged its guns to within 400 yards of an inner wall which had to be breached. Hall volunteered to replace a missing man in the crew of a twenty-four-pounder. When the initial bombardment had little effect, Peel ordered two guns to move within twenty yards of the wall. Unsurprisingly, the enemy concentrated its fire on these two gun crews. One was wiped out, but in the other Hall and Lieutenant Thomas Young, who was wounded, kept firing until they triggered the charge that breached the walls. Hall later recalled: 'I remember that after each round we ran our gun forward, until at last my gun's crew were actually in danger of being hurt by splinters of brick and stone torn by the round shot from the walls we were bombarding.' Peel recommended Hall and Young for the VC, and they both went on to receive the award.

Hall, who in his latter years had a full head of white hair and a white beard, served on numerous ships until he retired in 1876 with the rank of quartermaster. He moved back to Nova Scotia to live with two of his sisters on a farm in Avonport overlooking the Minas Basin and died in Hantsport on 25 August 1904. His remains lay in an unmarked grave for forty-one years, but after a public campaign they were reinterred in front of Hantsport Baptist Church.

MAJOR (LATER LIEUTENANT GENERAL AND SIR) JOHN CHRISTOPHER GUISE

Army: 90th Regiment (later the Cameronians – Scottish Rifles)
DATE OF BRAVERY: 16/17 NOVEMBER 1857
GAZETTED: 24 DECEMBER 1858

John Guise was born in Highnam, Gloucestershire, on 27 July 1823, the fifth son of General Sir John Guise. He was commissioned ensign in the 90th Regiment a month before his twentieth birthday and was promoted to captain in November 1846. He served briefly in the Crimea in December 1854 when he was present at the siege of Sebastopol, became a major in July 1855 and returned with his regiment from the Crimea in

June 1856. In July of the following year, he was on board HMS *Transit* when it struck a rock in the Straits of Banca, leaving its crew shipwrecked on an island until they were rescued a fortnight later. By then, the Mutiny had broken out, so Guise and his comrades were transferred in other ships to India.

His great act of bravery came in the build-up to and during the relief of Lucknow. In October 1857, he and a small force of men crossed the Ganges and arrived at Alum Bagh, a garden house two miles from Lucknow where 280 men were guarding sick and wounded British soldiers. Captain (later Field Marshal Viscount) Wolseley, Guise's commanding officer, wrote of the fighting on 24 October:

> I had no one but my own company near me for a long time, but even my ninety or a hundred men were too much for the cowardly rascals . . . Our detachment had a few men wounded: Captain Guise was one of them. He had already lost his right arm, but, daring to a fault, he nevertheless would engage one of the enemy in single combat with a right-handed sword, in which encounter he nearly lost his left hand also.

Guise's latest wounds healed quickly. Sir Colin Campbell arrived outside Lucknow on 12 November with his 4,000-strong army, and two days later Guise joined in their relief of the city with 600 bayonets of Major Roger Barnston's battalion. On the morning of 16 November, the British forces stormed the heavily fortified garden of Secundra Bagh and the Shah Nujif mosque beyond it. Guise was involved in the successful attempt to take Secundra Bagh and during fierce hand-to-hand fighting he rescued from certain death Wolseley's 'old friend and best of comrades' Captain Irby of the 90th. With Sergeant Samuel Hill, Guise also went in under heavy fire to save two other wounded men. Barnston, though, was mortally wounded in the attack and Guise took over command of the battalion. The next day's fighting was no less fierce but just as successful, and once again Guise led from the front.

Such was Guise's courage on 16 and 17 November that over thirty officers from his regiment, including Wolseley, insisted that he (and Sergeant Hill) must receive the VC. Guise was also promoted to lieutenant colonel by brevet. Eventually, he took over the command of the Cameronians and, after retiring from the Army, went to live in Gorey, County Wexford, where he died on 5 February 1895.

LIEUTENANT (LATER LIEUTENANT COLONEL) THOMAS BERNARD HACKETT

Army: 23rd Regiment (later Royal Welch Fusiliers)
DATE OF BRAVERY: 18 NOVEMBER 1857
GAZETTED: 12 APRIL 1859

Thomas Hackett was born in Riverstown, County Tipperary, on 15 June 1836. He was commissioned ensign in the Royal Welch Fusiliers eight days before his eighteenth birthday. The following year, in February 1855, he was promoted to lieutenant and joined his regiment in the Crimea, where he served at Sebastopol and was present at the assault on the Redan. In 1856, he returned home with his regiment but the following year, while en route to China, he was diverted to India to help put down the Mutiny.

The deed for which Hackett received his VC was performed on the outskirts of Lucknow on 18 November 1857 as Sir Colin Campbell's force attempted to relieve the beleaguered British residency. At Secundra Bagh, Hackett saw a corporal from his own regiment lying badly wounded on open ground where he was exposed to heavy fire. He asked for volunteers to help him rescue the corporal and, accompanied by four men, crossed a road, reached the wounded man and brought him back to safety while all the time under heavy musket fire. Lieutenant Colonel Crawford reported in a dispatch: 'I there [at Secundra Bagh] witnessed a most gallant and humane act performed by Lieutenant Hackett . . . It was . . . deserving of good reward.'

Hackett saw further action and was present at the defeat of the Gwalior Contingent at Cawnpore on 6 December 1857. Early in 1858, he also took part in the final siege, storming and capture of Lucknow.

He was promoted to captain in January 1858 and major in September 1870. Three years later, he sailed for the west coast of Africa to take part in the Ashantee Campaign. However, he sold his commission in April 1874 and retired with the rank of lieutenant colonel, returning to his home town of Riverstown. Later he was made a JP for Tipperary. His life was cut short by a shooting accident, his gun exploding in his face at Arrabeg on 5 October 1880.

PRIVATE ROBERT NEWELL

Army: 9th (the Queen's Royal) Lancers
DATE OF BRAVERY: 19 MARCH 1858
GAZETTED: 24 DECEMBER 1858

Robert Newell was born in Seaham, County Durham, in 1835. He was therefore twenty-two or twenty-three when he rescued a comrade whose horse had fallen during the fighting at Lucknow. He managed to bring the man to safety despite coming under heavy musket fire from the enemy. His courage was mentioned in a dispatch dated 8 April 1858 from Major General Sir James Hope Grant, who praised his 'conspicuous gallantry'. Still in India, Newell died just three months later, on 11 July 1858, five months before his VC was gazetted.

PRIVATE JAMES DAVIS (ALSO KNOWN AS JAMES DAVIS KELLY)

Army: 42nd Regiment (later the Black Watch/Royal Highlanders)

DATE OF BRAVERY: 15 APRIL 1858
GAZETTED: 27 MAY 1859

James Davis was born in Edinburgh in February 1835. He saw action at the battles of the Alma, Balaclava and Sebastopol in the Crimea, but it was while serving in India in April 1858 that he performed the act of bravery for which he was awarded the VC. During the attack on Fort Ruhya, an officer – Lieutenant Bramley – was killed close to the gate of the fort. Davis volunteered to fetch Bramley's body 'under the very walls of the fort', in close proximity to the enemy and at great risk to himself. He began his journey in the 'midday sun' and ended it, still carrying the body, some miles away in the jungle. He received his medal the following year 'for conspicuous gallantry'. He died in his home town on 2 March 1893.

LIEUTENANT (LATER LIEUTENANT GENERAL) HARRY HAMMON LYSTER

Indian Army: 72nd Bengal Native Infantry

DATE OF BRAVERY: 23 MAY 1858
GAZETTED: 21 OCTOBER 1859

Harry Lyster was born in Black Rock, County Dublin, on 25 December 1830 and, aged just sixteen, served as a special constable during the Chartist riots in London in 1847. In

September the following year, he received a commission into the East India Company's private army. Before Lyster sailed for India, his father took him to buy a sword at Wilkinson's in London. The father and son were unable to come to a decision on which weapon to choose when a man stepped forward and said to Lyster Snr: 'I think I can assist you. I am a good judge of swords.' They went with the stranger's advice and only later learned that he was Prince Napoleon, who would go on to become Emperor Napoleon III.

Lyster arrived in India in November 1848 and after a few months was posted to the 72nd Bengal Native Infantry. He saw active service in the Punjab at the siege of Mooltan and served with the 72nd for the next seven years, until being promoted to lieutenant in November 1856. After the outbreak of the Mutiny, he served as interpreter and aide-de-camp on the staff of General Sir Hugh Rose (later Lord Strathnairn) during the Central India Campaign from December 1857 to June 1858.

In Baroda, as the enemy was retreating, Rose ordered Lyster to take command of a troop of Hyderabad cavalry because they had no European officer with them. At one point, Lyster called on the cavalry to charge, leading from the front, but only one native officer obeyed the order. Nevertheless, Lyster carried on and thrust through the enemy's rearguard, killing three men, although his horse was wounded by a sword. He then instructed the sole native cavalry officer who had followed him to charge through the enemy, but the man stopped to fight and was killed. Shortly afterwards, Lyster saw the enemy's cavalry in the distance, advancing towards him. The rebel commander then rode ahead of his men, which Lyster took as a challenge to one-to-one combat, so he, too, advanced. They met at a gallop and Lyster thrust his sword through his adversary's body, killing him, while receiving a wound to his own right arm. The enemy's cavalry saw what had happened and fled. This confrontation was mentioned by Rose in his dispatches.

In the spring of 1858, Lyster again excelled himself. Rose was by now preparing to storm the town of Jhansi, where the rebels were holding out against the British. The commanding officer told Lyster: 'It will be necessary to have the place reconnoitred and situations chosen for the batteries, but the task is so dangerous that I do not like to order anyone to undertake it.' Lyster replied: 'If you will allow me, sir, I will undertake, if I can do it my own way, and without a guard.' Shortly afterwards, Lyster set off wearing an old shooting jacket and accompanied only by a boy on a pony. When they reached the edge of Jhansi, he left the boy and told him to conceal himself and the pony but to come if he heard a whistle. Lyster crept to the gate of the town, put his ear to it and overheard guards talking on the other side. He was then seen, fired at and pursued, but the boy arrived with his pony and they escaped.

When the siege took place, the batteries were erected on the positions chosen by Lyster as a result of his survey, and when the town was stormed on 4 April, Lyster took part in the action. He later fought in the Battle of Betwa, and in the action at Koonch on 11 May, which saw the town fall. Twelve days later, Rose sent Lyster with an order to the cavalry to charge, but once again Lyster ended up charging alone into the fleeing sepoys, killing two or three of them. This time he escaped injury himself. It was for this act of bravery, rather than any of his earlier exploits, that Lyster received his VC.

He went on to lead a long and eventful life before dying in London on 1 February 1922, aged ninety-one. He is one of three uncle-and-nephew teams who have received the VC, his nephew, Hamilton Reed, winning the VC in 1899 during the Boer War.

PRIVATE (LATER SERGEANT) JOHN PEARSON

Army: 8th (the King's Royal Irish) Hussars

DATE OF BRAVERY: 17 JUNE 1858
GAZETTED: 26 JANUARY 1859

John Pearson was born in Seacroft, near Leeds, on 19 January 1825. Initially he worked as a gardener but he enlisted as a private in the 8th King's Royal Irish Hussars in January 1844. He served throughout the Crimean War, and was present at the battles of Balaclava and Sebastopol. He sailed from Cork for India in October 1857, five months after the outbreak of the Mutiny.

Pearson, who was a formidable figure with his dark, bushy beard and moustache, won his VC for an act of bravery in June 1858 when a force from the 8th Hussars, along with the 9th Regiment and the Bombay Horse Artillery, charged the rebels at Gwalior, central India. During the battle, the Rani of Jhansi, a fearless female leader of the mutineers, was killed. Charging through a rebel camp into two batteries, the Hussars captured two of the enemy's guns despite coming under heavy fire. Four VCs were awarded for the collective bravery of the entire group of men. It was the soldiers themselves who decided that Pearson, along with a captain, a sergeant and a farrier, should receive the medals for their roles in the rout of the enemy. Pearson's VC was presented to him by Lieutenant General Sir Henry Somerset, the commander-in-chief of the Bombay Army.

Pearson was promoted to corporal in July 1858 but five years later was transferred to the 19th Hussars as a private, although within a month he was back up to corporal. He became a sergeant in August 1865, but two years later was invalided home to England from Meerut. Thereafter he lived with his wife and two sons in Halifax until 1880, when they emigrated to Canada to start a new life as farmers. He died in Ontario on 18 April 1892.

LIEUTENANT (LATER COLONEL) WILLIAM FRANCIS FREDERICK WALLER

Indian Army: 25th Bombay Light Infantry

DATE OF BRAVERY: 20 JUNE 1858
GAZETTED: 25 FEBRUARY 1862

Frederick Waller was born in Dagoolie, India, on 20 August 1840 and was commissioned ensign in the 25th Bombay Light Infantry in February 1857. Despite his youth, he saw action in central India from June to December of that year, and in 1858 he was detailed to the 1st Brigade of Sir Hugh Rose's Central India Field Force. Waller took part in a protracted campaign as the force swept the country from Mhow to Calpee in order to suppress the Mutiny. During this time, he was present at the siege and storming of Chanderi, the siege of Jhansi, the defeat of rebel forces under Tantia Topi on the Betwa River and the capture of Jhansi, all in March and April 1858.

In June, there was a crucial battle at Gwalior when three rebel leaders gathered their forces for a showdown after they had suffered a series of military setbacks. Initially, Gwalior fell to rebel forces but Rose's men had recaptured most of the town by sunset on 19 June. The following morning, Waller and another officer, Lieutenant Rose, a relative of Sir Hugh, heard laughter from enemy soldiers coming from a fort. The two officers, in charge of a small force of Indian soldiers, attacked and a blacksmith succeeded in forcing open the gates of the stronghold. After the sixth gate was opened, the rebels raised the alarm and there was fierce hand-to-hand combat in and around the fort. At one point, a handful of men climbed on to

ners below them. In the heat of the
utineer. Waller raced to his friend's
bel but he was too late to save his
ritish reinforcements arrived, the fort

the VC for his courage; Rose would
but this was in the days before it was
y. Waller, who had been promoted to
n the month, received his medal in India
William Mansfield. He was later promoted to
ying in Bath on 29 January 1885.

E BELL CHICKEN

dian Naval Brigade

OF BRAVERY: 27 SEPTEMBER 1858
TED: 27 APRIL 1860

Chicken, who was awarded the only naval VC to be
horseback, is believed to have been born on 6 March
in Bishopswearmouth, Co Durham. His father, also
George, was a master mariner, hence the young
Chicken's interest in the sea. However, other historical research
suggests he may have been born at Howden Pans,
Northumberland, on 2 March 1833.

When Chicken won his VC, he was not even serving in the
Navy. Instead, he was a civilian – a volunteer serving with the
Indian Naval Brigade. On 27 September 1858, Chicken
attached himself to a mixed party of fifty-four troopers of the
3rd Sikh Irregular Cavalry and sixty-eight men of Captain
Thomas Rattray's mounted police. They were all under the
command of Lieutenant Charles Baker, of the Bengal Police,
and, when action loomed, Chicken apparently told his
comrades of his determination to win the VC that day.

Baker's men attacked a force of 700 mutineers
encamped at a village called Suhejnee, near Peroo, in
The mutineers were routed and quickly fled, pur
horseback by Chicken and others. Chicken forged ahe
driving his horse recklessly across rivers, through sug
and thick jungle. He eventually caught up with a party
twenty armed mutineers, but by now he was alone. Fearl
his own safety, he charged the group, killing five wi
sword. Chicken was now set upon by the others in the
knocked off his horse and badly wounded. He would cert
have been killed had it not been for the arrival of four na
troopers from the 1st Bengal Police and 3rd Sikh Irregul
They galloped up to Chicken and pulled him clear.
receiving the despatches of a senior cavalry officer, Sir Co
Campbell (later Lord Clyde) recommended Chicken and Bake
the volunteers' commanding officer, for the VC and both wer
eventually approved.

Chicken, who continued to serve against the mutineers for
the next two years, was only eligible for the medal because
Queen Victoria signed a Royal Warrant on 13 December 1858
which made volunteers who had borne arms against the
mutineers at Lucknow and elsewhere entitled to win the VC.
The *London Gazette* of 27 April 1860 said the VC had been won
for 'great gallantry' and added that Chicken would have been
'cut to pieces' had it not been for his rescuers' timely arrival.

However, it is unlikely that Chicken ever knew that he had
been awarded the VC. He had been given command of a
schooner, *Emily*, which was lost with all hands during a violent
storm in the Bay of Bengal in May 1860. It is believed that the
original cross prepared for Chicken was sent to India, intended
for presentation. But it subsequently vanished – lost or stored
somewhere in India – rather than returned to the War Office as
should have happened when Chicken died. The War Office

later posted a replacement VC – similarly engraved because Chicken had no rank – to his father's home in Shadwell, east London, on 4 March 1862.

Intriguingly, the medal bought by the trust is almost certainly *not* the medal sent to Mr Chicken senior. It was therefore offered for sale at auction as the 'original but unawarded' VC, and it was acknowledged that a 'duplicate but official cross' had also been presented to Chicken's next of kin.

†LIEUTENANT (LATER FIELD MARSHAL AND SIR) HENRY EVELYN WOOD

Royal Navy and Army: 17th (Duke of Cambridge's Own) Lancers

DATE OF BRAVERY: 19 OCTOBER 1858 AND
   29 DECEMBER 1858
GAZETTED: 4 SEPTEMBER 1860

Evelyn Wood was born in Cressing, Essex, on 9 February 1838, the youngest son of Sir John Page Wood. He joined the Royal Navy as a midshipman in 1852 and fought in the Crimea, where he was aide-de-camp to Captain William Peel (see Peel's entry above). Wood quickly distinguished himself under fire and in attacks on several Russian positions. He also had an early lesson in the fact that there is little room for sentimentality in war. When looking at the Russian positions through a telescope that he was resting on the head of a sailor, an enemy shell took off the man's head. Wood, stunned by the horror of the moment and by his own near miss, stood motionless. However, another sailor shouted over: 'What the hell are you looking at? Is he dead? Take his carcass away. Ain't he dead? Take him to the doctor.' He took part in the ill-fated attack on the Redan fort in June 1855, during which all naval officers were either killed or wounded. Wood himself was hit twice, once in the elbow and once in the sword, but charged on weaponless. Doctors wanted to amputate his arm, but Wood persuaded them otherwise.

Over the next half century, Wood enjoyed a reputation as 'the most accident and sickness prone officer in the British Army'. It was said that he had never once served in a campaign in which he was not injured – if not by the enemy then by himself. He was not recommended for the VC during the Crimean War despite seeing plenty of action. After the Redan attack, he convalesced in Britain. However, he then left the Royal Navy to join the army, becoming a cornet in the 13th Light Dragoons and afterwards a lieutenant in the 17th Lancers. He later suffered from typhoid when back in the Crimea and his mother travelled to the war zone to bring him home.

During his long service career, Wood suffered many more ailments, including fever, sunstroke, indigestion, toothache, internal complaints, neuralgia and inflammation of the ear. He was badly battered when trying to ride a giraffe for a bet and broke his nose and elbow when his horse ran into a tree. However, on 19 October 1858, he displayed great bravery in Sinwaho, India, one of two actions for which he won the VC. When in charge of a troop of light cavalry, he almost single-handedly attacked a group of rebels and routed them. Subsequently, at Sindhora on 29 December, Wood heard that a group of some eighty rebels had captured an informant, Chemmum Singh, and intended to hang him. Wood led a small party in pursuit of the rebels and came across them sleeping in the jungle beside a camp fire. He and two others, a duffadar and a sowar, launched a ferocious attack on the enemy, killing some and forcing the others to flee. The informant emerged unharmed.

With the gazetting of his VC, Wood had amassed six medals at the age of just twenty-two. Later, he served in the

Ashantee War (1873–4) and the First Boer War (1880–1). In the former, the head of a nail fired from a musket entered his chest fractionally above his heart. The surgeon treating him thought he would die, yet within three weeks he was back serving with his regiment. He was made a Knight Grand Cross of the Order of the Bath (GCB) at the end of the war.

Wood helped negotiate the peace at the end of the First Boer War, by which time he was a statesman as well as a soldier. He was on good terms with Queen Victoria and with two prime ministers from opposite ends of the political spectrum – William Gladstone and Benjamin Disraeli. He remained in Natal until February 1882, and received the Order of St Michael and St George (GCMG).

After serving with distinction in Egypt, he was made a lieutenant general in 1891, full general in 1895 and field marshal in 1903. On his retirement from active service, he became chairman of the Association for the City of London and, in March 1911, Constable of the Tower of London. Field Marshal Sir Evelyn Wood, VC, GCB, GCMG, died on 2 December 1920 at Harlow, Essex, aged eighty-two.

Post-Mutiny India

Once the Mutiny had been suppressed, British troops launched several campaigns in a bid to expand the empire away from central India. Meanwhile, fierce tribes were trying to spread their influence in the other direction.

The Umbeyla Campaign lasted for just three months but cost nearly 1,000 casualties on the British side. This made it the largest of the forty-two expeditions to the North-West Frontier between 1849 and 1890. Two VCs were awarded in the course of this campaign, of which the trust now owns one.

Another expedition to pacify truculent indigenous tribes, the Bhootan (Bhutan) Campaign of 1864–5, also led to the award of two VCs. The trust has one of them.

LIEUTENANT (LATER COLONEL) GEORGE VINCENT FOSBERY

Indian Army: 4th Bengal European Regiment

DATE OF BRAVERY: 30 OCTOBER 1863
GAZETTED: 7 JULY 1865

George Fosbery, a vicar's son, was born near Devizes, Wiltshire, in 1833. He was educated at Eton and joined the Bengal Army in 1852. As well as being a fine and courageous soldier, he had a brilliantly creative mind and over the years invented new guns and bullets.

While serving on the subcontinent several years after the Mutiny had been suppressed, Fosbery was chosen by Sir Hugh Rose, the commander-in-chief in India, to accompany a force of 5,600 men under the leadership of Sir Neville Chamberlain. Their task was to drive a raiding group of Pathans out of the plains beyond the Chamla Valley. However, as the force moved to attack the Pathans in the autumn of 1863, it encountered difficulties getting its elephants and men through the Umbeyla Pass. With the invading army grinding to a halt, the local Bunerwal tribe feared its land was about to be annexed so it attacked the British force. His original battle plan suddenly in tatters, Chamberlain decided to build a defensive fort at the head of the pass and await reinforcements. On 25 October, Fosbery was involved in a desperate defence of the fort against the Bunerwal which saw 124 members of the British expedition killed or wounded.

The key to Chamberlain's position was Crag Picquet, a high, rocky hill commanding the lower defences. This fell to the enemy on 30 October and Fosbery was immediately put in charge of a special detachment of marksmen who were instructed to recapture it. The Highlanders and Fusiliers were armed with one of Fosbery's inventions – the exploding bullet. Fosbery led the attack on the crag with total disregard for his own safety as he climbed the narrow, steep face: he was the first man to reach the top on his side of the assault. In a fierce day of attacks and counter-attacks, the enemy was finally routed, but the British force also suffered fifty-five casualties. Fosbery and another officer, Lieutenant Henry Pitcher, were awarded VCs for their courage, with Fosbery praised for his 'coolness and intrepidity'.

Throughout November, he saw further action as the crag was lost again and recaptured in fierce fighting. He then continued his distinguished career as a soldier and inventor before retiring from the Army in 1877, as a colonel, to devote himself to 'the perfecting of the machine-guns', weapons that eventually changed the face of warfare. Among his other inventions were the 'paradox gun' and the automatic Fosbery revolver. He died in Bath on 8 May 1897.

LIEUTENANT (LATER CAPTAIN) JAMES DUNDAS

Indian Army: Bengal Engineers

DATE OF BRAVERY: 30 APRIL 1865
GAZETTED: 31 DECEMBER 1867

James Dundas, the son of a judge, was born in Edinburgh on 12 September 1842. At seventeen, he was appointed a lieutenant in the Bengal Engineers. Following training at Chatham, he sailed for India in March 1862. He was part of a punitive expedition into Bhootan, a mountainous region close to the border with Tibet. Four columns advanced and overcame modest resistance offered by the Bhooteas, who were equipped only with primitive weapons, including bows and arrows. However, shortly before the end of the campaign, the rebels routed Colonel Campbell's force at Dewan-Giri, forcing him to abandon the British garrison. This was one of several defeats suffered by the occupying forces and the authorities in Calcutta decided to form a Bhootan Field Force under Brigadier General Sir Harry Tombs to tackle the problem. Dundas and Captain William Trevor were among the force on 30 April 1865 that tried to recapture the Bhooteas' position at Dewan-Giri. The story is taken up by Trevor, in a letter to his brother:

> Here we are all safe at last, covered in blood & glory. I have a broken head and something of a lump from a slight spear wound in my thigh . . . In compensation for these little troubles I am informed that the General is going to recommend Dundas and myself for the Victoria Cross as being the first two to climb into the principal stockade. [They had been the first to advance into a blockhouse defended by 200 men. In doing so, they had scaled a fourteen-foot-high wall before going through an opening two feet wide.] We killed 63 . . . inside and took some 25 wounded prisoners; a lot more who jumped over were shot or bayoneted outside . . . I was first in, Dundas second, and Garnault [another comrade] third; who came afterwards I don't know. Just as our heads came level with the top Dundas got a clap on the head with a stone which sent him to the bottom again, knocking over Garnault in his fall. At the same time a fellow cut at me with a sword and another chucked a stone at me: I succeeded in guarding both with my sword . . . but a man on the left hit me a whack on the head with a stone which brought out a perfect deluge of blood and nearly blinded me. Just as I was going to get it

again Dundas reappeared on the field and blew out my stoner's brains.

Trevor estimated the enemy had 150 killed and many other injured, while the British force had 6 killed and 50 wounded.

At the end of the expedition, Dundas joined the Public Works Department. Several years later, in the summer of 1878, he again displayed his courage when, as a passer-by, he rescued an Indian from a blazing house after part of the roof had collapsed. In doing so, he received severe burns to his hands. In the spring of 1879, he was chosen to work for the secretariat of the Government of India. However, he was eager to see action again and went to the battlefront in the renewed war in Afghanistan. Two days before Christmas 1879, he was helping to destroy enemy forts when a mine exploded, killing him instantly. His body was recovered later in the day and he was given a soldier's burial. Sir Alex Taylor wrote a warm tribute to his friend, saying: 'The Corps has lost one of its "very best". A man of high abilities, well cultivated – modest, high-minded English [*sic*] gentleman, brave, gentle, and courteous. I do not know that he ever gave offence to anyone; far less do I believe that he had an enemy. To me he was an invaluable personal assistant, he was a greatly valued and respected personal friend.'

The Afghan War

In the middle of the nineteenth century, Afghanistan had ambitions of expanding its territory and power, while other countries, notably Britain and Russia, wanted to gain influence in the area. The threat of an expanding Russian Empire in Afghanistan placed pressure on British India, in what became known as the 'Great Game'. This also involved Britain's repeated attempts to impose a puppet government in Kabul.

The First Anglo-Afghan War rumbled on from 1838 to 1842 and was widely regarded as a disaster, even though it achieved its aim of overthrowing Dost Mohammad, the Afghan ruler. After thirty-six years of uneasy peace, tensions reached boiling point again in the summer of 1878, when Russia sent an uninvited diplomatic mission to Kabul. Sher Ali, the Amir, reluctantly allowed the Russian envoys access to the city on 22 July. Three weeks later, the British demanded that he also accept a British mission, but this time he refused. Nevertheless, a British diplomatic mission set out for Kabul in September 1878, but it was turned back at the entrance to the Khyber Pass. This act of defiance triggered the Second Anglo-Afghan War. A British force of about 40,000 fighting men split into columns which penetrated Afghanistan at three different points. An alarmed Sher Ali appealed to Russia for help, but when it was refused he fled.

British forces occupied much of the country and Sher Ali's son and successor, Yaqub Khan, signed the Treaty of Gandamak in May 1879 to prevent a total British invasion. He relinquished control of foreign affairs to the invaders, and British representatives were installed in Kabul and other locations. Afghan uprisings opposed to the treaty were foiled in October and December 1879, and the British won a deciding victory at the Battle of Kandahar in September 1880. However, in 1881, they left, having gained some territory and retaining some influence over Afghan affairs. They had earlier installed Abdur Rahman Khan on the throne, who was unique in that he was acceptable to the British, the Russians and the Afghan people.

The war led to the award of sixteen VCs, of which the trust now owns four.

CAPTAIN (LATER MAJOR) JOHN COOK

Indian Army: Bengal Staff Corps and 5th Gurkha Rifles

DATE OF BRAVERY: 2 DECEMBER 1878
GAZETTED: 18 MARCH 1879

John Cook was born in Edinburgh on 28 August 1843, the second son of Alexander Shank Cook, a respected advocate and sheriff. He was educated at Edinburgh Academy, then attended the Scottish Naval and Military Academy, and Addiscombe College, near Croydon. At seventeen, he went to India and was posted to the 3rd Sikhs. He quickly distinguished himself on the battlefield, being mentioned in dispatches for his service in the Umbeyla Campaign, as well as being thanked by his colonel for leading a courageous and effective bayonet charge. He was promoted to captain in 1872 and for the next six years served largely in India.

At the end of 1878, he joined the 5th Gurkhas in Afghanistan, part of Brigadier General Thelwall's 2nd Brigade. He was involved in the reconnaissance of Peiwar Kotal, the first pass leading into Afghanistan on the Kurrum side, then served under Major General Frederick Roberts (who already had the VC and became a field marshal) in a force which made a long night march in order to attack the enemy's left flank at dawn. However, the operation on 2 December 1878 was sabotaged when two Afghans serving in the British force let off their rifles to warn their countrymen. The 5th Gurkhas had the lead position, and on reaching the enemy Cook – in the words of his brother, Lieutenant Colonel Walter Cook – 'charged out of the breastworks with such impetuosity that the enemy broke and fled'. Nevertheless, there was still some fighting to be done. At one point Cook saw that one of his comrades, Major Galbraith, and a huge Afghan were battling with each other. He distracted the Afghan, then engaged him in hand-to-hand combat, allowing his fellow officer to escape. The fight ended when Galbraith shot the giant Afghan in the head at close range.

He received his VC in Ali Khel at a parade of 6,450 men to mark the Queen's birthday on 24 May 1879. Later that year, during the advance on Kabul, he distinguished himself again at the Battle of Charasia. Afterwards Cook, by now promoted to brevet major, narrowly escaped death when a gunpowder store exploded, killing several men. He described the incident as the 'most appalling sight I have ever witnessed'.

In skirmishes with the Afghans in December 1879, during which the Cook brothers led a bayonet charge, both men were wounded: John was brought to his knees by a heavy blow to the head, while Walter was shot in the chest. John recovered sufficiently to fight the next day but was again wounded, this time when a bullet passed through the bone of his left leg just below the knee. He had to spend the night on a hill in the open and, in the words of his brother, 'the effect of this delay and exposure was to prove fatal'. Initially, John thought he would lose his leg and joked that he would get a job in the Pay Department and still 'be able to shoot the snipe off an elephant'. However, his doctors procrastinated over the amputation and his condition deteriorated over the next few days. He died in hospital in Sherpur on 19 December 1879.

LIEUTENANT (LATER GENERAL AND SIR) REGINALD CLARE HART

Army: Corps of Royal Engineers

DATE OF BRAVERY: 31 JANUARY 1879
GAZETTED: 10 JUNE 1879

Reginald Hart, whose extraordinary life was littered with brave acts, was born in Scarriff, County Clare, on 11 June 1848, the eighth child of Lieutenant General Henry Hart. He was educated at Marlborough, Cheltenham and the Royal Military Academy, Woolwich, before being commissioned as a lieutenant in the Royal Engineers. Aged nineteen and on leave in France, he was strolling along the pier at Boulogne-sur-Mer with his future wife when a drunken Frenchman got into difficulties in the sea. Another Englishman dived in to save the man, but soon he too was floundering. As the crowd on the shore grew, Hart removed his jacket and dived into the sea, but he struck his head on a submerged object and was dazed and bleeding heavily. Nevertheless, he reached the two men and dragged the drowning Frenchman ashore, while the Englishman managed to make his own way to the beach. A Frenchman in the crowd decided that the drowning man should be resuscitated by being held upside down. Hart disagreed and argued that, as the rescuer, he should have a say in the matter. The altercation was settled when Hart punched the obdurate Frenchman. He later received the Silver Medal of the Royal Humane Society for his courage, along with a similar bravery award from the French President.

In 1872, accompanied by his new bride, he went to India, where he spent the next six years before going on leave to Ireland. However, he was recalled on the outbreak of war with Afghanistan in 1878 and on arrival there was attached to the 24th Bengal Native Infantry, which set out with the Jumrood Column in January 1879.

Hart, who was always enthusiastic about seeing action, joined a force of 500 men escorting a supply column from Ali Musjid. On the way back, the rearguard, including Hart, was delayed and isolated from the rest of the force by some Afghan fighters. Late in the afternoon, gunfire was heard and a party of sowars (Indian mounted troops) came into view. The British rearguard saw one of the sowars fall into the water and thirty or forty Afghans closing in on him. Hart received permission to go to the stricken man's aid, and with ten sepoys ran 1,200 yards to where the wounded cavalryman lay in the water. He then directed three or four sepoys to keep the tribesmen at bay before carrying the sowar to the cover of a cliff while being fired on from both flanks and from the river. At one point, a tribesman came to within thirty yards of the two men but missed with his shot. Eventually, reinforcements arrived to see off the Afghans. However, despite Hart's efforts, the sowar, from the 13th Bengal Lancers, died before reaching the British camp.

When he was gazetted, Hart was praised for 'his gallant conduct in risking his own life in endeavouring to save the life of a private soldier'. He received his decoration from Queen Victoria at Windsor Castle, and his son later recalled that the pins of the brooch from which the VC was suspended were pushed not just into his father's tunic but into his flesh.

Despite recurrent ill health, including bouts of malaria, Hart served with distinction in the Army for many more years and, as was his wont, had at least two further narrow scrapes with death. In 1882, while serving in Egypt and out at night searching for a 'lost' battalion, he rode into two enemy horsemen and was fired upon from point-blank range. When his assailants realised they had missed, they pursued Hart until he reached a battalion of marines. Two years later, he saved the life of a gunner who had fallen into the Ganges as his battery was crossing a bridge. The gunner, in his desperation, almost drowned both of them, but a sergeant helped them reach a boat which was tied to the bank.

Hart received a bar to go with his Royal Humane Society Medal, was knighted by Edward VII in 1904 and became a full general in 1914. In November 1914, he was made Lieutenant Governor and General Officer Commanding, Guernsey and

Alderney. He remained in the Channel Islands until June 1918, when, aged seventy, he finally retired from the Army. He spent his final years in Bournemouth, where he died on 19 October 1931.

LIEUTENANT WALTER RICHARD POLLOCK HAMILTON

Indian Army: Bengal Staff Corps/Corps of Guides

DATE OF BRAVERY: 2 APRIL 1879
GAZETTED: 1 SEPTEMBER 1879

Walter Hamilton was born in Inistioge, County Kilkenny, on 18 August 1856. He was the fourth son of Alexander Hamilton, a JP, and a great-nephew of General Sir George Pollock. In 1874, he joined the 70th (Surrey) Regiment as a second lieutenant and was posted to the regiment's Rawalpindi headquarters in India later the same year. After being promoted to full lieutenant, he was appointed in August 1876 as officiating wing subaltern in the Queen's Own Corps of Guides. In February the following year, he was detailed to the Cavalry Section of the corps. He saw action from 1877 to 1878 as aide-de-camp to Brigadier C.P. Keyes.

On 21 November 1878 – the very day that war was declared against the Amir of Afghanistan – Hamilton was involved in the fighting. He was part of the front attack on the stronghold of Ali Musjid, which was abandoned by the enemy and occupied. When this defeat was followed by another at Peiwar Kotal, Sher Ali fled Kabul in December and left his son, Yakub Khan, in command. In March 1879, Hamilton was chosen to command fifty sabres of the Guides Cavalry who joined a hundred rifles of the 45th Sikhs under Lieutenant Barclay to provide an escort for a survey party. The party was attacked at Maidanak, and Barclay and several others were killed before Hamilton and his men saw off the onslaught.

Around this time, the situation in Afghanistan worsened, with talk of thousands more natives rising against the British. Brigadier General Charles Gough, VC, was sent out with a force that included Hamilton to disperse an enemy force, believed to be 1,500 strong, at Futtehabad. Gough's column left Jellalabad at 1 a.m. on 2 April, formed a camp at Futtehabad before dawn, and within a few hours was confronted by 5,000 Afghans. A fierce battled ensued and, at the first suitable opportunity, Gough ordered the cavalry of both the Guides and the 10th Hussars to charge. When Wigram Battye, who was commanding the Guides, was shot through the chest and killed, Hamilton assumed command. He proved to be an inspirational leader, cheering on his men to avenge the death of their commanding officer. The horsemen burst into the breastworks and drove out the enemy, who fled in all directions. During the battle, a sowar fell from his horse and was attacked by three of the enemy. Hamilton rushed to his comrade's aid and cut down all three assailants, thereby saving the sowar's life. It was for this act and the manner in which he led his men that Hamilton was awarded the VC. Shortly after the action at Futtehabad, the first campaign of the Second Afghan War was brought to a conclusion.

By June, the British Army had started to withdraw from the country. However, those pulling out did not include Hamilton, who was given a most dangerous and delicate role. Sir Louis Cavagnari was appointed as envoy and minister plenipotentiary to the Court of Kabul. It was decided he should have only a tiny staff and escort: Mr Jenkyns, a civil assistant; A.H. Kelly, a surgeon; and Hamilton, who would act as military attaché 'in charge of a carefully picked Escort of 20 Cavalry and 50 Infantry of the Guides Corps'.

Initially, the mission received a cordial welcome in Kabul, and was given a base 250 yards from the Amir's palace. However, tensions began to build throughout July and August, and Hamilton was in no doubt that he and his men were in danger. On 3 September, the situation reached crisis point when an Afghan regiment that was owed two months' pay shouted threats to do away with the British mission. General Daud Shah, who was in charge of giving the men a month's pay, was cut down and bayoneted: the mutiny of the Ardal Regiment had begun. Some mutineers moved on to the British residency and started stoning troopers, one of whom suffered fatal injuries. For the next twelve hours, Hamilton and those around him showed astonishing courage as they repeatedly held off a far larger force of Afghans. About halfway through the battle, the residency was surrounded and burning, and the mutineers had positioned two field guns outside the barrack walls. From his rooftop position, Hamilton sent out his third and final appeal to the Amir for help, promising the mutineers no less than six months' pay. An hour later, after one of the guns had been fired into the barracks, Hamilton collected his few surviving men and charged headlong in an attempt to capture the guns, but they were forced back. When the guns were fired again, Hamilton led a second charge, briefly capturing them but failing in his bid to bring them back to the barracks. He then decided to try to seize just one of the guns. Charging yet again, he shot three men with his revolver, cut down two more with his sword and finally reached the gun. However, he was overwhelmed and hacked to pieces. It was a tribute to the standing of Hamilton – who was aged just twenty-three – that the twelve remaining men in his little garrison were now offered the chance to surrender, but refused. Instead, they died fighting to the last man. By the time all seventy had been dispatched, six hundred mutineers lay dead around the residency. The treachery of the Afghans and the massacre reignited the Second Afghan War.

Hamilton was killed just two days after his VC had been announced in the *London Gazette*. Shortly afterwards, a statue showing his final act of bravery was erected in Kildare Street, Dublin. He was also the inspiration for a leading character in M.M. Kaye's bestseller, *The Far Pavilions*.

CAPTAIN (LATER BRIGADIER GENERAL AND SIR) ARTHUR GEORGE HAMMOND

Indian Army: Bengal Staff Corps/Corps of Guides

DATE OF BRAVERY: 14 DECEMBER 1879
GAZETTED: 18 OCTOBER 1881

Arthur Hammond was born in Dawlish, Devon, on 28 September 1843, the son of Major Thomas Hammond, and was educated at King Edward VI School, Sherborne, and at Addiscombe College. He was commissioned in June 1861, and was soon sent to India, arriving in Calcutta on New Year's Eve. In October 1862, he joined the 12th Native Infantry, and after reaching the required standard in Hindustani, was posted to the Corps of Guides in September 1863. At the time, the Guides formed part of the force that was being prepared for the Umbeyla Campaign in north-west India. In June 1867, he was placed in the Bengal Staff Corps and, after rejoining the Corps of Guides, served as wing commander during the whole of the Jowaki Campaign of 1878–9. He was mentioned twice in dispatches and was 'specially thanked for gallant conduct' by General Keyes.

Hammond won his VC during the storming of Asmai Heights. The *London Gazette* reported: 'For conspicuous coolness and gallantry . . . in defending the top of the hill, with a rifle and fixed bayonet, against large numbers of the enemy, while the 72nd Highlanders and Guides were retiring; and again, on the retreat down the hill, in stopping to assist in carrying away a wounded sepoy, the enemy being not 60 yards off, firing heavily all the time.'

Thereafter, his time in the Army was as lively and as full of distinguished service as his earlier years. During the Hazara Campaign in north-west India in 1888, he commanded the 3rd Sikhs, was mentioned in dispatches, and as a result was created a Companion of the Distinguished Service Order in April 1889. He was again mentioned in dispatches in the Hazara Campaign of 1891 and the Tirah Campaign (see below). From 1890 to 1898, he was also aide-de-camp to Queen Victoria. He was knighted by Edward VII in 1903. He died in Camberley, Surrey, on 20 April 1919.

The Tirah Campaign

The Tirah Campaign was a frontier war fought in north-west India from 1897 to 1898. For sixteen years, the Afridis had received a subsidy from the government of British India in return for safeguarding the Khyber Pass. Then, without warning, the tribesmen rebelled, capturing all the posts in the Khyber held by their own countrymen, and attacked the forts on the Samana Ridge, near Peshawar. It was estimated that the Afridis and another tribe, the Orakzais, could raise up to 50,000 men if they united.

A force under General Sir William Lockhart, commanding the Punjab Army Corps, was sent to quell the rebellion. There were some long marches and several fierce battles in late 1897. When the Afridis saw the size of the force mounted against them, they resorted to guerrilla tactics, but by early 1898 they had been worn down. Peace negotiations began, and under the threat of another expedition into

Tirah the Afridis agreed to pay fines and surrender their rifles. The expeditionary force was disbanded on 4 April 1898, having achieved its objectives.

Seven VCs were awarded for this campaign, of which the trust owns one.

LIEUTENANT HECTOR LACHLAN STEWART MACLEAN

Indian Army: Staff Corps and Corps of Guides

DATE OF BRAVERY: 17 AUGUST 1897
GAZETTED: 9 NOVEMBER 1897 AND
   15 JANUARY 1907

Hector Maclean was born in Bannu, on the North-West Frontier of India, on 13 September 1870. He won his VC for his actions in the Battle of Nawa Kili during the Tirah Campaign. Along with two other officers and five men of the Corps of Guides, Maclean set out to rescue a lieutenant from the Lancashire Fusiliers who had been shot and was about to be butchered by enemy swordsmen when the eight Guides arrived on the scene. However, as the Fusilier was being dragged to safety, he was shot again and killed, while Maclean was also fatally wounded.

His was one of the six VCs awarded posthumously in 1907.

India after the Great War

Ten VCs were awarded between the end of the First World War and the start of the Second. Half of these were won in the campaign in Russia, which was effectively a 'mopping-up' operation after the Great War. Most medal experts therefore consider there were only five 'proper' inter-war medals: four awarded because of action on the North-West

Frontier and one as a result of bravery in Mesopotamia. Of these VCs, two, both won in India, are in the trust's collection.

In May 1919, the Amir of Afghanistan declared war on the British Empire and sent his regular army across the Indian border. The Afghans were pushed back over the border but other tribes in Waziristan and north Baluchistan rose in sympathy. Local militias recruited by the British to defend the area then defected, taking their weapons and ammunition with them. As a result, by 1920 Britain was facing a full-scale frontier war against tribesmen who had long been spoiling for a fight but who were now better armed than ever before. When the British government demanded reparations for the raids, murders and kidnappings perpetrated since 1914, some tribes – notably the Utmanzai (northern) Wazirs – accepted the terms, but the formidable Mahsuds rejected them and others prevaricated.

When RAF bombing raids failed to bring the Mahsuds into line, it was decided to send in ground forces to inflict a serious defeat. The 43rd and 67th brigades were formed into the Derajat Column to carry out this task. In early December 1919, it began its advance along a river valley in the full knowledge that the mission ahead was a daunting one. The Mahsuds were fearless and aggressive fighters. Indeed, Sir John Smyth, brigade major of the 43rd, considered that, armed with modern rifles, they were the most formidable opponents he had ever encountered. Over the next two years, the Mahsud Rebellion was largely suppressed but not before they had shown their ability as awesome guerrilla fighters. There were sporadic incidents of unrest, however, up to 1924: several bloody encounters left 639 British soldiers dead and 1,683 wounded.

LIEUTENANT WILLIAM DAVID KENNY

Indian Army: 4/39th Garhwal Rifles

DATE OF BRAVERY: 2 JANUARY 1920
GAZETTED: 9 SEPTEMBER 1920

William Kenny was born in Saintfield, County Down, on 1 February 1899 and was commissioned into the Garhwal Rifles towards the end of the First World War. By October 1919, he was serving with his regiment on the North-West Frontier as part of the 43rd Brigade's attempt to quell local unrest in the area.

Sir John Smyth later paid a warm tribute to Kenny's courage in his autobiography:

> Kenny was as good a young Subaltern as any Battalion could wish to have. He was tall, strong, red-haired, always smiling, and his men would have followed him anywhere. Kenny's broad smile was the last I ever saw of him.
>
> As soon as the general withdrawal started the Mahsuds pressed him from all sides, but his Company fought back fiercely and did not give an inch. When the rest of the Battalion was well away, and at last he got the order to withdraw his own Company, he trickled three Platoons away very cleverly, remaining behind with the fourth to give them cover: but when he started to withdraw he saw that one of the other Platoons was having difficulty in getting several wounded men away. Obeying the Frontier Code of never leaving a wounded man to the tender mercies of the tribesmen, he at once ordered the Platoon he was with to about turn, fix bayonets and charge the pursuing enemy. It was of course certain death and Kenny was awarded a very well-deserved posthumous VC. The 4/39th had displayed

the greatest gallantry and the Mahsuds ever afterwards treated them with considerable respect.

The *London Gazette* provided further evidence of Kenny's heroism:

> For most conspicuous bravery and devotion to duty near Kotkai . . . when in command of a Company holding an advanced covering position, which was repeatedly attacked by the Mahsuds in greatly superior numbers. For over four hours this Officer maintained his position, repulsing three determined attacks, being foremost in the hand-to-hand fighting which took place, and repeatedly engaging the enemy with bomb and bayonet. His gallant leadership undoubtedly saved the situation and kept intact the right flank, on which depended the success of the operations and the safety of the troops in the rear. In the subsequent withdrawal, recognising that a diversion was necessary to enable the withdrawal of the Company, which was impeded by their wounded, with a handful of his men he turned back and counter-attacked the pursuing enemy, and, with the rest of the party, was killed, fighting to the last. This very gallant act of self-sacrifice not only enabled the wounded to be withdrawn, but also averted a situation which must have resulted in a considerable loss of life.

SEPOY (LATER CAPTAIN) ISHAR SINGH
Indian Army: 28th Punjab Regiment
DATE OF BRAVERY: 10 APRIL 1921
GAZETTED: 25 NOVEMBER 1921

Ishar Singh, the first Sikh to win the VC, was born at Nenwan in the Punjab on 30 December 1895. In April 1919, he was serving with his regiment in the tribal territory of Waziristan – on the India–Afghanistan border. In early 1921, he was part of an Indian column that was sent into the Mahsud heartland to quell the rebellious tribesmen.

Britain had begun the first stages of a road-building programme that was intended to make the North-West Frontier more accessible. On 10 April, Singh was part of a company that was escorting a group taking supplies between Haidari Kach and Shakan. The party was attacked from both sides of a valley by a hundred-strong group of Mahsuds, and during this ambush Singh won his VC. The *London Gazette* reported:

> When the convoy protection troops were attacked, the Sepoy was No. 1 of a Lewis-Gun Section. Early in the action he received a very severe gunshot wound in the chest, and fell beside his Lewis-Gun. Hand-to-hand fighting having commenced, the British Officer, Indian Officer, and all the Havildars [Indian Army officers] of his Company were either killed or wounded, and his Lewis-Gun was seized by the enemy. Calling up to other men, he got up, charged the enemy, recovered the Lewis-Gun, and although bleeding profusely, again got the gun into action. When his Jemadar [another rank in the Indian Army] arrived he took the gun from Sepoy Ishar Singh and ordered him to go back and have his wound dressed. Instead of doing this the Sepoy went to the Medical Officer, and was of great assistance in pointing out where the wounded were, and in carrying water to them. He made innumerable journeys to the river and back for this purpose. On one occasion, when the enemy fire was very heavy, he took the rifle of a wounded man and helped keep down the fire. On another occasion, he stood in front of the Medical Officer who was dressing a wounded man, thus shielding him with his body. It was over three

hours before he finally submitted to being evacuated, being then too weak from loss of blood to object. His gallantry and devotion to duty were beyond praise. His conduct inspired all who saw him.

Shortly after the announcement of Singh's VC, the *Madras Mail* published a telegram from George V to the commanding officer of the 28th Punjabis: 'Please convey to Ishar Singh and his Regiment my warm congratulations on this the first occasion on which a Sikh soldier has won the Victoria Cross. It was well and gallantly won.'

Singh died in his home town on 2 December 1963.

4

SOUTH AFRICA

The Zulu War

The Zulu War, or the Anglo-Zulu War, was fought between Britain and a large indigenous tribe of southern Africa. It occurred as a direct result of British expansion into Africa, aimed at gaining more territory and securing control of the region's natural riches. The result – a victory for the might of the British Empire over poorly equipped but formidable tribesmen – signalled the end of the Zulus as an independent nation.

In 1854, the disputed territory was proclaimed the Republic of Utrecht. This led to twenty-five years of tension between Dutch settlers and the native Zulus. When Cetshwayo became absolute ruler of the Zulus upon his father's death in 1873, he set about arming his people and preparing to resist the settlers, and tensions intensified when Britain annexed the Transvaal in 1877. Further disputes – and a quarrel picked by the British – led to a state of war from 11 January 1879.

A British force of 5,000 Europeans and 8,200 Africans under Lord Chelmsford, a lieutenant general, invaded Zululand, while two other forces were employed in guarding the frontier of Natal and safeguarding Utrecht. Cetshwayo's army numbered 40,000 men but they fought with spears and shields against an army equipped with guns and muskets. On 22 January Chelmsford's centre column of

1,600 *Europeans and* 2,500 *Africans was encamped near Isandhlwana, having advanced from Rorke's Drift, a mission station in Natal, situated near a natural ford on the Buffalo River. That morning Chelmsford split his forces and moved out to support a reconnoitring party. After he had left, the camp was surprised by a 20,000-strong Zulu army. The plumed and chanting warriors swept to a brutal victory, butchering everyone they came across, including their own wounded. Every man who stood his ground was killed. There were 806 European and 471 African casualties on the British side. Chelmsford and the reconnoitring party arrived at the battlefield that evening to discover the massacre. The next day the survivors retreated to Rorke's Drift.*

After the victory at Isandhlwana, several regiments of Zulus who had missed the battle had moved on to attack Rorke's Drift. The garrison stationed there under Lieutenants John Chard and Gonville Bromhead was tiny, and at least a quarter of those few men were sick even before the battle began. Late in the afternoon they were attacked by about 4,000 Zulus, who got within the entrenchments six times. However, on each occasion they were driven back at bayonet point. At dawn, the Zulus withdrew. This battle inspired Zulu, *the epic film from* 1964 *starring Stanley Baker and Michael Caine.*

Over the next few months, the British, aided by reinforcements, wore down the Zulu Army. The Battle of Kambula on 29 *March* 1879, *where the Zulus suffered massive losses, was a turning point. By July, the tribesmen were defeated, and on* 28 *August Cetshwayo was captured.*

The Zulu War led to the award of twenty-three VCs, two of which are in the trust's collection. Rorke's Drift alone accounted for eleven of these VCs, the largest number awarded for a single military action.

LIEUTENANT (LATER COLONEL) JOHN ROUSE MERRIOTT CHARD

Army: Corps of Royal Engineers

DATE OF BRAVERY: 22/23 JANUARY 1879
GAZETTED: 2 MAY 1879

PRIVATE ROBERT JONES

Army: 2nd Battalion, 24th Regiment (later the South Wales Borderers)

DATE OF BRAVERY: 22/23 JANUARY 1879
GAZETTED: 2 MAY 1879

John Chard was born in Pathe, near Bridgwater, Somerset, on 21 December 1847 and educated at Plymouth New Grammar School, Cheltenham and Woolwich. He entered the Royal Engineers at the age of nineteen and for a time was stationed in Bermuda, but he went to South Africa at the outbreak of the Zulu War.

Robert Jones, a farmworker's son, was born into an agricultural community in Raglan, Monmouthshire, on 19 August 1857. At the age of eighteen he grew restless with life on the farm and enlisted, whereupon he quickly became known as '716 Jones'. This was because his surname was so common in the regiment that the soldiers' numbers were used to distinguish them from their comrades. In February 1878, with two years of military service under his belt, he sailed for South Africa, and early the next year he marched through Natal as part of the British force that was seeking to invade Zululand.

At 3.15 p.m. on 22 January 1879, the garrison at Rorke's Drift saw two men 'riding hell for leather' towards them. One of the horsemen, Lieutenant Adendorff, came into the camp and informed Chard, the officer in charge, about the disaster at Isandhlwana. At about the same time, Chard received another urgent message from Lieutenant Bromhead, who had also been notified of the disaster. Bromhead's instruction left no room for doubt – Rorke's Drift had to be held at all costs.

Chard, Bromhead and Assistant Commissary Dalton discussed tactics. They agreed the best course of action was to abandon the ford and concentrate on defending the nearby mission. By 3.30 p.m. this process had begun, with the guard at the ford recalled and construction beginning on a four-foot-high wall of maize bags at the mission. Then came what appeared to be welcome news – an officer and 100 troops from Colonel Anthony Durnford's force arrived as reinforcements. They were positioned ahead of the mission and instructed to delay the Zulu force for as long as possible.

One of the most difficult decisions was what to do with the sick men, who were in a makeshift hospital at the mission. It was decided that those unable to fight should remain where they were because, if the mission were to be overrun, this would be one of the last places to be taken. The windows and doors of the hospital building, which measured sixty-by-eighteen feet, were barricaded with tables and mattresses, and its defence was left to Surgeon James Reynolds, who was given 716 Jones and five other privates to assist him.

By 4.15 p.m., when firing was heard from over the hills to the south, everyone was in position and ready to fight. However, shortly afterwards the officer from Durnford's force rode in and announced that the enemy was advancing but that his men would not stand and were making off. With this news, the Natal Native Contingent (NNC) also withdrew, leaving Chard with the command of just 139 men, of whom 35 were sick (although some estimates put the number of sick soldiers nearer to 80). As Chard rearranged his defences, the heart-stopping shout went up: 'Here they come!' Bromhead sent Private Frederick Hitch on to the roof to observe, and when

Hitch reported that the enemy was massing, Bromhead asked: 'How many?' 'Four to six thousand,' came the reply. 'Is that all? We can manage that lot very well,' said Bromhead, who was eager to inspire confidence in his men.

716 Jones was stationed in a room at the back of the building which contained a barricaded external door and window. It was occupied by a patient, Corporal Jessy Maher, of the NNC. From their room, the men would have been able to see the Zulu force's iNdluyengwe Regiment approach along Oscarberg Hill. As the Zulus neared the maize-bag wall, they came under sustained fire and a fierce battle was soon raging all around the front of the mission. The initial assault was beaten off but soon the Zulu attackers were reinforced by the uDhloko and uThulwana regiments, while snipers kept up a steady fire on the British force from Oscarberg Hill.

A sustained attack followed on the northern maize-bag wall and Chard was forced to order the men holding it to retreat behind another defensive line – a wall made from wooden biscuit boxes – at the eastern end of the enclosure. This left those in the hospital, including 716 Jones, isolated and highly vulnerable. Zulus swarmed all over the building, trying to break down the barricades, and set fire to the thatched roof. When he ran out of ammunition, 716 Jones helped Maher into the adjoining kitchen, where 593 Private William Jones was positioned with six more patients. The situation was desperate and the two Joneses returned to the original room, where they crossed bayonets and took up a position at the doorway. Trooper Lugg, who was in a loophole in the kitchen wall, managed to pick off several Zulus as they came into the room. 716 Jones and 593 Jones managed to bayonet every other Zulu who broke through, although the former received three wounds from an assegai (a stabbing spear). In a short lull in the fighting, the Joneses went into the kitchen and helped the patients through a high window which led to the area between the north and south maize-bag walls. Once most of the injured men had escaped, the two Joneses held the Zulus back in the doorway, while at the same time trying to dress the last patient in the room, Sergeant Robert Maxfield, who was delirious with fever.

At this point, a pickaxe smashed through the wall behind them. It was 1395 Private John Williams making an escape route for Private Harry Hook and their patients, who had been in the western end of the building. The two men managed to get their eight surviving patients through the hole while fighting off pursuing Zulus. By now, Maxfield was dressed but he refused to move. The two Joneses took over guarding the escape hole from Hook and Williams, who were helping their patients out of the window. With the roof smouldering and Zulus starting to force their way through the hole, the Joneses retreated to join Hook and Williams. As the four men prepared to leave the building, 716 Jones – having already passed his .577 Martini-Henry rifle through the window – made a final attempt to save Maxfield. However, he was only in time to see the patient being repeatedly stabbed by the Zulus. As he clambered out of a window to relative safety, the roof of the burning building collapsed. The four rescuers and fourteen patients then had to race across the enclosure and into the biscuit-box area. Privates Thomas Cole and 1398 Joseph Williams had been killed: the latter was stabbed and, as was the Zulu tradition at the time, had his stomach ripped open.

It was now, with daylight fading, that the fight to hold the retrenchment began under the command of Lieutenant Chard. The Zulus launched a series of assaults but each one was repulsed by the British force. The fact that the thatched roof of the building was on fire enabled the defenders to take good aim at their newly lit targets. By 10 p.m., however, the flames were dying down and the men of B Company had to use their bayonets to prevent Zulus forcing their way over the ramparts. By midnight, after nearly eight hours of relentless fighting, the onslaughts had ceased, although occasional rifle fire continued until 4 a.m.

Dawn revealed the full extent of the carnage. When the Zulus began to pull back to Oscarberg Hill, the British force thought the fighting was over. Chard began rebuilding defences and ordered the thatch to be taken from the store-house roof. The Zulus then appeared on the hills to the south-west, yet, just as a new onslaught seemed inevitable, they melted away without launching a fresh attack. Shortly afterwards, Lord Chelmsford and his men, fresh from surveying the scenes at Isandhlwana, came across 'the survivors of as gallant a defence as the annals of the British Army have ever known'. Lying on the ground were 350 dead Zulu warriors, with a further 500 wounded. (The latter were subsequently killed by the British.) The British garrison lost just seventeen killed and ten wounded (two of whom died later of their wounds).

Chard mentioned 716 Jones's sterling acts in his report, dated 25 January 1879. The private received his decoration from Sir Garnet (later Lord) Wolseley at Utrecht, Transvaal, on 11 September that year, and was also singled out in a special account that Chard was asked to write for Queen Victoria in January 1880. As he left South Africa, 716 Jones still bore one bullet and four assegai wounds, injuries from which he never fully recovered. On 26 January 1888, he was finally discharged from the Army and thereafter worked as a labourer on a country estate in Peterchurch, Herefordshire. A decade later, at the age of forty, he suddenly collapsed. He seemed to recover quickly but his wife detected a change in his personality and he started drinking heavily. The next month, on the morning of 6 September 1898, his wife found him acting strangely, but he left for work as normal and on arriving at the estate asked for a shotgun and two cartridges in order to shoot vermin. A gunshot was heard shortly afterwards in the garden and Jones was found dead. An inquest decided that he had taken his own life while of unsound mind.

The *London Gazette* praised John Chard for setting a fine example and conducting himself with great gallantry in 'most trying circumstances' at Rorke's Drift. This was unsual praise for the thirty-one-year-old lieutenant because up to that point he had not enjoyed a good reputation as an officer and was regarded as somewhat slow witted. However, even the award of the VC did not win him the respect of his fellow-officers. General Wolseley later remarked: 'I presented Major [he was promoted after Rorke's Drift] Chard RE with his Victoria Cross; a more uninteresting or stupid fellow I never saw. [Colonel Sir Evelyn] Wood tells me he is a most useless officer, fit for nothing.' Soon after the defence of Rorke's Drift, Chard fell ill with a fever, but he recovered sufficiently to fight against the Zulus at the Battle of Ulundi. At the end of 1879, he was ordered home and was greeted at Plymouth with a telegram from the Queen, who later received him at Balmoral.

In spite of the disdain of his fellow-officers, Chard eventually rose to the rank of colonel before retiring from the Army in August 1897. He died three months later at his home in Hatch Beauchamp, Somerset.

While the most that the trust has paid at auction for a VC was £200,000 for Sergeant Norman Jackson's in 2004, I am prepared to reveal here that we paid considerably more for Chard's when we acquired it in a private sale. However, it was worth every penny because it records arguably the most heroic stand in British military history.

The Basuto Gun War

After the end of the Zulu War in 1879, there were still some sporadic conflicts in the region. The Transvaal War of 1880–1, sometimes called the First Boer War, was the result of British and Dutch competition over who should control southern Africa.

At the same time, the so-called Basuto Gun War was fought from 1880–1 in Basutoland, later Lesotho. At the termination of the fighting in 1879, the African population was ordered to hand in its firearms. Although most complied, some did not and this led to inter-tribal conflict and tensions between the British and local Africans. Certain tribal chiefs, including Jonathon and Letsi, had complied with the firearms order. However, no sooner had they done so than they were attacked by Chiefs Lerothodi, Masupha, Moletsane and others. In September 1880, some of these tribes also attacked white administrators, and troops and volunteers were soon mobilised. A detachment of Cape Mounted Riflemen was then attacked by Chief Lerothodi. When the detachment reached Mafeking, it was attacked again. Between October 1880 and February 1881, there were several skirmishes between the British and the tribesmen. In May, a peace was concluded, although Chief Masupha did not surrender finally until September. Eventually, the British decided that Basutoland should become a crown colony and this was effected in March 1884.

Six VCs were awarded during the war, of which the trust has one.

SURGEON (LATER SURGEON MAJOR) JOHN FREDERICK McCREA

South African Forces: 1st Cape Mounted Yeomanry

DATE OF BRAVERY: 14 JANUARY 1881
GAZETTED: 28 JUNE 1881

John McCrea was born at St Peter Port, Guernsey, on 2 April

1854. He became a Member of the Royal College of Surgeons in 1878 and joined the Cape Yeomanry in August 1880. A few months later, he was one of a handful of men who escaped with their lives after an unexpected attack on their regiment by the Basuto Cavalry. This occurred as the 1st Capes attempted to relieve Colonel Carrington and his force of 200 Cape Mounted Rifles, who by that stage had been besieged for six weeks at Mafeteng.

In early January 1881, Carrington again engaged with the Basutos, this time at Tweefontein. Several confrontations led to heavy casualties on both sides. Amid the heat of battle on 14 January, McCrea performed heroically, as the *London Gazette* recorded:

> after the enemy had charged the burghers in the most determined manner, forcing them to retire with the loss of sixteen killed and twenty-one wounded, Surgeon McCrea went out for some distance, under a heavy fire, and, with the assistance of Capt Buxton, of the Mafeteng Contingent, conveyed a wounded burgher named Aircamp to the shelter of a large ant-heap, and, having placed him in a position of safety, returned to the ambulance for a stretcher. Whilst on his way thither Surgeon McCrea was severely wounded in the right breast by a bullet, notwithstanding which he continued afterwards to attend the wounded during the remainder of the day, and scarcely taking time to dress his own wound, which he was obliged to do himself, there being no other medical officer in the field. Had it not been for this gallantry and his devotion to duty on the part of Surgeon McCrea, the sufferings of the wounded would undoubtedly have been much aggravated and greater loss of life might very probably have ensued.

McCrea, who sported a bushy moustache, is one of very few people to receive no other medal, save for the VC. The campaign medal for the conflict – the Basuto War Medal – was issued some twenty years later, but by then McCrea had died, on 16 July 1894 in Kokstad, East Griqualand, aged forty.

The Matabeleland Rebellion

Matabeleland is a region in the west and south-west of modern-day Zimbabwe, between the Limpopo and Zambezi rivers. It is named after its inhabitants, the Ndebele people, who took control of the area in 1834 after being pushed out of other parts of southern Africa. The rebellion by tribesmen against their colonial 'masters' was suppressed by the British in 1896.

It led to the award of two VCs, one of which is in the trust's collection.

TROOPER FRANK WILLIAM BAXTER
Army (Local Forces): Bulawayo Field Force

DATE OF BRAVERY: 22 APRIL 1896
GAZETTED: 7 MAY 1897 AND 15 JANUARY 1907

Frank Baxter was born in Woolwich, south-east London, on 29 December 1869 and emigrated to South Africa in 1887. He accompanied the Pioneer Column into Rhodesia (now Zimbabwe) in 1890, was discharged the following year, and then began farming at Umtali. He also had several mining interests in and around Bulawayo, and was a member of Grey's Scouts, a local defence force. During the Matabeleland Rebellion, he was part of Captain Bisset's patrol that went to confront the rebels, who had grouped on the Umguza River, some five miles from the centre of Bulawayo.

The battle, which took place on 22 April 1896, was the fourth attempt to defeat the rebels. It was ultimately successful, but it cost Baxter and several others their lives, while many more were wounded. The Scouts managed to drive away the rebels, but as they pursued them they were suddenly fired upon by some warriors hiding in the bush. One of Baxter's fellow-troopers was shot in the back and fell to the ground, but Baxter immediately dismounted, put his injured comrade on his own horse and sent them to safety. That left Baxter standing alone with the rebels in the bush firing at him from very close range. Several of the Scouts attempted to rescue him, but he was eventually shot in the side and killed by the rebels.

Baxter had made the ultimate sacrifice: he had given up his own life to save a comrade. At the time, though, it was impossible to win the VC posthumously. However, that would soon change, and Baxter was one of the six men gazetted in 1907 for acts of bravery that had occurred the previous century. His cross was subsequently sent to his father.

The Second Boer War

The Second Boer War – generally known simply as the Boer War – was fought at the turn of the twentieth century between the British Empire and the two independent Boer republics: the Orange Free State and the South African Republic (the Transvaal). After a long and hard-fought campaign, the two republics were defeated and were absorbed into the British Empire. The war cost around 75,000 lives, including 22,000 British soldiers.

After the discovery of gold in the Transvaal, thousands of British and other prospectors and settlers streamed over the border from the Cape Colony as well as further afield. Johannesburg sprang up and there were tensions between the newcomers and locals. There was gamesmanship too between Joseph Chamberlain, Britain's Colonial Secretary, and the leaders of the Orange Free State and the Transvaal.

War was declared on 11 October 1899, with the Boers striking first by invading Cape Colony and Natal Colony before the end of January 1900. In a period known as Black Week, 10 to 15 December 1899, the British forces led by General Redvers Buller suffered devastating losses at Magersfontein, Stormberg and Colenso. The Boers also besieged the towns of Ladysmith, Mafeking and Kimberley, where the townspeople all suffered terrible hardship.

There were further defeats for the British in the first five weeks of 1900, but when reinforcements arrived on 14 February troops under the command of Field Marshal Lord Roberts launched a series of successful counter-offensives. Kimberley was relieved the very next day, and there were further victories before the relief of Ladysmith. However, it was the relief of Mafeking in May that prompted the biggest celebrations in Britain. As 250,000 British troops, under the overall command of Lord Kitchener, gained control of both republics, the enemy resorted to guerrilla tactics, while the British built large-scale concentration camps to hold refugees, including women and children, created by their 'scorched earth' policy. The war rumbled on until the Boers finally conceded defeat in 1902.

Seventy-eight VCs were awarded during the Boer War, of which the trust owns fifteen.

CAPTAIN (LATER BRIGADIER GENERAL) CHARLES FITZCLARENCE

Army: the Royal Fusiliers

DATE OF BRAVERY: 14 OCTOBER–26 DECEMBER 1899
GAZETTED: 6 JULY 1900

Charles 'Fitz' FitzClarence, a brilliant, fearless soldier, was born in Bishopscourt, County Kildare, on 8 May 1865. His paternal grandfather, George, 1st Earl of Munster, was the eldest of five illegitimate sons born to King William IV by his mistress, 'Mrs Jordan', while his father and uncles all served in the Army or Navy. FitzClarence was educated at Eton and Wellington colleges before becoming a lieutenant in the Royal Fusiliers on 10 November 1886. Later, he was 'grievously disappointed' to miss active service in Egypt, while his twin brother, yet another soldier from the FitzClarence family, made the trip. Tragically, he was killed at Abu Hamed in 1897. The following year, Charles was promoted to captain and was sent on 'special duty' to South Africa. After the outbreak of the Boer War in 1899, he quickly distinguished himself on the battlefield, winning his VC for three separate acts of bravery during the siege of Mafeking, which lasted from October 1899 to May 1900.

On 14 October 1900, FitzClarence was in command of a squadron from the Protectorate Regiment, consisting of only partially trained men who had never seen action, when it was sent to the assistance of an armoured train which had left Mafeking. The squadron was surrounded by a far larger force of enemy soldiers and it looked as if they would be massacred. FitzClarence, however, showing coolness and courage, inspired his men so they not only relieved the train but inflicted a heavy defeat on the Boers, who lost fifty men and had many others wounded. The *London Gazette* said: 'The moral effect of this blow had a very important bearing on subsequent encounters with the Boers.'

Thirteen days later, FitzClarence was leading his men into action again. This time his squadron traversed the open space from Mafeking to make a night-time attack on the enemy's trenches. The sortie was so secret that not even the army doctor was told, although he was warned that he must have an ambulance ready for the wounded. There was hand-to-hand fighting in the enemy trench and FitzClarence, the first man into it, killed four men with his sword, beheading one with a clean blow. The British force was also firing on the enemy from the rear and the Boers suffered a heavy defeat, while the squadron had only six men killed and nine wounded. FitzClarence was twice wounded but was saved from serious injury by his compass case.

Major Robert Baden-Powell, later the founder of the Scout Movement, said of the two incidents in October that had it not been for FitzClarence's 'extraordinary spirit and fearlessness, the attacks would have been failures, and we should have suffered heavy loss both in men and prestige'.

On Boxing Day 1899, FitzClarence distinguished himself yet again during the action at Game Tree, near Mafeking, despite being seriously injured by a bullet which passed through both his legs.

The siege was finally raised by Colonel Mahon on 17 May 1900. By then, FitzClarence was considered so brave and dashing that he had been nicknamed the 'Demon of Mafeking' or simply the 'Demon', a sobriquet which stuck until his death. He served as a brigade major in South Africa from August 1900 to February 1901 and was mentioned in dispatches, receiving the Queen's Medal with three clasps and becoming a brevet major on 29 November 1900. He was transferred to the Irish Guards on their formation, and from 1903 to 1905 was brigade major to the 5th Brigade at Aldershot. In 1909, he succeeded to the command of the 1st Battalion Irish Guards, and four years later was given the command of the regiment and regimental district, positions he held until the outbreak of the Great War.

In September 1914, he was handed the command of the 1st (Guards) Brigade, 1st Division, in France, with the rank of Brigadier General. The following month, the Germans launched a fierce attack on the British Expeditionary Force at

Pilckem, north of Ypres. The Scots Guards lost 10 officers and had a further 370 men killed or wounded. However, the Germans also suffered heavy losses and the line was held until the end of the month, when the Welsh Guards and the Queen's were shelled out of their trenches before the Battle of Gheluvelt. The position was lost at 11.45 a.m. on 31 October, yet at noon FitzClarence decided that the last of his reserves – the surviving half of the 2nd Battalion – must be thrown in to prevent an overwhelming defeat. He personally rode over to the Worcesters and ordered Major E.B. Hankey to advance and retake Gheluvelt. The Worcesters were fearless and determined, and eventually drove the Germans from the village. Hankey later said: 'I feel perfectly certain that by shoving us in at the time and place he did, the General saved the day.'

However, by 8 November, the Germans were attacking again. Two days later, the Prussian Guard, the pride of the Kaiser's army and thirteen battalions strong, advanced, their officers with drawn swords. There were huge casualties on both sides as the 1st (Guards) Brigade was forced out of its trenches. At 3 a.m. on 12 November, FitzClarence began the operation to try to retake these trenches. He ordered the Guards to move up in cold rain and thick mud and with little idea of where the enemy was positioned. It was a dangerous mission and one officer said: 'We're going in nine wickets down with a sprung bat.' FitzClarence, now aged forty-nine, was at the head of his men. They advanced steadily until a man at the rear of the Guards fired his rifle into the air, thereby betraying their position and causing the enemy to open fire. FitzClarence halted his men and advanced alone. The column then heard more firing and tentatively advanced again. A little later, they found FitzClarence lying on the ground. Three men carried his body back to safety, but the 'Demon' had had his final brush with the enemy.

CORPORAL (LATER BUGLE MAJOR) JOHN DAVID FRANCIS SHAUL

Army: 1st Battalion, the Highland Light Infantry

DATE OF BRAVERY: 11 DECEMBER 1899
GAZETTED: 28 SEPTEMBER 1900

John Shaul was born in King's Lynn on 11 September 1873, the son of Sergeant John Shaul of the Royal Scots. He was educated at the Duke of York's School in Chelsea, and at the age of fifteen joined the 1st Battalion, Highland Light Infantry. In 1898, he served in Crete, then went with his regiment to South Africa the following year.

He won his VC while serving as a corporal bandsman, his official role during battles being command of the battalion's stretcher-bearers. The Battle of Magersfontein came about as a result of the British forces' attempt to clear a path through the Boer lines. However, the British met fierce resistance all day on 11 December 1899 and were ultimately repulsed at a cost of nearly 1,000 men killed, wounded or missing, 700 of them from the Highlanders.

However, Shaul performed magnificently in the battle, showing courage far beyond anything that anyone could have expected. The *London Gazette* reported:

> Corporal Shaul was observed . . . to perform several specific acts of bravery. [He] was in charge of stretcher-bearers; but at one period of the battle he was seen encouraging his men to advance across the open. He was most conspicuous during the day in dressing men's wounds, and in one case he came, under a heavy fire, to a man who was lying wounded in the back, and, with the utmost coolness and deliberation, sat down beside the wounded man and proceeded to dress the wound. Having done this, he got up and went quietly

to another part of the field. This act of gallantry was performed under a continuous and heavy fire, as coolly and quietly as if there had been no enemy near.

Shaul was presented with his VC on 11 August 1901 at Pietermaritzburg by the Duke of Cornwall, the future George V. He was later promoted to band sergeant and in 1903–4 served in Egypt and the Sudan. He then went to India before leaving the Army in 1909, having completed twenty-one years' service. He emigrated to South Africa in 1910 and initially worked in the East Rand Proprietary Goldmine in Boksburg; he also joined the Imperial Light Horse as a bandmaster. After the outbreak of the Great War, he enlisted and served with the 5th South African Infantry in East Africa in 1916 before being invalided out with dysentery later in the year. In 1948, he finally retired from the East Rand Proprietary Goldmine after nearly four decades with the company. He died on 14 September 1953.

CAPTAIN (LATER MAJOR GENERAL) HAMILTON LYSTER REED

Army: 7th Battery, Royal Field Artillery

DATE OF BRAVERY: 15 DECEMBER 1899
GAZETTED: 2 FEBRUARY 1900

Hamilton Reed, who was born in Dublin on 23 May 1869, was the son of Sir Andrew Reed, the Inspector General of the Royal Irish Constabulary. He was also the nephew of Harry Lyster, who won a VC in 1858 during the Indian Mutiny. Only three uncle-and-nephew teams have won the VC, and the trust owns the decorations of this pair. Reed joined the Royal Field Artillery in 1888 and was promoted to captain in 1898. He served in South Africa from 1899 to 1901, took part in numerous actions and was mentioned in dispatches three times. It was for his courage at Colenso that he won the VC.

On 15 December 1899, the British relief expedition for Ladysmith, under the command of Sir Redvers Buller, arrived at the Tugela River at Colenso. The enemy, which had managed to conceal itself, ambushed the British troops and brought a heavy fire down on the men. The British response was to order a frontal attack over open ground. Meanwhile, the guns of the 14th and 66th Field Batteries were attacked by a second, concealed Boer force. There was no route available for a withdrawal and it looked as if both batteries would be lost, so volunteers were called for to help save the guns.

Reed had heard what was going on and had already brought down three teams of men from his 7th Battery to see if they could be of use. They agreed to ride out and try to save the guns from falling into the hands of the Boers, but the shell and rifle fire that they met was intense. Reed and five of the other fourteen men were wounded, as were thirteen of their horses, including Reed's. When a further horse was killed, the men were forced to abandon their mission. Six men eventually received the VC for their actions at Colenso (see following entries for Roberts and Schofield), with Reed accepting his from Buller at Ladysmith on 18 March 1900.

He went on to serve with distinction in the First World War, and his decorations included the Order of the Bath (military division), the Order of St Michael and St George, and the French Legion of Honour and Croix de Guerre. He was mentioned in dispatches eight times and was promoted to major general in 1919. He died in London in March 1931.

†LIEUTENANT THE HON FREDERICK HUGH SHERSTON ROBERTS

Army: the King's Royal Rifle Corps

DATE OF BRAVERY: 15 DECEMBER 1899
GAZETTED: 2 FEBRUARY 1900

CAPTAIN (LATER LIEUTENANT COLONEL) HARRY NORTON SCHOFIELD

Army: Royal Field Artillery

DATE OF BRAVERY: 15 DECEMBER 1899
GAZETTED: 30 AUGUST 1901

Frederick Roberts, whose bravery led to the VC becoming a posthumous award, was born in Umballa, India, on 8 January 1872. He was the son of Field Marshal Earl Roberts, who himself had won the VC for bravery during the Indian Mutiny. Roberts Jnr entered the King's Royal Rifle Corps on 10 June 1891, aged 19, and for the next four years was on active service on the North-West Frontier, India, where he received several medals and clasps and was mentioned in dispatches.

Harry Schofield, the recipient of one of the most controversial VCs ever awarded, was born in Audenshaw, near Ashton-under-Lyne, Lancashire, on 29 January 1865. He entered the Royal Artillery via the Royal Military Academy, Woolwich, in 1884, and was promoted to captain in 1893. Six years later, he became aide-de-camp to General Sir Redvers Buller, the commander of the 1st Army Corps, and accompanied the general to South Africa after the outbreak of the Boer War. On arrival, Buller and his staff went to Natal, where a force of 20,000 men and five field batteries was awaiting them. Their initial task was to relieve Ladysmith, but first they had to cross the heavily defended Tugela River at Colenso. This was proving difficult enough, but then news arrived of the Boers' assault on the guns of the 14th and 66th Field Batteries. At this point, three men showed incredible courage, emerging as 'one of the most gallant trios ever to win the Victoria Cross' by riding to the batteries in a bid to rescue the guns. They were Roberts, Schofield and Captain Walter Congreve of the Rifle Brigade.

Schofield, who kept a pocket diary during the Boer War, later wrote:

> We went to the back donga [gully] where all the horses and drivers were, which was under a hot fire and the General personally tried to get some of them (men and horses) out to try and recover the guns but there were no officers there; so General and Congreve (RB) and self set to work to get some out and we got two teams and a corporal and hooked in the teams to limbers [two-wheeled ammunition carriers] just in front; doing this was no easy matter as it was rather difficult without NCOs to get men on foot to come and help to hook in; Gerard was coming out when I shouted to him to send me a man or two to help; we got the teams hooked in somehow, I forget how (except I saw Congreve doing his) and then I started off at a gallop with the limbers for the two guns on the right and Roberts, 60th, joined in; also Congreve came on tho' I did not find this out til after; the impression I had going on was galloping on a carpet spotted thick with spots, it was a very hot fire; after we had gone about 400 yards young Roberts on my left was shot and fell backwards, he had just before been looking at me and smiling, waving his stick in a circular motion like one does one's crop sometimes when one goes away from covert, thinking to have a good burst; Congreve tells me he himself was shot before this and also his

horse and the latter plunging badly, threw him; so the Corporal and self were left.

When on the way, I saw the lead driver of the right guns riding very wildly; I shouted to him to keep his horse in hand, which I think took them off thinking of the bullets, as it did me a little; on getting to the guns I howled out 'wheel about on your guns', which they did quite splendidly, as if on parade; Corp. Nurse and self jumped off our horses and ran to hook on the guns, I found mine rather too far to drag up alone so told the Corporal to come up and help me, which he did and then he put his own gun on which was just in the right place; while he was doing this my wheel driver turned round and said 'elevate the muzzle Sir', which I did; they all kept their heads most admirably; we then mounted, galloped for the centre sunken road running across the far donga and I left them in a place of safety some way behind; after crossing the donga a spent bullet hit me on the thigh, only a tap and didn't leave a mark. Corporal Nurse, drivers Henry Taylor, Young, Potts, Rockall, Lucas, Williams, all of the 66th battery were not touched; 3 or 4 horses got hit; luckily not enough to make them falter or we should not have got off that particular plain I think.

Congreve, who had crawled into the donga, then returned to the stricken Roberts and pulled him to shelter. Roberts survived for several hours but eventually died from his injuries. Two more attempts were made to retrieve the remaining guns but Buller was eventually forced to accept their loss.

Less than two months later, on 2 February 1900, and on Buller's recommendation, four men were awarded the VC for their bravery on 15 December, including Roberts, who therefore became the first man to receive the medal post-humously. Nineteen others received the Distinguished Conduct Medal, while Schofield was awarded the Distinguished Service Order (DSO). In justifying his actions, Buller said: 'I have differentiated in my recommendations because I thought that a Victoria Cross required proof of initiative, something more in fact than mere obedience to orders.' He concluded that Schofield, though courageous, had merely followed orders.

As has been detailed earlier, Roberts' VC aroused intense debate because he seemed to have received preferential treatment on account of who his father was. But there was another element to the controversy: Schofield seemed to have been treated unfairly in comparison with his fellow-officers, including Roberts. The press started a campaign on his behalf, highlighting his gallant actions and identifying him as the officer who had actually saved the guns. A letter from his stud groom dated February 1900 summed up the mood of dissatisfaction: 'I think it's a great shame you did not get the VC, perhaps you will get it yet. I hope you will. Everyone says you ought to have it.' The groom enclosed several newspaper cuttings, one of which referred to the 'Missing VC'. Around this time, Schofield himself was bitterly disappointed because he had assumed that he had been recommended for a VC. His diary entry for 4 March 1900 reads: 'Very angry and I must admit the dispatch astonishes me very much indeed.'

Eventually, the tide of public opinion won the day. On 30 August 1901, Schofield was awarded his long-overdue VC (his DSO was cancelled). He had been promoted to major the previous year, but retired from the Army in December 1905. However, he returned to the Colours during the First World War, ending up as a commandant of the lines of communication in France and Flanders. He finally left the service for good in 1918 with the rank of lieutenant colonel and died in London on 10 October 1931.

SERGEANT (LATER LIEUTENANT) HORACE ROBERT MARTINEAU

South African Forces: Protectorate Regiment (North-West Cape Colony)

DATE OF BRAVERY: 26 DECEMBER 1899
GAZETTED: 6 JULY 1900

TROOPER HORACE EDWARD RAMSDEN

South African Forces: Protectorate Regiment (North-West Cape Colony)

DATE OF BRAVERY: 26 DECEMBER 1899
GAZETTED: 6 JULY 1900

Horace Martineau was born in Bayswater, London, on 31 October 1874 and enlisted in the 11th Hussars at the age of sixteen. The next year he set off for Natal with his regiment. He was then stationed at Rawalpindi, India, from 1892 until 1895, when he bought his discharge and returned to South Africa. But that was far from the end of his military career: he served in the Matabele Rebellion of 1896 with Colonel Robert Baden-Powell, then in the Cape Police and, after the outbreak of the Boer War, as a volunteer in the Protectorate Regiment.

Horace Ramsden, one of only four men to receive the VC for saving the life of his brother, was born in Chester on 15 December 1879. His family emigrated to the Cape Colony in 1891, settling in Cape Town, and while there Horace and his younger brother Alfred completed their education at St George's Grammar School. Horace was seventeen when he joined Prince Alfred's Own Cape Volunteer Artillery and saw action as the battery's cook in the Langeberg Campaign in

Bechuanaland during 1896–7. Two years later, he enlisted in the new Protectorate Regiment, which was raised for the defence of Mafeking. However, he was upset that his brother wanted to join him in the regiment, a view shared by their mother who, when she learned that Alfred was enlisting, searched a troop train in order to try to get him to stay at home. Alfred hid beneath a seat to avoid his frantic mother, and the brothers were duly enrolled as Troopers 87 and 88 of C Squadron.

Mafeking was besieged by 10,000 Boers from 13 October 1899, but Baden-Powell's force of just 745 men was able to hold out due to superior firepower from its modern artillery. Then, on 18 November, Commandant General 'Piet' Cronje took two-thirds of his men to besiege nearby Kimberley. As a consequence, Baden-Powell planned an audacious attack on the reduced Boer force, reasoning that Boxing Day would be the best date due to the fact that many of the besiegers who were left would be given a pass to take a Christmas break. News of the attack leaked, however, and the enemy was waiting when 260 men from C and D squadrons of the Protectorate Regiment attacked the fort on Game Tree Hill at dawn. British casualties were heavy: 24 killed, 23 wounded and 3 missing. Men started to drop 200 yards from the fort, and even when some had reached their target they were milling around because they could not gain entry. Nothing less than a slaughter followed: two-thirds of the sixty men from C Squadron, including their commanding officer, lay dead or wounded. The command to retreat to a nearby armoured train was given, but too late.

However, amid the carnage, there were some fine examples of individual bravery, and none better than those shown by Martineau and Ramsden. After the order had been given to withdraw from the fort, Martineau saw that a comrade,

Corporal Le Camp, had been shot and wounded some ten yards from the base. Initially, Martineau managed to half drag, half carry the injured man to a bushy area some 150 yards away, where he staunched the bleeding and bandaged the corporal's wounds, despite being hit by a bullet in his own side. As the enemy kept up a relentless fire, Martineau then set off again but was shot a second time and sank to the ground, unable to carry the corporal any further. Finally, he was shot a third time, this time so seriously that his left arm had to be amputated at the shoulder.

Another of the many casualties was Alfred Ramsden, who had been shot and seriously wounded only ten yards from the Boer parapet. He later described the mayhem, and his brother's courageous response to the crisis:

> I was shot through both legs. My elder brother, Trooper Horace Ramsden, then came to me and lay down and made me roll myself back. He then carried me for a long way, putting me off [his back] to rest three or four times, til we met some men of D Squadron who then helped him to carry me to the Armoured Train. He was quite exhausted from carrying me. I am sure that I owe my life to his having carried me away as there was no cover where I fell, and I should have been left exposed to the very heavy fire, which continued for a long time afterwards, if he had not done so. I begged him several times to leave me to die as my wounds were intensely painful, but he said I must come along and that he was determined to get me to safety.

Trooper Walter Dufton described how he looked around when he heard someone call to him. It was Horace Ramsden carrying his brother:

Lieutenant Edward St John Daniel won his VC for three separate acts of bravery in the Crimean War. He later became the first man – and, indeed, the only officer – to forfeit his medal for dishonourable conduct under Clause 15 of the original 1856 Warrant.

After winning his VC on a daring commando raid in 1855, Commander John Commerell gained successive promotions culminating in the rank of Admiral of the Fleet in 1892. This portrait shows him wearing his numerous medals in the rather haphazard manner of his day.

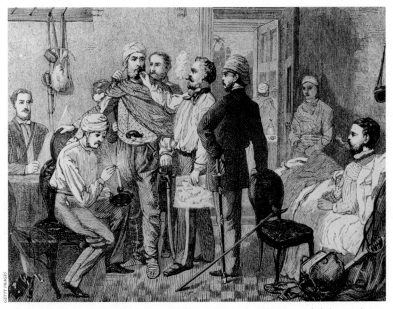

Mr Thomas Henry Kavanagh, one of only four civilians to have been awarded the VC, being disguised as a native Indian during the Indian Mutiny. He then slipped out of the Residency in Lucknow to locate the relief force camped outside the city and guide it back to the beleaguered garrison.

Lieutenant John Chard (*seated right, wearing medal*) shown relaxing with other officers of the Royal Engineers, in camp towards the end of the Zulu War in 1879.

This *Boy's Own Paper* illustration shows Lieutenant Walter Hamilton winning his VC leading a cavalry charge against a much larger enemy force at the battle of Futtehabad during the Afghan War in 1879.

'These Ruthvens are a daring race, renowned in Scottish History and in military annals.' Captain the Hon Alexander Hore-Ruthven was awarded his VC for saving the life of an Egyptian officer during the campaign in the Sudan in 1898. An extremely distinguished soldier who amassed a veritable chestful of awards, he crowned his long career as a highly successful Governor-General of Australia.

Captain Charles Fitzclarence was one of three men awarded the VC for the heroic Defence of Mafeking in 1899–1900. A fearless soldier descended from an illegitimate son of King William IV, 'Fitz' was killed in action in Flanders in 1914.

Recommended – unsuccessfully – for the VC on the Chitral Expedition in 1895, Lieutenant 'Frank' Maxwell finally won the medal in South Africa in 1900. An aide-de-camp to Lord Kitchener, with whom he got along famously well, Maxwell is shown here (*back row, second from right*) between the British commander and the Boer envoys at the conclusion of the Anglo–Boer War.

Midshipman Basil Guy was one of only two men to win the VC in China in 1900 during the so-called Boxer Rebellion. Later, during the Great War, Guy commanded one of the famous Q-ships that decoyed enemy submarines into capture and for which he was awarded the DSO.

Still managing a smile for the photographer despite his severe wounds, Captain John Liddell won his VC for an aerial battle over Ostend in 1915.

Belgian airmen attempting to extricate Liddell from his battered plane before the doctor arrived. He died a month later.

Private George Peachment was one of the youngest winners of the VC at only eighteen years of age. Despite his baby face, Peachment unhesitatingly risked his life to tend his wounded company commander during a withdrawal but was mortally wounded in the attempt.

Winner of the first VC ever awarded to an airman, Lieutenant William Rhodes-Moorhouse was fatally wounded during a bombing raid over Belgium and died from his injuries the next day.

One of the most celebrated incidents of multiple VCs awarded for the same action was the so-called 'Six Before Breakfast', won by men of the Lancashire Fusiliers during the ill-fated Gallipoli Landings on 25 April 1915. One of the famous six was Sergeant Alfred Richards, known as 'The Lonely VC' because he lived alone and had no family. He finally married the following year.

GALLIPOLI V.C. MARRIED.

Captain Noel Chavasse was the only man to win a double VC during the Great War. He risked his life to tend wounded men on the Western Front, firstly in August 1916 and again exactly a year later. On the second occasion he was severely wounded and succumbed to his own injuries shortly afterwards.

An early media star in the modern sense, Lieutenant 'Billy' Leefe-Robinson achieved instant celebrity when he shot down the first German airship over England on the night of 2/3 September 1916. The menace of the Zeppelin raids was causing widespread panic amongst the general public until Leefe-Robinson proved the airships were not invincible and became a national hero overnight. The Zeppelin relics *(top right)* are also in the Ashcroft VC Collection.

When plucky sixteen-year-old Jack Cornwell died at his gun on the deck of HMS Chester during the battle of Jutland, it seemed that the whole nation was consumed with grief at the loss of his young life.

Lance-Corporal Thomas Bryan, who won his VC for single-handedly silencing an enemy machine-gun near Arras in April 1917, receives his award from King George V at a field investiture.

When Major Stewart Loudoun-Shand won the VC rallying his men until he was mortally wounded on the first day of the battle of the Somme, his sacrifice as well as his achievement were both overshadowed by the carnage of 60,000 other casualties in those first hours of the bloodiest campaign of the war.

Over 6 feet tall and weighing 20 stones, Corporal Edward Foster, inevitably nicknamed 'Tiny' by his comrades, was awarded his VC for a daring attack on two enemy machine-guns in Flanders. A pre-war dustman with Wandsworth Borough Council, he was promoted after the war – as a mark of respect – to Dusting Inspector.

Looking far more apprehensive than when he won his VC in 1917, Petty Officer Ernest Pitcher here tries to make conversation with King George V, Queen Mary and the Dowager Queen Alexandra when the royal party visited a naval exhibition in 1918.

When Commander Daniel Beak won his VC fighting ashore with the Royal Naval Division in August/ September 1918, he was already an almost legendary figure who had previously been awarded a DSO and two MCs. Demobbed in 1919, he found civilian life so suffocating that he joined the Army and enjoyed a second military career culminating in his appointment as General Officer Commanding at Malta in 1942.

He asked me if I would take the rifle and bayonet he was carrying. He was about 20 yards away from me then and I was about to get up to go and help him, when he coolly laid his brother down and walked across to where I was lying and gave me the rifle. He then walked back to where his brother was lying, put him on his back again, and came along with me back to the Armoured Train carrying him . . . All the way I offered to help him but he said 'Never mind old man, you are utterly done yourself. I can manage all right.' I was completely exhausted. Trooper Horace Ramsden's coolness and bravery under the very heavy fire was wonderful. He seemed quite indifferent to it. The only thing he seemed to think about was his determination to carry his brother back to safety.

Ramsden had carried his younger brother perhaps half a mile on his back and thereby saved his life, although Alfred later had to have one of his legs amputated.

After losing his left arm, Martineau saw no further action in the Boer War and later worked for the government in Cape Town. Despite his handicap, though, he served in the Bambata Rebellion of 1906 and also worked for the African Boating Company. During the First World War, he was commissioned as a lieutenant and served in the Australian and New Zealand Army Corps (ANZAC) Transport Service at Suez and Gallipoli. However, he fell ill and was invalided to New Zealand. He died at Dunedin in April 1916.

Ramsden received his VC in October 1900 from Lord Roberts, his commander-in-chief, in Pretoria. He then returned home to Woodstock, Cape Town, where he was fêted by locals during his short spell of leave and attended a reception hosted by the mayor. He was also promoted to lieutenant in Lord Roberts' bodyguard and then served in the

Johannesburg Mounted Rifles until the end of the Boer War in 1902. Thereafter, he lived in Grahamstown while serving as a member of the South African Police, and was a corporal during the First World War in Hartigan's Horse, seeing action during the German South-West African Campaign. In April 1915, he was captured by the enemy at Hunsat but was released in July and returned to police duties. He died in Wynberg, Cape Town, on 3 August 1948.

PRIVATE (LATER SERGEANT) ALBERT EDWARD CURTIS

Army: 2nd Battalion, the East Surrey Regiment

DATE OF BRAVERY: 23 FEBRUARY 1900
GAZETTED: 15 JANUARY 1901

Albert Curtis, one of the few men to write in detail about how he won his VC, was born in Guildford, Surrey, on 6 January 1866. His act of bravery took place in General Sir Redvers Buller's final attempt to relieve the siege at Ladysmith. During this action, the East Surreys' charge at Wynne's Hill was repelled by the Boers and the British force was driven back, which meant that the wounded lay where they had fallen, close to the Boer trenches. Colonel Harris, the regiment's commanding officer, was one of those lying injured in full view of the enemy. After at least two unsuccessful attempts, Curtis finally managed to reach the colonel, bound his wounds and gave him his flask, all under heavy fire. He then sought the assistance of another comrade, Private T.W. Morton, and they tried to move the officer to shelter. The colonel, who feared both men would be killed, urged them to leave him but they refused and managed to get him to safety. Immediately after the battle, Curtis and Morton reported back to their company but neither mentioned the courageous act they had performed.

As a result, it was another eight months before Curtis was recommended for the VC, after Colonel Harris's successor investigated the incident. Morton was also recommended for the medal, but it was decided that his role was secondary, so he received a Distinguished Conduct Medal instead.

Curtis must have been asked for his version of events once he had been tracked down and identified as the hero of the day. The resulting handwritten testimony is still in existence, and while it may not be grammatically perfect, it provides a vivid account of the horrors of the Boer War:

> Just as we rose from our cover the Boers put in a most deadly fire you couldn't see nothing but men being knocked over. Then someone gave the order to get under cover so we dropped down where we were and behind any stone that was near us. All day some of the chaps tried to get away but every time they rose they would go a few yards and be knocked over. I saw Lt. Hinton go to where I knew the Colonel was laying. He had no sooner got to him than he was shot dead. I did not know the Colonel was wounded at this time but about four in the afternoon I heard someone groaning in the direction where the Colonel was laying so [I] came to the conclusion that he was wounded. So I rose up from my cover and made for the Colonel but had to get under cover again as the fire became too heavy and the way I got to whim [*sic*] was to dodge from stone to stone until I reached him. I asked him if he was hurt and he said I am hit all over the body but he said who are you and I said one of your own Regiment come to try and get you away. I then sat him up but he was too weak to remain. So I called Pte. Morton of the same Regt. to help me he came at once and between us we managed to get him back up and took a handkerchief from his breast pocket and

tied his right arm close to his body and then tried to make a stretcher with our rifles but did not have time so [we] put our hands together and made a chair and the Colonel put his left arm around my neck to steady himself and we then carried him back to a place where some more of our Regiment was. Myself and Morton had to go back for our equipment and rifles and went back to where the Colonel was lying. I then told Morton to look after the Colonel while I looked about for a stretcher. I was away about half an hour. When I came back they were just taking the Colonel away on a stretcher belonging to the Queen's Regiment.

Curtis was presented with his VC at Pietermaritzburg on 14 August 1901. Nine years later, he became a yeoman warder at the Tower of London, a position he held for the next twenty-one years. He died in Barnet, Hertfordshire, on 28 March 1940.

SERGEANT JAMES FIRTH

Army: 1st Battalion, the Duke of Wellington's (West Riding) Regiment
DATE OF BRAVERY: 24 FEBRUARY 1900
GAZETTED: 11 JUNE 1901

James Firth was born in Jarrow, County Durham, on 15 January 1874 and joined the Army in July 1889. He had been promoted to Sergeant by the time the Boer War broke out. In recommending Firth for his VC, Lieutenant Umfreville of the 1st West Riding Company, 15th Mounted Infantry, described the scene:

On the 24th February 1900, in the vicinity of Plewman's Farm, six miles N.W. of Arundel, Cape Colony, the 1st

West Riding Mounted Infantry Company had driven the Boers out of one range of koppies [low hills] and followed them up to another – but arriving at the crest of this second range they found themselves under a very heavy fire from higher koppe's [*sic*] to their direct front and also their right and left fronts from a vastly superior force. No. 4673 Lance-Corpl. Blackman was hit just over the crest and lay exposed to the enemy's fire (at a range of 4 to 500 [yards]). Sergt. Firth picked him up and carried him under the shelter of the rocks.

Shortly afterwards, the enemy attempted to rush our position, covered by the fire from the dominating koppe's [*sic*], they reached the ridge and 2nd Lieut. Wilson (now Lieut.) was shot thro' the head in a most exposed place. Sergt. Firth carried him over the crest to shelter, but was himself shot thro' the nose and eye and fell beside his Officer – the remains of his eye had to be subsequently removed.

Firth, who wore an eyepatch for the rest of his life, died in Sheffield on 29 May 1921.

DRIVER HORACE HENRY GLASOCK

Army: Q Battery, Royal Horse Artillery

DATE OF BRAVERY: 31 MARCH 1900
GAZETTED: 26 JUNE 1900

Henry Glasock was born in Islington, north London, on 16 October 1880. At the age of just nineteen he was at Korn Spruit in South Africa with two batteries of the Royal Horse Artillery, travelling from Thabanchu towards Bloemfontein. This British force was ambushed by the enemy with the loss of most of the baggage column and five out of the six guns of the leading battery. When the alarm was raised, Q Battery went into action some 1,150 yards from the spruit (a small watercourse) until the order to retire was received. At this point, the major commanding the battery ordered the guns and their limbers (two-wheeled ammunition carriers) to be run back by hand to a safe place. This was an incredibly dangerous and exhausting task, performed by Glasock and several others. It was not until all but one of the guns and one limber had been moved to safety that the battery was re-formed. Four separate attempts were then made to rescue the final gun and limber but they eventually had to be abandoned.

It was decided that all members of Q Battery had been equally courageous, so their heroism was treated as a case of collective gallantry under the thirteenth rule of the Victoria Cross Warrant. Glasock, whose name was decided by ballot, was one of the four men chosen from the battery to receive the decoration. He was discharged from the Royal Horse Artillery on 25 January 1911 and died in South Africa on 13 February 1920.

LIEUTENANT (LATER BRIGADIER GENERAL) FRANCIS AYLMER MAXWELL

Army: Indian Staff Corps, attached to Roberts' Light Horse
DATE OF BRAVERY: 31 MARCH 1900
GAZETTED: 8 MARCH 1901

Francis Maxwell was born in Guildford, Surrey, on 7 September 1871, the son of Surgeon-Major Thomas Maxwell. He was educated at Sandhurst and joined the Royal Sussex Regiment in India in 1891. He served on the subcontinent for four years before being attached to the Guides Infantry in time for the Chitral Expedition. At one point on this expedition, after some confusion over orders, Lieutenant Colonel Frederick Battye and his troops advanced too far into enemy territory – away from the main British force – and were confronted by an enemy contingent of up to 10,000 men. As he attempted to withdraw amid intense fighting, the colonel received a serious gunshot wound. Maxwell and his comrades dragged him from the battlefield but he later died from his injuries. Maxwell was recommended for the VC for this act of bravery, but this was turned down. Instead, he was presented with the Distinguished Service Order from Queen Victoria at Windsor Castle in June 1898. By then, he had earned a reputation as a cavalryman who 'never lost an opportunity of putting to the test his exceptional skill in swordsmanship, mounted combat, and shooting'. In January 1900, he volunteered to serve in the Boer War and was attached to an irregular unit – Roberts' Light Horse.

Once in South Africa he immediately covered himself in glory on the battlefield. At Korn Spruit, he came across a force commanded by Brigadier General Broadwood which was retreating under a ferocious enemy attack after being ambushed. 'My Squadron was leading,' he later informed his mother, 'when about a quarter of a mile from the stream, an excited man galloped up and said the Boers were right in the wagons disarming our men . . . I galloped up to the wagons and sure enough, without the smallest noise or confusion, were Boers, thick as peas, collecting arms from our men. There was no mistake, for I almost rode one swine over.' He was soon in the midst of fierce fighting as he tried to save the British guns from falling into enemy hands. On five separate occasions, he went out to recover two guns and three limbers. In one instance, Maxwell, another officer and some gunners dragged a limber by hand. 'Never was anything more magnificent than the way these men fought,' Maxwell said later of his comrades. The ambush was a military disaster for the British, but the courage of Maxwell and the others was outstanding. This time the recommendation that he should receive the VC was approved, and he collected his decoration from the Duke of York at Pietermaritzburg in August 1901.

By then, Maxwell was serving as aide-de-camp to Lord Kitchener in South Africa. The two men got on famously well: Kitchener admired Maxwell's dashing and straight-talking manner so much that he affectionately called him the 'Brat'. After the war ended, Maxwell returned to England with Kitchener before accompanying him to India. Over the next twelve years, he worked in senior posts there, in Britain and in Australia. From 1910, he was military secretary to the Viceroy, Lord Hardinge, and his subsequent work in Australia prevented him from reaching Europe until two years after the start of the Great War.

Despite his cavalry background, in May 1916 he was given command of the 12th Middlesex Battalion, who were then building roads in France, a task said to have been 'mishandled' by a previous commanding officer. Maxwell, on the other hand, led the battalion with distinction at Trones Wood and later in the taking of Thiepval. For his outstanding leadership, he was given a bar to his DSO and command of the 18th (King George's Own) Lancers in October 1916. Soon afterwards, he was promoted to Brigadier General, commanding the 27th Infantry Brigade, 9th (Scottish) Division. At around this time, he wrote: 'I don't believe in running from shells . . . nor does bobbing appeal to me as being useful, while it certainly is quite undignified. If men are about, a pipe and upright posture show a better example.'

He was killed, aged forty-six, while on reconnaissance near Ypres, Belgium, on 21 September 1917. Two weeks later, his grieving Scots orderly movingly described his master's death in a letter to his widow:

We were from 80 to 100 yards in front of our front line. A Captain of the Scottish Rifles came along with us . . . The General was showing him the land . . . I was about five yards in front watching for any movement in shell-holes. I was lying flat with my rifle ready to shoot. The first bullet that was fired by the Huns went right into the ground below my left elbow. I shouted to the General to get down . . . He sat for about two minutes, then got up again to show what he was saying to the Captain, and was just opening his mouth to speak when he got shot. I caught him as he was falling, and jumped into a shell-hole with him. I held his head against my breast til it was all over. Madam, I cried til my heart was like to burst . . . He was a King among men.

CORPORAL (LATER LIEUTENANT COLONEL) FRANK HOWARD KIRBY

Army: Corps of Royal Engineers

DATE OF BRAVERY: 2 JUNE 1900
GAZETTED: 5 OCTOBER 1900

Frank Kirby was born in Thame, Oxfordshire, on 12 November 1871, and educated at Alleyn's School, Dulwich, south-east London. He entered the Royal Engineers on 8 August 1892 and later served throughout the Boer War. He was awarded the Distinguished Conduct Medal for blowing up the Bloemfontein Railway in March 1900, and just three months later he won the VC for his part in a raid north of Kronstadt with General Hunter Weston.

Near the Delagoa Bay Railway, the party was retreating while being pursued by a larger enemy force. One man whose horse had been shot was spotted running after his comrades, but he was a long way behind and under brisk fire as the enemy closed in on him. Suddenly Kirby rode out from the retiring troops in order to assist the desperate man. By the time he reached him, they were under even heavier fire, but he managed to get his comrade on to the back of his horse and they rode to safety. The *London Gazette* reported: 'This is the third occasion on which Corpl. Kirby has displayed gallantry in the face of the enemy.'

He became a warrant officer in December 1906, and in April 1911 was commissioned from the ranks. His first posting as an officer was to the Air Battalion, Royal Engineers, at Farnborough when it was still not known whether the aeroplane would be an effective weapon of war. The following year, he joined the Royal Flying Corps, becoming a squadron commander, and during the Great War he served in France during 1916 and 1917. He was promoted to captain and then to temporary lieutenant colonel before retiring. He died in Sidcup at the age of eighty-four.

SERGEANT (LATER LIEUTENANT COLONEL) BRIAN TURNER TOM LAWRENCE

Army: 17th (Duke of Cambridge's Own) Lancers
DATE OF BRAVERY: 7 AUGUST 1900
GAZETTED: 15 JANUARY 1901

Tom Lawrence was born in Bewdley, Worcestershire, on 21 October 1873 and educated at King Charles I's School in Kidderminster. At the age of twenty he enlisted into the Duke of Cambridge's Own Lancers, and was promoted to corporal in November 1897. He left for South Africa on the outbreak of the Boer War.

On arriving, Lawrence took part in operations in the Orange Free State in the first half of 1900, including actions at Vet River and Zand River. He then became involved in operations in the Transvaal, near Johannesburg, Pretoria and Diamond Hill. At daybreak on 7 August 1900, he and three other men were sent out on patrol near Essenbosch Farm. Lawrence and Private Hayman were scouting about two or three miles in front of the main force when they came under fire from a group of perhaps fourteen Boers. Hayman's horse was hit and fell, pinning the rider underneath and dislocating his shoulder. Lawrence dismounted, dragged Hayman from his injured mount and helped him on to his own horse. He then fastened the reins to the saddle, told Hayman to hold on for dear life, pointed the horse in the direction of the picket and gave it a kick to start it off. Once horse and rider had galloped away, Lawrence used his own rifle and Hayman's carbine to keep up a steady fire until his comrade was out of range. He then made a two-mile withdrawal by foot, firing regularly to deter the pursuing Boers. Captain D'Arcy Legard, also of the 17th Lancers, who had witnessed the incident, said that without the 'gallant conduct and ready comprehension of Sergt. Lawrence, Private Hayman would certainly have been captured by the enemy'.

In the remainder of the war, Lawrence took part in many more operations in Orange River Colony and Cape Colony, so it was over two years before he received his VC, on 12 August 1902, when Edward VII presented it to him in London. He became squadron sergeant-major at the Cavalry Depot, Canterbury, where he was given the nickname 'Posh' because it was said to reflect his character. After more than ten years in the ranks, he was appointed riding master in the 18th Hussars on 15 October 1904 and given the honorary rank of lieutenant. He was a fine horseman and became respected in competitive equestrianism, representing his country at the International Horse Show and the 1912 Olympic Games in Sweden, when he won a silver medal.

He served during the Great War but was badly wounded in the first few months of the conflict. However, he recovered sufficiently to work with the general staff. In April 1918, while serving with the Egyptian Expeditionary Force, he was mentioned in one of Major General Edmund Allenby's dispatches. Lawrence's name appeared on a list of those 'whose distinguished and gallant services and devotion to duty I consider deserving of special mention'. He received the brevet of major in 1917 and later was promoted to lieutenant colonel. In the early 1920s, he raised a Kurdish cavalry regiment and commanded a mobile column unit during operations in eastern Kurdistan. During the Second World War, he helped with the war effort and was made a Military Knight of Windsor in recognition of his various services for his country. He died in retirement in Nakuru, Kenya, on 7 June 1949.

LIEUTENANT (LATER MAJOR) ALEXIS CHARLES DOXAT

Army: 3rd Battalion, Imperial Yeomanry

DATE OF BRAVERY: 20 OCTOBER 1900
GAZETTED: 15 JANUARY 1901

Alexis Doxat was born in Surbiton, Surrey, on 9 April 1867 and educated at Norwich Grammar School and Philberd's, Maidenhead. He was working in the Stock Exchange at the outbreak of the Boer War in 1899 but left his job to travel to South Africa with Lord Scarborough's detachment. In May 1900 he took part in the advance of Lord Methuen's force from Boshof, and four months later he joined General Douglas's column as the commander's aide-de-camp, working largely as a reconnaissance officer.

The following month, near Zeerust, Doxat and a party of

mounted infantry were reconnoitring a position held by a hundred Boers on a ridge of small hills. When Doxat's group got to within 300 yards of the position, the enemy opened fire. The British were forced to retire but Doxat, seeing that one of his comrades had lost his horse, galloped back under heavy fire and brought the man to safety.

He received his VC from Edward VII at Marlborough House, London, on 17 December 1901, and died in Cambridge on 29 November 1942.

PRIVATE JOHN BARRY

Army: 1st Battalion, the Royal Irish Regiment

DATE OF BRAVERY: 7/8 JANUARY 1901
GAZETTED: 8 AUGUST 1902

John Barry was born in St Mary's, County Kilkenny, on 1 February 1873 and enlisted into the Royal Irish Regiment at the age of seventeen. He saw active service in India before being posted to South Africa.

On 7 January 1901, Major Orr's detachment at Monument Hill was relieved by Captain Fosbery, who was in command of his own A Company and D Company. Shortly before midnight, in dense fog, the ninety-three men in Fosbery's party came under attack, with eighteen of them in a gun sangar (lookout post) becoming involved in fierce hand-to-hand combat. The defenders used bayonets, picks and axes to fend off the enemy in what was described as 'the father and mother of a fight'. The action continued for half an hour before the Boers made a second rush in their attempt to get the Maxim gun that was in the sangar. Barry, though wounded, realised the enemy was about to capture the vital weapon, so he picked up an axe and smashed it into the breech of the gun, thus rendering it useless. As he did so, he was hit by a hail of bullets fired by a dozen burghers who were surrounding him. At the age of twenty-seven, he had died a hero.

Barry's posthumous VC was one of the six awarded by Edward VII on 8 August 1902 – two years after the controversy surrounding the decision to award a VC to the Hon Frederick Roberts, the son of Earl Roberts. Roberts Jnr had died just hours after the act of bravery that won him the medal and he therefore became the first ever posthumous VC. Barry's VC was sold in 2000 with a newspaper cutting of the announcement and some fascinating correspondence, including a letter written by Major General Smith-Dorrien, dated 12 January 1901, in which he said: 'Truly poor Barry died a noble death for his country's good.'

CORPORAL (LATER SERGEANT) JOHN JAMES CLEMENTS

South African Forces: Rimington's Guides

DATE OF BRAVERY: 24 FEBRUARY 1901
GAZETTED: 4 JUNE 1901

John Clements was born in Middleburg, Cape Colony, on 19 June 1872 and enlisted in Rimington's Guides at the age of twenty-seven. According to his commanding officer, Colonel Rimington, he was 'of splendid physique, a good boxer and always ready for a "scrap"'.

Clements was in a scouting party with six other men about five miles south of Strijdenburg when they heard that a group of Boers was near. They captured a man, who told them that five of the enemy were watching them from a koppie. Leaving one man in charge of the prisoner, the remaining six Guides charged the hill, but both Clements and the officer in command, Lieutenant Harvey, were badly injured in the attack. Clements had been shot through the lungs and was called on to surrender, yet he threw himself into the middle of the Boers and shot three of them, which caused the others to surrender to him.

Major General Bruce Hamilton proposed Clements for his VC:

> Lieut. Harvey . . . told me that when he and Clements were wounded there only remained two of his party against five unwounded Boers at close quarters, and that the former would probably have been obliged to surrender had not Clements with conspicuous courage and devotion, and although dangerously wounded, dashed amongst them and shot three of them with his revolver . . . I am very strongly of the opinion that this was an act for which the Victoria Cross should be awarded, and I strongly recommend it for the favourable consideration of the Commander-in-Chief.

After the Boer War, Clements became a farmer in Natal, but he enlisted in Botha's Scouts for the German South-West Africa Campaign at the beginning of the First World War and served there until the autumn of 1915. He then returned to farming and died in Newcastle, Natal, on 18 June 1937.

SERGEANT MAJOR (LATER LIEUTENANT) ALEXANDER YOUNG

South African Forces: Cape Mounted Police

DATE OF BRAVERY: 13 AUGUST 1901
GAZETTED: 8 NOVEMBER 1901

Alexander Young was born in Ballinona, County Galway, on 27 January 1873 and joined the 2nd Dragoon Guards (Queen's Bays) in May 1890. Thereafter, he established himself as the best rough rider in the British Army, which led to him performing equestrian feats for Queen Victoria. He went with his regiment to the Egyptian capital of Cairo and, while there, became a favourite of the Irish soldiery for his riding skills. He was undefeated in any contest of horsemanship, and Private O'Heir, of the 2nd Connaught Rangers, noted: 'Ringing Irish cheers always welcomed him to the arena, and enthusiastic outbursts cheered his prowess, and inspired his genius for daring feats of horsemanship to wonderful achievements which excelled anything ever beheld there on these great public occasions.' These achievements led to him being nicknamed the 'Terror'. However, when he returned to Canterbury, Kent, to take charge of a riding school, he received a severe kick from a temperamental horse and was forced to retire from the service.

He returned to Galway to live with his sister but soon became restless and set off for South Africa. At the outbreak of the Boer War, he was serving in the Cape Mounted Police and, because of his knowledge of the country and the enemy, was placed in command of a force covering a large district. He took part in many actions and was once shot in the leg but still managed to ride back to hospital.

He won his VC for bravery at Ruiter's Kraal. Together with a handful of men, he dislodged some twenty Boers, under Commandant Daniel Erasmus, from their koppies. The Boers sped back to another koppie but Young, who by now was alone, charged after them, firing at the gallop. He shot one of the enemy dead and then squared up to Erasmus at point-blank range. The Boer commander fired three rounds but missed with all of them, which enabled Young to overwhelm the enemy position single-handedly and take Erasmus prisoner.

After the war, Young remained in the Cape Police until 1906. Next he served in the suppression of the Herero Rebellion, which broke out in German territory. Although the Germans put down the unrest, they were unable to capture the rebel leader. However, Young apprehended him, which led one contemporary to comment that he 'did for the Germans in a week what they had failed to do for themselves in three years'. Young was awarded a special decoration by the Kaiser for this service – which he burned publicly in Cape Town after the outbreak of the Great War. He also served in the Zululand Rebellion, when he was again wounded, and for the next four years he finally started to live a quiet life, working as a farmer in Natal. However, he rejoined the Cape Mounted Police when De Wet's Rebellion broke out, serving as a regimental sergeant major, and was later commissioned first lieutenant in the 4th South African Mounted Rifles, taking part in General Smuts's successful expedition into German East Africa.

After demobilisation at Durban, Smuts called for 10,000 volunteers for the British forces in France. Typically, Young was one of the first to offer his services, and after being commissioned into the South African Scottish, he sailed for Europe. He visited his native Galway from his regiment's base in Aldershot and had clearly become something of a celebrity during his absence as he received a warm welcome. Soon he was fighting under Sir John Maxwell in Egypt against the Sudanese and the Turks. Back in Europe, he went to France with the South African Brigade to participate in the 'Big Push' on the first day of the Somme. Fifteen days later, he was wounded at Devil's Wood and was invalided to hospital in Brighton. Remarkably, though, he was back at the front in September. However, the *Galway Express*, which was always keen to write about its local hero, reported his death the following month: 'with the hardy boys from the veldt, now well inured to war . . . he kept the Hun on the move until the 19th [of October 1916] when he was killed, dying as he had lived on the battlefield, facing the foe'.

5

OTHER IMPERIAL CONFLICTS AROUND THE WORLD

While Britain was extensively engaged in India and southern Africa in the second half of the nineteenth century, her troops were also involved in a number of other spats – both large and small – mostly as a result of successive governments' expansionist policies. Many acts of bravery were performed in these theatres, and the trust now possesses several of the VCs that were awarded as a result.

The Maori Wars

In total, fifteen VCs were awarded in the two Maori Wars: the Taranaki War of 1860–1 (when two were earned); and the Waikato–Hauhau War of 1863–6 (for which thirteen were presented). The trust now owns three of these medals. These bloody conflicts were the result of Maori resentment over British expansion in New Zealand and the rapid rise in the number of British settlers in the islands around the middle of the nineteenth century.

LIEUTENANT (LATER COLONEL) ARTHUR FREDERICK PICKARD

Army: Royal Regiment of Artillery

DATE OF BRAVERY: 20 NOVEMBER 1863
GAZETTED: 22 SEPTEMBER 1864

Arthur Pickard was born in Forest Hill, Northamptonshire, on 12 April 1841 and served with the Royal Regiment of Artillery as part of a force that suppressed the Maori uprisings in New Zealand. He won his VC during an assault on the enemy's position at Rangiriri. Along with William Temple, an assistant surgeon in the regiment who was also awarded the medal, Pickard crossed to the entrance of the Maori Keep, a point upon which the enemy was concentrating its fire, in order to tend to wounded soldiers. In fact, he crossed and recrossed the parapet several times to fetch water for the wounded men, putting his life on the line on each occasion. The *London Gazette*, recording the VCs, said that 'testimony is borne to the coolness displayed by him and Assistant-Surgeon Temple under the trying circumstances to which they were exposed'.

Pickard later became a colonel, was created a Companion of the Bath (civil division), and was awarded the Order of Leopold from Austria and the Order of St Stanislaus from Russia. He worked as equerry to the Duke of Connaught and to Queen Victoria before dying from consumption in Cannes on 1 March 1880, aged just thirty-eight.

COLONEL (LATER MAJOR GENERAL AND SIR) JOHN CARSTAIRS McNEILL

Indian Army/Army: 107th Regiment (Bengal Infantry) later the Royal Sussex Regiment

DATE OF BRAVERY: 30 MARCH 1864
GAZETTED: 16 AUGUST 1864

John McNeill was born on Colonsay, Argyllshire, on 29 March 1831. He entered the Bengal Army in 1850. During the Indian Mutiny, he served as aide-de-camp to Sir Edward Lugard, with whom he took part in the final siege and capture of Lucknow. During a lull in military operations in March 1858, he and another officer were exploring the virtually deserted streets near the Kaiser Bagh when they were approached by a native Indian who informed them that two Englishwomen were in hiding near by. In fact, Annie Orr and Madelaine Jackson had been held for five months by the rebels. In a daring operation that captured the imagination of the British public, McNeill and his fellow-officer rescued the two women. Jackson, recalling the rescue twenty years later, wrote of hearing shells and cannonballs: 'I flew out to see what was happening and there was a tall Englishman! We were saved!' McNeill was twice mentioned in dispatches for his actions against the mutineers.

It was in the Maori War of 1863–6 that McNeill, by then a colonel, next saw active service, being mentioned no fewer than five times in dispatches and winning the VC. While acting as aide-de-camp to Sir Duncan Cameron, the commander-in-chief, he was tasked with taking a message to the commanding officer at Te Awamatu. McNeill and two privates delivered the message successfully, but on their return they encountered fifty Maoris. McNeill sent one of the privates for reinforcements, then retreated with the other private when the enemy attacked. However, as he galloped away, McNeill turned to see that the private had been thrown from his horse. Rather than saving himself, McNeill caught the runaway horse and returned, under heavy fire, to rescue the stricken private moments before the enemy reached him.

McNeill's adventures did not end there. On returning to the British Isles, he was appointed to the command of the Tipperary Flying Column, which stood in readiness during the Fenian Conspiracy of 1866–7. Then, as brevet lieutenant colonel, he was appointed military secretary to the Governor-General of Canada in 1868. He helped organise Garnet Wolseley's Red River Expedition in 1870, and was made a Companion of the Order of St Michael and St George for his efforts. His actions meant that when Wolseley was given the command of the Ashantee Expedition in West Africa in 1873, he chose McNeill – who had been knighted in 1871 – as his chief of staff. Wolseley praised McNeill later the same year, describing him as 'daring, determined, self-confident and inde-fatigable . . . He was not a man I should have liked to meet as my enemy in action.' When McNeill was badly wounded at Essaman in October 1873, Wolseley saw him emerge from the fray supporting his badly injured arm – with muscles, tendons and sinews standing out 'like strands of an unravelled rope's end' – with his good one. However, McNeill seemed to be more angry than hurt, and he said indignantly: 'An infernal scoundrel out there has shot me through the arm.' He was twice mentioned in dispatches during the Ashantee Campaign, but his injury forced him to return to England.

McNeill's otherwise unblemished military career was tarnished a little when, as a major general, he commanded the 2nd Brigade in Sir Gerald Graham's Suakin Expedition to eastern Sudan in 1885. An Anglo-Indian force was ambushed by 5,000 indigenous warriors, then known almost universally by the politically incorrect British force as 'Fuzzy-Wuzzies'. Altogether 130 British and Indian troops were killed and, although Graham exonerated McNeill from blame, the latter's reputation still took a knock.

He retired from the Army in 1890 to become an equerry to the future Edward VII and died in his apartment at St James's Palace in May 1904.

CAPTAIN (LATER LIEUTENANT COLONEL) FREDERICK AUGUSTUS SMITH

Army: 43rd Regiment (later the Oxfordshire and Buckinghamshire Light Infantry)

DATE OF BRAVERY: 21 JUNE 1864
GAZETTED: 4 NOVEMBER 1864

Frederick Smith was born in Dublin on 18 November 1826 and was commissioned ensign into the 1st Regiment of Foot on 1 January 1849. Three years later he was promoted to lieutenant. He served during the Crimean War and fought at three large battles: Alma, Inkermann and Sebastopol. He was promoted to captain in March 1855 and six years later transferred to the 43rd Light Infantry, with whom he served during the 1863–6 Maori War.

The 43rd Regiment suffered a setback in the spring of 1864 when it attempted to storm the Maori fort of Gate Pah. After a bombardment, the regiment and a naval brigade managed to force its way into the fort, which had been built on a narrow strip of land with swamps on either side. There was little resistance from the defenders and the British soon broke ranks to search for food, valuables and other spoils of war. However, the Maoris then launched an ambush against the largely unarmed British, who were forced to withdraw, leaving behind their dead, dying and wounded.

The 43rd was determined to make amends for this catastrophe and an opportunity arose on 21 June. A reconnoitring column, led by Colonel Greer, had advanced some three miles inland from Gate Pah to Tauranga, where it came across the Maoris making new entrenchments. Greer engaged the Maoris with his force of 600 men, while at the same time sending for reinforcements. The battle had been raging for two hours when the reinforcements arrived and Greer ordered a full-scale assault on the position. Smith led the advance in what the *London Gazette* later described as 'the most gallant manner'. He was wounded even before he reached the rifle pits – the defensive enemy trenches – but when he got there he leapt down and began fierce hand-to-hand combat, 'thereby giving his men great encouragement, and setting them a fine example'. The fighting was particularly vicious and the Maoris who survived the initial bayonet charge fought back with their gun butts and tomahawks. However, the British eventually routed them, killing many while others fled. By contrast, the British suffered only thirteen fatalities in the encounter.

Smith was then promoted in rapid succession and became a lieutenant colonel in 1875. He retired from the Army three years later and died in Duleek, County Meath, on 22 July 1887.

Japan

In the 1850s, the Japanese had agreed to open their borders to trade with Western countries. However, the daimyos (Japanese feudal princes) were angered by this agreement and preferred to continue Japan's traditional international isolation. In 1863, HMS Euryalus was fired on by shore batteries close to Kagoshima Harbour, forcing the thirty-five-gun frigate to retreat as the band played 'Oh Dear, What Can the Matter Be'. Britain was unhappy about this attack and plotted revenge. The Shimonoseki Expedition of 1864 was the result, and led to the award of three VCs. The trust now possesses one of them.

MIDSHIPMAN DUNCAN GORDON BOYES

Royal Navy

DATE OF BRAVERY: 6 SEPTEMBER 1864
GAZETTED: 21 APRIL 1865

Duncan Boyes was born in Cheltenham on 5 November 1846 and was educated at Cheltenham College. He is believed to have joined the Royal Navy when he was seventeen, serving in HMS *Euryalus.*

In late summer 1864, Vice-Admiral Augustus Kuper was placed in overall command of an international force of British, French, Dutch and American warships which anchored in the Straits of Shimonoseki opposite the Japanese stronghold of Choisiu. On 5 September the international force bombarded and silenced the shore batteries, and the next morning Boyes landed with a naval brigade, two battalions of Royal Marines and a battalion of Dutch Royal Marines. Their task was to spike and dismount the enemy guns, dismantle their platform and blow up their ammunition. However, that afternoon, with their mission nearly completed, they were ambushed by a large Japanese force. The Japanese were eventually driven back and the British then discovered a large fort, defended by guns, at the head of the valley. HMS *Perseus* had grounded during the previous day's bombardment and it was vital to take the fort before nightfall.

Boyes carried the Queen's Colour of the leading company as the naval brigade advanced up one side of the valley and the Royal Marines advanced up the other. They encountered heavy fire and seven men were killed and twenty-six wounded.

Commander John Moresby, of HMS *Argus*, who witnessed the attack, later wrote: 'Our men never checked, and rushing on, swarmed over the wall and won the stockade, the enemy disappearing into the bush.' Boyes, in particular, never wavered, despite being a clear target for the Japanese defenders, and his Colour was pierced six times by musket balls. During the onslaught, one colour sergeant was killed and another wounded. Yet even when Boyes and the wounded sergeant, Thomas Pride, were ordered to halt their advance, they hesitated, such was their determination to rout the enemy. The fort was eventually captured and destroyed, Boyes and Pride won VCs for their daring, and the Queen arranged a presentation parade on their return to Britain. Boyes, still only eighteen, and Pride received their VCs on 22 September 1865, in the presence of other VC holders and a crowd of thousands. The next day *Euryalus* was paid off and Boyes left her for another ship.

The remainder of his life was less praiseworthy. He was court-martialled for breaking into a naval yard in Bermuda and dismissed from the service for what appears to be little more than a childish prank. He took the disgrace badly, became depressed and began drinking heavily. In a final attempt to improve his mental state and his health, he went to work in New Zealand, where his brother had a sheep station at Kawarau Falls in Otago Province. However, he suffered a nervous breakdown and took his own life at Dunedin on 26 January 1869, aged just twenty-two.

West Africa

A British Expeditionary Force led by Sir Garnet Wolseley captured Kumasi, the capital of Ashantee (Ashanti), on the Gold Coast of West

Africa in 1873. This led to the Ashantee War of 1873–4 after Kofi Karikari, the King of the Ashantee, raised a force of up to 60,000 to defend his lands. Wolseley, a veteran of the Crimean War and the Indian Mutiny, fought a short but brilliant campaign to ensure victory at the battles of Amoaful and Ordahsu. Four VCs were awarded as a result of this conflict, of which the trust now owns one.

LANCE SERGEANT (LATER SERGEANT) SAMUEL McGAW

Army: 42nd Regiment (later the Black Watch/Royal Highlanders)

DATE OF BRAVERY: 21 JANUARY 1874
GAZETTED: 28 MARCH 1874

Samuel McGaw was born in Kirkmichael, Ayrshire, in 1838. He saw action during the Indian Mutiny, then served with his regiment during the Ashantee War in West Africa. At one point his regiment marched 180 miles from Cape Coast Castle to the capital of Ashantee prior to the Battle of Amoaful, showing great courage on 31 January 1874. The *London Gazette* noted his VC was granted 'For having at the Battle of Amoaful, led his section through the bush in the most excellent manner, continuing to do so throughout the whole day, although badly wounded early in the engagement.'

A contemporary later described how 'for nearly eight hours the savage Ashantees withstood the combined movements of our troops, and it seems that as a last attempt to turn the foe from his bush and forest lair the 42nd was ordered to advance . . . the section of sixteen men with McGaw at their head, went on and on through hundreds and thousands of the foe, and although wounded and bleeding, he yet dauntlessly accompanied his section'.

McGaw received his VC from Queen Victoria at Osborne House, Isle of Wight, on 20 April 1874. Shortly afterwards, the people of Kilmarnock, near where he was born, sent him a 'purse filled with sovereigns' in recognition of his courageous deeds. He later served with the Royal Highlanders in Cyprus, where he developed a fever and died on 22 July 1878.

The occupation of Egypt

The British occupation of Egypt in 1882 marked the culmination of a policy that had been actively pursued since 1798. This involved the de facto *separation of Egypt from the Ottoman Empire and conflicting attempts by several European powers to influence or control the country: France and Britain, in particular, sought ascendancy. A large military demonstration in September 1881 forced Khedive Tawfiq, the local ruler, to dismiss his prime minister. France and Great Britain sent warships to Alexandria in April 1882 in a show of support for the Khedive but this merely prompted the fear of invasion throughout the country. The Khedive moved to Alexandria for fear of his own safety, leaving army officers to take control of the government. By June, Egypt was in the hands of nationalists opposed to European domin-ation of the country, and when a British naval bombardment of Alexandria had limited effect, an expeditionary force landed at both ends of the Suez Canal in August 1882. The British force succeeded in defeating the Egyptian Army at Tel El Kebir the following month and thereafter assumed control of the country, reinstating the Khedive as a puppet ruler.*

The occupation of Egypt led to three VCs being awarded, of which the trust owns one.

GUNNER (LATER CHIEF GUNNER) ISRAEL HARDING

Royal Navy

DATE OF BRAVERY: 11 JULY 1882
GAZETTED: 15 SEPTEMBER 1882

Israel Harding was born in Portsmouth on 21 October 1833, appropriately enough Trafalgar Day. But it was not just his date and place of birth which pointed towards a naval career. He had a formidable naval heritage: his grandfathers were a King's pilot and a master mariner, while his father was Queen's pilot at Portsmouth for several years. He began his own naval career at the age of fourteen when he became a cabin boy on his father's ship, the steam vessel *Echo*, and spent his late teens on HMS *Arrogant*. Next he joined HMS *Excellent*, where he was part of a team testing a new gun. Then he spent two years on active service in the Baltic and won the Baltic Medal after being present at the bombardment of Sveaborg. On his return to home waters he first displayed his exceptional courage: while serving in the Channel Squadron he jumped into a stormy sea to save two men who had been swept overboard.

In 1860, he became a warrant officer and was assigned to the *Barracouta* as gunner on an expedition to Mexico. While there, he took part in the occupation of Vera Cruz and the rescue of the gunboat *Plover*. For the latter action he was recommended for promotion to lieutenant, although for some reason this was not approved. His long and varied naval career took a new turn during the Ashantee War, when he served on board HMS *Victor Emmanuel*, a hospital ship. Then he spent three years in command of the *Castor*, a drill ship for naval reservists on the Tyne. In May 1882, came the posting that would lead to him earning the VC, when he was appointed to HMS *Alexandra*, one of sixteen Royal Navy ships dispatched to Alexandria.

Once in Egyptian coastal waters, the *Alexandra* steamed to a position opposite the guns of Fort Ras-el-Tin. When an ultimatum from Admiral Sir Beauchamp Seymour to Arabi Pasha expired, the bombardment of the forts of Alexandria began on 11 July 1882. Harding's ship soon came under returning fire, and eventually a ten-inch shell penetrated its armour plating. Some men raised the alarm and Harding responded immediately, rushing up a ladder from below decks. He could see that the shell's fuse was still burning, so he doused it with some water from a nearby tub. Then he single-handedly picked up the shell and placed it in the tub. His actions undoubtedly saved many lives as well as severe damage to the ship. Later, he modestly attributed his actions to 'early training in a hard school'. Altogether the *Alexandra* was hit about sixty times, but casualties were relatively light, with one man killed and three wounded.

Harding's final posting, before retiring in 1885, was as officer in charge of naval recruitment at Portsea. He died on 22 May 1917 while on a visit to Billingshurst, Sussex. After his death, his son Joseph received a letter of condolence from Admiral Lord Charles Beresford, who had also distinguished himself at Alexandria in 1882. The letter was a tribute to 'your gallant father, he was a grand old gentleman and a brave seaman, the heroic act he performed at Alexandria justly earned him the Victoria Cross. He was a very old friend of mine and I always regarded him with respect and esteem.'

The First Sudan Campaign

Britain campaigned in the Sudan from 1881 to 1885 after a jihad – or holy war – was declared by Muhammad Ahmad ibn as Sayyid Abd Allah, a Muslim leader more commonly known as the Mahdi.

After raising an army in 1881, he led a successful war of liberation from Ottoman–Egyptian military occupation. Britain was determined to retain its influence in the area after the opening of the Suez Canal in 1869 but had no desire to get drawn into a full-scale war. After challenging the Mahdi for a couple of years, the British forces, under General Charles Gordon, attempted to withdraw in December 1883. However, this proved far from straightforward because their exit to the north was blocked by the Mahdi's forces. With no escape route, they were besieged for ten months at Khartoum, and the city finally fell to the Sudanese just two days before British reinforcements arrived on 28 January 1885.

Three VCs were awarded during the campaign, of which the trust has one.

LIEUTENANT (LATER COLONEL AND SIR) PERCIVAL SCROPE MARLING

Army: 3rd Battalion, the King's Royal Rifle Corps, attached Mounted Infantry

DATE OF BRAVERY: 13 MARCH 1884
GAZETTED: 21 MAY 1884

Percival Marling was born into a privileged background at King's Stanley, Gloucestershire, on 6 March 1861. He was the eldest son of Sir William Henry Marling and was educated at Harrow and the Royal Military College, Sandhurst. He joined the 3rd Battalion of the King's Royals as a second lieutenant on 11 August 1880 and soon saw action, serving in South Africa in 1880–1 and near Alexandria, Egypt, in 1882. Two years later, he was in the Sudan: he was a member of the British Mounted Infantry in the Suakin Campaign against the Mahdist forces and was present on 29 February at the Battle of El Teb, one of the few successes for the British forces in the campaign. After the relief of Tokar the next day, he joined the main army heading for Suakin. Shortly after the troops reached their destination, the British received intelligence that a large force of Dervishes had assembled some six miles away at the village of Tamaai.

On 11 March, the 42nd Regiment marched out of Suakin and formed an entrenched camp halfway towards Osman Digna's position. Reinforcements from Suakin joined them the next day and the British force advanced again, halting just two miles from the enemy. At 8 a.m. the following morning, a combined force of more than 4,000 men started to move towards the enemy lines, but the Dervish Army advanced too. Fierce fighting involving foot soldiers and cavalry from both sides ensued. During the confrontation, a Private Morley, of the Royal Sussex Regiment, was shot and seriously wounded. Marling lifted the injured man on to his horse but he immediately fell off. As the fighting raged all around them, Marling dismounted, let his horse loose and carried Morley to safety. The battle continued throughout that day and into the next, with the end result a British victory. The Dervishes lost an estimated 3,000 men from a force of 12,000. The British losses totalled just 217, killed and wounded. Marling's gallant rescue of Morley at Tamaai was the subject of an oil painting by Major Godfrey Douglas Giles, the war artist, which was hung at the Royal Academy Exhibition in London in 1887.

Marling continued to serve in Egypt for the next five years before going to India in 1889. He then returned to South Africa to serve in the Boer War (1899–1902), but was invalided to England with enteric fever in the first year. Having recovered, he was back in South Africa in early 1901 and was twice mentioned in dispatches, as well as being promoted to the command of the 18th Hussars. He was also created a Companion of the Bath for his services in South Africa.

Marling retired from the Army as a colonel in 1910 because of injuries he sustained when falling from his horse. Yet, at the outbreak of the Great War in 1914, he volunteered for active service and went to France. However, the following year, he was invalided home with congestion of the lungs. In 1928, he became High Sheriff of Gloucester, and three years later he published his reminiscences, *Rifleman and Hussar*. Around the same time, he toured some of the old battlefields in Egypt and the Sudan where he had seen action. Unsurprisingly, top of his list of places to see was Tamaai, where he had won his VC half a century earlier. Marling wrote: 'I never thought I should return some 50 years later to the places in the comfort of a motor-car and with whisky-and-soda to drink instead of water which had to be carried in goatskins for days.' He died in Stroud, Gloucestershire, on 29 May 1936.

The Crete Rebellion

After Greece achieved its independence from Turkish rule in 1832, Crete became an object of contention, and its Greek population revolted twice against the Ottomans – in 1866 and 1897. In the latter uprising, 1,500 Greek troops landed on the island to hoist their national flag in defiance of Turkish sovereignty, and in response Turkey declared war on Greece. The crisis was considered so serious that Britain, France, Russia, Italy, Germany and Austria – the six superpowers of the day – all sent warships to the area. Eventually a situation arose that was similar to that in modern-day Cyprus, but more chaotic: the Christian Cretans held the countryside, while the Muslim Turks, assisted by bands of Bashi Bazouks (irregular mercenary troops drawn from all over the Ottoman Empire), were in control of the towns. There were occasional skirmishes between the two sides – and sometimes the observing superpowers were involved, too – but eventually the crisis was resolved in 1898.

Just one VC was awarded as a result of the troubles in Crete, and the trust now owns it.

SURGEON (LATER STAFF SURGEON) WILLIAM JOB MAILLARD

Royal Navy

DATE OF BRAVERY: 6 SEPTEMBER 1898
GAZETTED: 2 DECEMBER 1898

William Maillard was born in Banwell, Somerset, on 10 March 1863. He was the son of a Wesleyan minister and supposedly a distant descendant of Sir Francis Drake. Family lore says that his forebears adopted the unusual surname – a corruption of *mallard*, the French for drake – when they settled on Guernsey. William was educated at Dunheved College, Launceston, Cornwall, and Kingswood School, Bath, before studying medicine at Guy's Hospital, London, from 1882 to 1889, when he won the Gold Medal.

He was posted to the torpedo gunboat HMS *Hazard* in 1897, shortly before it was sent to Crete. In September 1898 the tense situation on the island reached crisis point. A detachment of 130 men from the Highland Light Infantry (HLI) attempted to install a new collector of taxes in the northern town of Candia, but a Muslim mob of several thousand rose in rebellion and massacred nearly 1,000 Christians. As the riots continued, the town was set on fire and the British vice-consul died in the blaze, while the HLI detachment was besieged in the customs house. The Turkish authorities did nothing to stop the mayhem, so an appeal for help was sent to *Hazard*, the only warship in the area. Two detachments of fifty men were sent ashore, and as the HLI began to suffer heavy casualties an appeal was made for medical help on 6 September.

Maillard, Lieutenant Lewes and Lewes's steward were rowed ashore by five sailors in the captain's gig. As they neared the harbour wall, they were greeted with heavy gunfire from a band of Bashi Bazouks, but they managed to land, ran ashore and headed for cover. But Maillard saw that one of the sailors, Ordinary Seaman Alfred Stroud, had collapsed in the boat with a gunshot wound and immediately ran back into the water, amid a storm of fire, in an attempt to bring the injured sailor ashore. The boat was drifting out to sea, however, and Maillard was eventually forced to leave Stroud, who was 'almost dead', and return to cover. Maillard's clothes were said to have been 'riddled with bullet holes' but he was unhurt.

The conflict at Candia, in which seventeen British lives were lost, ultimately led to the end of Turkish authority across the island. Seven Muslims were publicly hanged for the murder of two HLI privates during the rioting.

Maillard later maintained modestly that he should have been reprimanded for his folly: he was the only medical officer in the area and that night had to treat seventy HLI casualties on board *Hazard*. Yet, of course, he was also immensely proud of being the first (and so far only) naval medical officer to receive the VC. His decoration was unusual in two other ways. First, it was won in 'peacetime' because there had been no British declaration of war against anyone involved in the crisis in Crete – the so-called Cretan Question. Second, his recommendation for a VC took a new route. Previous naval VCs had been approved by the War Office, having first been passed to the monarch by the Secretary of State for War. On this occasion, the recommendation came from the First Lord of the Admiralty to the sovereign. Maillard was presented with his medal by Queen Victoria at Windsor Castle on 15 September 1898.

He was promoted to staff surgeon in 1899, but his health soon deteriorated, forcing him to retire in 1902. He died the following year, aged just forty.

The Second Sudan Campaign

The Second Sudan Campaign took place between 1896 and 1900. The British and French were still competing for influence in the area, and there was also resentment from the local inhabitants towards both sets of Europeans. By 1896, the French had a grip on several areas – Bahr el Ghazal and the Western Upper Nile up to Fashoda – and planned on annexing them to French West Africa. An international conflict known as the Fashoda Incident developed between France and Britain over this region, and in 1899 France agreed to cede the area to the UK.

From 1898, Britain and Egypt administered all of present-day Sudan, but with the north and south treated as separate colonies. Britain also hoped to add southern Sudan to its East African colonies.

Six VCs were awarded during the Second Sudan Campaign, of which the trust owns one.

CAPTAIN (LATER BRIGADIER GENERAL AND EARL OF GOWRIE) THE HON ALEXANDER GORE ARKWRIGHT HORE-RUTHVEN

Army: 3rd Battalion, the Highland Light Infantry

DATE OF BRAVERY: 22 SEPTEMBER 1898
GAZETTED: 26 FEBRUARY 1899

Alexander Hore-Ruthven, an eminent soldier and statesman, was born in Windsor on 6 July 1872, the second son of the 8th Baron Ruthven. He was educated at Eton, joined the Highland

Light Infantry (HLI) Militia – which did not have the status of the regular Army – in 1891 and was promoted to captain in 1896. Employed with the Egyptian Army from 1898 to 1903, he spent the first two years involved in the Second Sudan Campaign. On 22 September 1898, he took part in the Nile Expedition and commanded the Camel Corps detachment of Colonel Parsons' column during the attack on the last Dervish stronghold at Gedaref. Then, Parsons' force of 1,350 men – which was considerably outnumbered – captured the town of Nur Angora, leaving 500 Dervish casualties. Within six days, Ahmed Fadid, one of the Dervish leaders, had arrived with a force of 8,000 men. Yet, after a fierce battle, he too was repulsed.

During his time in the Sudan, Hore-Ruthven repeatedly distinguished himself on the battlefield, and he was mentioned in dispatches at least twice. He was also present at the final defeat of the Khalifa in 1899 (the Khalifa – Abdallahi ibn Muhammad – had eventually succeeded the Mahdi as the leader in 1891). By then, he had already won his VC, for an act of bravery during the attack on Gedaref on 22 September 1898. In the heat of battle, he saw that an Egyptian officer had been wounded and that the advancing Dervishes were fifty yards from where he lay. Although the enemy was firing and charging, Hore-Ruthven picked up the wounded officer and carried him towards the 16th Egyptian Battalion. Because he was progressing more slowly than the advancing Dervishes, Hore-Ruthven stopped two or three times, put down the wounded man and fired on the enemy to check their advance. Nobody who witnessed the incident was in any doubt that the Egyptian officer would have been killed but for Hore-Ruthven's bravery.

He received his decoration from Queen Victoria at Windsor Castle on 11 May 1899. Six days later, he joined the Cameron Highlanders as a second lieutenant and was promoted to full lieutenant the following year. Thereafter, he became a special service officer to the Somaliland Field Force and took part in an action at Jidballi in January 1904. From 1905 to 1908, he was military secretary to two successive Lord Lieutenants of Ireland, Lord Dudley and Lord Aberdeen. In 1908, he was promoted to captain in the 1st Dragoon Guards (he had to go through the promotion system again after switching from the militia to the regular Army), and worked as military secretary to the Governor-General and Commander-in-Chief of Australia until 1910.

During the First World War, Hore-Ruthven continued to cover himself in glory. From November 1914 to March 1915, he served as a brigade major in France. In April 1915 he was promoted to major in the Welsh Guards and two months later was employed with the Mediterranean Expeditionary Force. However, he was seriously wounded at Gallipoli, becoming the first casualty of the newly formed Welsh Guards Regiment. He won the Distinguished Service Order (DSO) in May 1916 for his services at Gallipoli, and over the next two years was mentioned five times in dispatches and was made a Companion of the Bath, a Companion of St Michael and St George and received two bars to his DSO. His second bar was announced in the *London Gazette* on 10 December 1919:

> He commanded his brigade with conspicuous gallantry and judgement throughout the operations east of Ypres from 28 Sept. to 27 Oct. 1918 inclusive. His presence and personal bearing at critical times during the fighting was of decisive value, especially during a strong enemy counter-attack. On 20 Oct. at St Louis, he went forward among the attacking troops at a critical juncture, and inspired them to the final effort, whereby the high ground of great tactical value was captured.

Furthermore, Hore-Ruthven was one of the few men to win the Croix de Guerre from both France and Belgium.

As a full colonel, he commanded the Welsh Guards from 1920 to 1924 and for the following four years the Guards Brigade at Aldershot. In 1928, he succeeded his friend Lieutenant General Sir Tom Bridges as Governor of South Australia, before taking up the same post in New South Wales seven years later. Later in 1935, he was given a peerage, becoming Baron Gowrie of Canberra and Direleton for his services to Australia. On 23 January 1936, he was sworn in as Governor-General and Commander-in-Chief of Australia. His war record and his charming personality made him immensely popular in Australia and the surrounding Commonwealth territories. His term of office was due to end in 1939 but his successor, the Duke of Kent, then accepted a naval appointment on the outbreak of the Second World War, so Baron Gowrie agreed to stay on in Australia and supervise the Commonwealth's war effort. His experience as a soldier was invaluable and he received personal approval to launch Operation Jaywick, the famous commando raid on Japanese ships in Singapore in 1943. The following year, he was finally succeeded as Governor-General by the Duke of Gloucester and received an astonishing show of affection from the Australian people for his years of service. He died eleven years later in Shipton Moyne, Gloucestershire, at the age of eighty-two.

When his medals came up for sale at Christie's in 1989, the auction house needed nearly two full pages to list and photograph all twenty of them.

The Boxer Uprising

By the end of the nineteenth century, several Western powers and Japan had established wide interests in China, but the dowager empress, Tz'u Hsi, favoured a last effort to expel them through armed resistance. She therefore encouraged a nationalistic secret society called the Boxers, who rebelled against foreign influence from 1898 to 1900.

In June 1900, some 140,000 Boxers occupied Beijing and for eight weeks besieged both foreigners and Chinese Christians. The siege was lifted in August by an international force of British, French, Russian, American, German and Japanese troops. The Boxer Uprising was over and the following year China was ordered to pay multi-million-pound reparations.

Two VCs were awarded for actions during the uprising and the trust now has one of them.

MIDSHIPMAN (LATER COMMANDER) BASIL JOHN DOUGLAS GUY

Royal Navy

DATE OF BRAVERY: 13 JULY 1900
GAZETTED: 1 JANUARY 1901

Basil Guy, the son of the vicar of Christchurch, Harrogate, was born in Bishop Auckland, County Durham, on 9 May 1882. He was educated at Aysgarth School in Yorkshire, Llandaff Cathedral School in south Wales, and on HMS *Britannia*, passing out to the *Barfleur* on 15 July 1898. He served in the Far East for many years, including during the Boxer Rebellion.

On 13 July 1900, during an attack on Tientsin, heavy crossfire was brought to bear on the naval brigade and there were many casualties. One of them was an able seaman, who was shot some fifty yards short of cover. Guy stayed with the man, then tried and failed to lift him under intense fire. As he was unable to carry his comrade to safety, Guy bandaged the wound, ran for help, mustered some stretcher-bearers, and returned with them to the injured man as quickly as he could. However, the man was shot again and died before he could be brought to safety.

The *London Gazette* reported: 'During the whole time a very heavy fire had been brought to bear upon Mr Guy, and the ground around him was absolutely ploughed up.' Edward VII presented Guy with his VC on 8 March 1902 at Keyham Barracks, Devonport. He also received the China Medal and, on 15 July 1903, was promoted to lieutenant for his services in China.

Later, he served in both the First and the Second World Wars, winning the Distinguished Service Order in the earlier conflict for his command of a decoy ship, HMS *Wonganella*, during an action with a U-boat. He was promoted to commander in 1918 and died in London on 29 December 1956.

The Third Somaliland Expedition

At the start of the twentieth century, the region now claimed by Somaliland – an independent but internationally unrecognised state in the Horn of Africa – was known as the British Somaliland Protectorate. There was unrest there from 1903 to 1904 and the British were forced to send an expedition to quell the disquiet.

Three men won the VC for their actions during this campaign, and one of these medals is now in the trust's collection.

CAPTAIN (LATER MAJOR) GEORGE MURRAY ROLLAND

Army (Bedfordshire Regiment): Indian Army, 1st Bombay Grenadiers

DATE OF BRAVERY: 22 APRIL 1903
GAZETTED: 7 AUGUST 1903

George Rolland was born in Wellington, India, on 12 May 1869, the son of a military father and a novelist mother. He was educated at Harrow and Sandhurst before joining the Bedfordshire Regiment in November 1889 as a second lieutenant. He was promoted to lieutenant in 1891 and captain in 1900, and joined the Indian Army the following year. In October 1902, he arrived in Somaliland to take up his roles as intelligence officer to the Berbera Bohottle Flying Column and staff officer to Major John Gough. He and two comrades won VCs at the Battle of Daratoleh, and one of Rolland's letters gives a vivid account of the events of the day:

> It was a grand fight, and for four hours our little band of 200 stood shoulder to shoulder in a tiny little square, barely thirty yards on each side, with a hail of bullets falling all round us. Our ammunition was running short, so at 2.30 p.m. [the action began at 10.30 a.m.] Major Gough decided to retire. A horde of savages followed us for three more hours, coming to within fifteen to thirty yards of us. It was a tight corner. Major Gough is a splendid soldier, so cool and calm; he is a grand fellow. Poor Capt. Bruce and I were on the rearguard together – both Harrow boys. The bush was so dense we could hardly see a yard in it. We were left behind with four men so Bruce called out: 'Rolland, come along with those men,' and we retired slowly firing as we went. A savage crept up close to the path along which we were marching; owing to

the dense grass and bush we did not notice it. Poor Capt. Bruce suddenly threw up his arms and fell on his face, shot through the body. The bullet entered his right side and passed out by the left. I saw the savage moving off; my carbine was on him in a second, and he rolled over. I can't tell whether he was actually the man who shot Capt. Bruce, but I saw no other, so think it must have been him.

I ran to Capt. Bruce and raised him up, turning him on his back. He was bleeding terribly, and I saw at a glance that it was a mortal wound. I dragged him a little out of the path, which was much exposed to the enemy's fire, and undid his collar, taking off his bandolier, revolver and belt, while the four brave men covered me with their fire and kept the enemy in check, who were yelling with delight as they saw one white man dying and another close to him, and they kept calling out to each other. (I was told later by the Somali who fought by me that they were saying they had got us all, and to come on and spear us.) Capt. Bruce was a very heavy man, of nearly fourteen stone, and I am only nine stone, so I could not lift him. None of the men could stop firing to help me, or the enemy would have been on us, so I shouted to the disappearing column, 'Halt in front!' It was then out of sight, slowly retiring along the winding path, and we were practically cut off. It was a moment of great despair, as I thought my shout had not been heard. The enemy were now pressing us very hard, so I had to stop attending to poor Capt. Bruce, and emptied the magazine of my carbine at them. Then I fired off my revolver and emptied that too. Suddenly Capt. Bruce stood up, and I rushed to hold him up. He walked two steps forward and fell on his face again. I tried to break his fall, and he brought me down too, as he was too heavy for me. I again turned him on his back. He opened his eyes and spoke to me (his last words): 'They have done for me this time, old man!' From now to his death he was practically unconscious. To my infinite relief I then saw Capt. Walker trekking towards me. He and I tried to carry Capt. Bruce, but it was no use and I then left them and ran back 400 yards or more to where the rearguard was, to fetch help. It was a terribly long run, and I thought I must get hit any moment, as the bullets fell splashing round me. I seized a Bikanir camel, and was running back with it, when Major Gough came up and asked what was the matter. I told him, and he rushed back to Capt. Bruce. I followed slower, as the led camel refused to step out, and I could not induce mine to hurry up – in fact, he was frightened, and did not like to leave his friends. I reached the little group, and made the camel sit down, and we lifted up Capt. Bruce, Major Gough at his head, and Capt. Walker and I at his feet. While doing so three bullets struck the ground between us. One went through poor Capt. Bruce's leg, but he was too far gone to feel it. Then the Sikh, who had done his duty nobly, had his arm smashed by a fourth bullet. We had to throw Capt. Bruce on the camel anyhow, and as we did so the poor fellow died . . . It was the hardest day of my life.

In 1906, Rolland joined the Nagpur Volunteer Rifles as adjutant, but four years later he died from injuries sustained in a fall, aged just forty-one.

6

THE FIRST WORLD WAR –
THE ARMY

The Great War was 'total war' and led to a scale of casualties that had never been seen before. By the end, more than ten million military personnel and civilians had been killed. It was eventually won by the Allied Powers: principally Britain, France and, latterly, the United States of America. They defeated the Central Powers, led by Germany, Austria-Hungary and the Ottoman Empire. Before America entered the war in 1917, the Allied Powers were sometimes referred to as the Triple Entente, and the Central Powers as the Triple Alliance. These pre-war diplomatic alliances were intended to make war less likely because no country would relish taking on three major powers. However, once the conflict broke out, the alliances made it more widespread. The 'spark' for the war was the assassination of Archduke Franz Ferdinand, the heir to the Austrian throne, in Sarajevo on 28 June 1914, which set off a rapid chain of events: Austria-Hungary declared war on Serbia, Russia mobilised its forces in defence of the Serbs, Germany declared war on France and Russia and invaded (officially neutral) Belgium en route to France, and Britain declared war on Germany.

The war took place in many theatres but much of it was fought on the Western Front: both sides 'dug in' along a meandering line of fortified trenches stretching from the Channel to the Swiss frontier with France. The conflict is perhaps best remembered for its trench warfare. Advances in military technology meant that defensive firepower outweighed offensive capability, yet military commanders persisted in using nineteenth-century tactics against twentieth-century technology: millions of men were sent 'over the top' to face barbed wire that slowed their advance, artillery that was far more lethal than ever before and machine-guns that were deadly against an advancing infantry. Furthermore, the Germans began using poison gas in 1915, and soon the Allies followed suit. Yet still thousands of men were sent to their deaths as military leaders desperately tried to make minuscule advances. On 1 July 1916, the first day of the Battle of the Somme, the British Army saw the bloodiest day in its history, suffering 57,470 casualties, of whom 19,240 were killed. Battles such as Ypres, Vimy Ridge, the Marne, Cambrai, Verdun and fruitless operations like Gallipoli also saw horrific levels of casualties. By the end of 1917, however, both sides had modernised considerably; wireless communications, armoured cars, tanks and tactical aircraft were all in wide use.

America joined the war on the Allied side in 1917 – the same year as the Bolshevik Revolution occurred in Russia. The United States had been angered by the fact that German U-boats had attacked its merchant ships, sinking three of them, so Congress declared war on Germany on 6 April 1917. The Americans' participation eventually proved decisive, more than making up for the withdrawal of Russia from the Allied side. The Allies managed to withstand the German Spring Offensive of 1918, then countered with their own Hundred Days Offensive from 8 August, during which they gradually gained the upper hand. The Central Powers collapsed in the autumn, and on 11 November the opposing armies on the Western Front agreed a ceasefire. The fighting did not start again, although a formal state of war persisted between the two sides until 1919, when the Treaty of Versailles was the first in a series of peace treaties to be signed between the various combatants.

The horrors of the First World War led to the award of 626 VCs – at the time of writing, almost half of the total number. The trust now has fifty-seven of these medals in its collection.

The Western Front

The Western Front is arguably the best-known battle line in history. During the Great War, it was a narrow battlefield some 460 miles in length and up to 20 miles in depth. Yet, during a period of 50 months, more than six million soldiers were killed and 14 million wounded along the Western Front alone. Thousands of men lost their lives day after day in often deadlocked trench warfare that saw endless offensives and counter offensives from both sides.

By the end of 1914, both sides had dug in along a meandering line of trenches – fortified by machine-gun nests, artillery and barbed wire – stretching from the North Sea to the Swiss frontier with France. This line remained largely unchanged for much of the war. Eventually, in 1918, the Allies, by this time supported by American troops, gained the upper hand in the Hundred Days Offensive beginning in August.

†LIEUTENANT MAURICE JAMES DEASE

Army: 4th Battalion, the Royal Fusiliers

DATE OF BRAVERY: 23 AUGUST 1914
GAZETTED: 16 NOVEMBER 1914

†PRIVATE SIDNEY FRANK GODLEY

Army: 4th Battalion, the Royal Fusiliers

DATE OF BRAVERY: 23 AUGUST 1914
GAZETTED: 25 NOVEMBER 1914

Maurice Dease was born in Coole, County Westmeath, Ireland, on 28 September 1889. He was the only son of Edmund and Katherine Dease. After attending the Royal Military College, Sandhurst, he joined the 4th Battalion, the Royal Fusiliers, as a second lieutenant in May 1910 and was promoted to a full lieutenant in April 1912.

Frank Godley, the first private to win the VC in the First World War, was born in East Grinstead, Sussex, on 14 August 1889 and was brought up by an aunt after his mother died when he was six. He was a talented sportsman: a good cross-country runner, footballer and cricketer.

Dease, who was a deeply religious young man, and Godley, who had fair hair and a thick moustache, embarked for France and Belgium in August 1914. Their battalion was one of the first to go to war and they arrived at Mons on 22 August. The next day, during heavy fighting, the Germans seized the initiative. Initially, Dease, in charge of a single company of Royal Fusiliers defending Nimy Bridge, had control of the machine-gun. Early in the fighting, he was wounded but he refused to leave the battlefield. It was a fellow officer, Lieutenant Steele, who wrote to Dease's family informing them of his courage:

> Poor Maurice got shot below the knee or thereabouts about 9 a.m. while he was attending to a machine-gun on the left side of the bridge. Ashburner and I begged him to go off and get fixed up at the hospital, but he refused. He then crawled over to the right-hand side gun. Almost as soon as he got there he was again shot somewhere in the side. I made him lie down near me and with great difficulty kept him quiet as he was worried about his guns. I promised to look after these for him and he settled down a bit quieter. I asked him if he was in any pain and he said, "No" and smiled more or less cheerfully. As soon as I managed to get the guns going again he seemed much more happy. He seemed to have been hit again while I was busy on his left. For the next two hours there was a perfect hail of machine-

gun fire as well as Artillery and Infantry fire. Maurice during this time became very quiet, and I fancy unconscious. When we retired Maurice had to be left behind . . .

Dease was hit five times and subsequently died from his wounds. It was only at this point that Godley, who had been helping him, took over. When he was then asked to stay on alone while his comrades retreated, it effectively meant almost certain capture by the Germans – dead or alive. Godley did not waver: for two hours, he sprayed the enemy with relentless machine-gun fire while his fellow Royal Fusiliers withdrew. Eventually having run out of ammunition, he destroyed the gun. By then he was wounded but managed to crawl to the nearby road where he was helped to hospital by two Belgian civilians.

The Germans later took over the hospital and Godley was taken prisoner. He refused to answer questions but was still well treated by the Germans, being sent to Berlin for skin grafts; his back alone required 150 stitches. When he was fit enough, he was transferred to Doberitz prisoner-of-war camp. While there a senior German officer told him that he had won the VC. Godley, along with Lieutenant Dease, had been gazetted for the medal on 25 November 1914. At the end of the war, with Godley having been a PoW almost for its entirety, the camp guards deserted and he and others made his way back to Britain.

Godley later became a school caretaker and retired in 1951, after thirty years' service. He died in Epping, Essex, on 29 June 1957, aged sixty-seven.

MAJOR (LATER MAJOR GENERAL)
ERNEST WRIGHT ALEXANDER

Army: 119th Battery, Royal Field Artillery

DATE OF BRAVERY: 24 AUGUST 1914
GAZETTED: 18 FEBRUARY 1915

Ernest Alexander was born in Liverpool on 2 October 1870, the son of a wealthy shipowner who was a director of the Suez Canal. He was educated at Cherbourg House, Malvern, Harrow and Sandhurst, where he received his first commission in July 1889. He twice served in India: from 1892 to 1900, and from 1903 to 1906, when he was promoted to major.

After Britain declared war on Germany on 4 August 1914, it took some time to make vital military preparations, so the first contact British troops had with their German opponents was not until the 22nd of that month. Alexander won his VC just two days later – which made it the third award of the war, two having been won the previous day. His act of bravery took place during the retreat from Mons, at Elouges. According to the *London Gazette*, Alexander showed great courage

> when the flank guard was attacked by a German corps . . . handling his battery against overwhelming odds with such conspicuous success that all his guns were saved, notwith-standing that they had to be withdrawn by hand by himself and three other men. This enabled the retirement of the 5th Division to be carried out without serious loss. Subsequently Lieutenant-Colonel Alexander (then Major) rescued a wounded man under a heavy fire with the greatest gallantry and devotion to duty.

Captain Grenfell, who was seriously wounded in the action, also received the VC for his part in rescuing the guns, while

Sergeants Turner and Davids were awarded the Distinguished Conduct Medal.

Alexander's courage and leadership resulted in a series of rapid promotions, culminating in command of the Royal Artillery (RA) of XI Corps from May 1917 until April 1918, and subsequent appointment as major general of the RA at the headquarters of the First Army. Later, he commanded the RA, Southern Area, Aldershot Command. During the course of the war, he was mentioned nine times in dispatches, was created a Companion of St Michael and St George in June 1915, received the Military Order of Savoy (Cavalier) in September 1918, became a Companion of the Bath in January 1919, received the French Croix de Guerre in August 1919, and was created Grand Officer of the Military Order of Avis on 21 August 1919. He died in Kingsbridge, Devon, on 25 August 1934.

DRIVER (LATER SERGEANT) FREDERICK LUKE

Army: 37th Battery, Royal Field Artillery

DATE OF BRAVERY: 26 AUGUST 1914
GAZETTED: 25 NOVEMBER 1914

Frederick Luke, who was born in West Tytherley, Hampshire, on 29 September 1895, was just eighteen when he won his VC on the seventh day of armed conflict between Britain and Germany. He was serving as a volunteer driver with the Royal Field Artillery at Le Cateau, France, when Sir Horace Smith-Dorrien's force came under attack. The German infantry commanded by General Alexander Von Kluck advanced along a twelve-mile front, supported by relentless fire from some six hundred guns. The British had only about a quarter of that number of guns, which were generally of a smaller calibre, so their batteries' losses were enormous. As the day wore on, Von

Kluck sensed victory and started a huge enveloping movement on both flanks. Smith-Dorrien knew he could not counter this, so between three and four o'clock the British troops were ordered to retire.

During the withdrawal, Captain Douglas Reynolds, of the 37th Battery, attempted to rescue a couple of his guns from the advancing enemy with the help of two teams of mounted volunteers. One of the teams was killed by the Germans, who were only about a hundred yards distant by this point, but Luke, Reynolds and Driver Drain succeeded in hauling the other gun to the safety of the British lines. All three men won the VC for their bravery.

Luke, who served as a sergeant later in the war, lived a long life, dying in Glasgow at the age of eighty-seven.

DRUMMER (LATER REGIMENTAL SERGEANT MAJOR) SPENCER JOHN BENT

Army: 1st Battalion, the East Lancashire Regiment

DATE OF BRAVERY: 1/2 NOVEMBER 1914
GAZETTED: 9 DECEMBER 1914

Spencer Bent was born in Stowmarket, Suffolk, on 18 March 1891. His father was killed in the Boer War, so young Spencer was brought up by his uncle and aunt, who lived near Ipswich. He was just fourteen when he joined the Army as a drummer in the East Lancashire Regiment. When he took up boxing, he was soon christened 'Joe' – a parody of 'Chow' Bent, a well-known professional boxer at the time. The nickname stayed with him until his death.

He arrived in France on 22 August 1914, the first day of armed conflict between Britain and Germany, and saw action at Le Cateau, but it was in the first Battle of Ypres where he won his VC. His platoon was holding one of the front-line trenches near Le Gheir after a ferocious day's fighting the previous day, and an exhausted Bent was trying to get some sleep. However, he awoke to find his comrades abandoning their positions. There was no officer in the trench to give the order to withdraw, nor even an NCO, as the platoon's sergeant was visiting an advance post, but someone had passed word down the line that the battalion had been ordered to retire. Bent started following the others, but then decided he could not do without his treasured French trumpet so made his way back for it. When he reached the trench, he spotted a soldier crawling around, raised his rifle and demanded that the man, whom he assumed to be a German, identify himself. It turned out to be the platoon's recently returned sergeant, who told him that no orders to retire had been given. Bent immediately ran after his comrades to call them back. While doing this, he met an officer who helped him round up the rest of the platoon.

Early the next morning, the German infantry advanced confidently towards the trench (some reports say that they were goose-stepping), clearly believing that it had been abandoned. When they got to within 400 yards, the British platoon's machine-gun and rifles opened fire, causing the advancing infantrymen to run for cover. However, soon the German artillery launched a heavy, continuous bombardment, and the officer, platoon sergeant and a number of the men were killed or injured. Bent therefore took command and repelled several more infantry attacks until he was relieved later in the day.

This was just one of several courageous actions by Drummer Bent in the autumn of 1914. On 22 October he had carried ammunition to a patrol that had been cut off by the Germans, and two days later he had brought food and ammunition to a front-line trench under very heavy shell and rifle fire. Then, on 3 November, he went into no man's land to rescue several wounded men. One of these, Private McNulty, was a full thirty yards from the British trench, and whenever Bent attempted to lift him the two men were met by a hail of bullets from the Germans. So, in order to get him to safety, Bent hooked his feet under McNulty's armpits and edged backwards, dragging the injured man behind him.

Shortly after this successful rescue, Bent himself was seriously injured, sustaining a gunshot wound to his leg, shrapnel injuries to both arms and hands, and a small wound to the head. He was sent back to England, where he received several months of medical care, and only learned he had won the VC when he read about it in his local paper. He was the first man from his regiment to win a VC in the Great War, collecting his decoration from George V at Buckingham Palace on 13 January 1915.

Bent was promoted to corporal and helped with the national recruitment campaign for six months before being promoted again, to sergeant. He returned to France in 1916 and rejoined his old battalion on the Somme. He remained there until November, when he again returned to England to convalesce from the stresses of life in the trenches. But in January 1917, he was back on the continent, this time with the 7th Battalion of his regiment. He took part in the battles of Messines Ridge and Passchendaele, then rejoined the 1st Battalion in time for the German Spring Offensive and the subsequent battles of summer and autumn 1918. In fighting around the village of Sepmeries, this formidable soldier won the Military Medal, notably for leading two patrols which attacked the enemy on 29 October.

He returned home for good in May 1919, left the Army in 1926 and went on to work as a caretaker and a commissionaire.

He died peacefully in his sleep in London at the age of eighty-six.

†LIEUTENANT (LATER BRIGADIER AND THE RT. HON SIR) JOHN GEORGE SMYTH

Indian Army: 15th Ludhiana Sikhs

DATE OF BRAVERY: 18 MAY 1915
GAZETTED: 29 JUNE 1915

John Smyth was born in Teignmouth, Devon, on 24 October 1893 and attended the Royal Military Academy, Sandhurst. He joined the Indian Army as a second lieutenant on 24 August 1912. The following year, he joined the 15th Ludhiana Sikhs, becoming a full lieutenant in November 1914. He distinguished himself while serving with the Lahore Division from September 1914 to August 1915.

The Allies had captured a trench, known as the 'Glory Hole', near Richebourg L'Aouve, France. Early on the morning of 18 May 1915, the Germans tried to recapture it. Efforts were made to supply two forward companies – one from the 15th Ludhiana Sikhs and the other from the 1st Highland Light Infantry – that had moved in under cover of darkness to relieve the men in the captured trench. However, those attempting to bring the supplies were shot down before they had covered half the distance. Groups sent back for supplies by both of the forward companies suffered the same fate.

In this desperate situation, Smyth asked for volunteers from his Sikhs and every man in the company stepped forward. He therefore chose the ten he considered to be the strongest. This little party gathered up bandoliers of ammunition and two boxes, each containing forty-eight bombs. After sneaking over the parapet, they quickly lost three men to shell fire. However, using smoke from the German shelling as cover, they continued to creep along a trench barely two feet deep and full of dead British, Indian and German bodies. They were only a third of the way to their target when they were spotted, and enemy machine-gunners and riflemen inflicted additional casualties. Further along, they had to wade through a chest-deep stream. Eventually, only Smyth and one other man, Sepoy Lal Singh, reached a shell hole close to their objective with one of the boxes of bombs. As they dashed over the last few yards, Singh was mortally wounded. Smyth was uninjured, although his tunic and cap had been pierced with bullet holes. All the Sikhs in his party had been killed or seriously wounded. It had been a high price to pay for getting one box of ammunition to within some twenty yards of the intended target. When Smyth received his VC at Buckingham Palace on 12 July 1916, he was the only man from a large group of recipients who could walk unaided.

He went on to serve on the North-West Frontier for nearly three years, being promoted to brigade major in 1918. In May the following year, two frontier tribes, the Wazirs and Mahsuds, rose up against the British. Smyth showed great courage when he helped save a convoy of supplies that had been ambushed by the Mahsuds. His commanding officer recommended him for a bar to his VC, but he was awarded the Military Cross instead. Thereafter, he remained in the Army and continued his illustrious career. He was mentioned in dispatches at least three times in three other conflicts: in Mesopotamia; quelling a riot in the Indian city of Peshawar; and in the Second World War, when he was involved in fighting prior to Dunkirk. Later in the war, he served in Burma and took part in several battles against the Japanese. In 1950, he became the Conservative MP for Norwood, and five years later he was created a baronet. In 1956, he was a co-founder of the

Victoria Cross and George Cross Association. He retired from Parliament in 1966 and died on 26 April 1983.

SECOND LIEUTENANT SIDNEY CLAYTON WOODROFFE

Army: 8th Battalion, the Rifle Brigade (Prince Consort's Own)

DATE OF BRAVERY: 30 JULY 1915
GAZETTED: 6 SEPTEMBER 1915

Sidney Woodroffe was born in Lewes, Sussex, on 17 December 1895 and was educated at Marlborough College, where he was a senior prefect and represented the school at rugby, cricket and hockey. He then attended Pembroke College, Cambridge, after gaining a classical scholarship. He joined the Rifle Brigade two days before Christmas 1914 and went to France in May of the following year before winning his VC for conspicuous bravery at Hooge, Flanders.

Woodroffe's father, who lost three of his four sons in the Great War, received a letter from Lieutenant R.C. Maclachlan which spelled out precisely how courageous Sidney had been:

> Your younger boy was simply one of the bravest of the brave, and the work he did that day will stand out as a record hard to beat . . . When the line was attacked and broken on his right he still held his trench, and only when the Germans were discovered to be in the rear of him did he leave it. He then withdrew his remaining men very skilfully right away to a flank, and worked his way alone back to me to report. He finally brought his command back, and then took part in the counter-attack. He was killed out in front, in the open, cutting the wire to enable the attack to be continued. This is the bald statement of his part of that day's action. He risked his life for others right through the

day and finally gave it for the sake of his men. He was a splendid type of young officer, always bold as a lion, confident and sure of himself too. The loss he is to me personally is very great, as I have learnt to appreciate what a sterling fine lad he was. His men would have followed him anywhere.

PRIVATE (LATER SERGEANT) HENRY EDWARD KENNY

Army: 1st Battalion, the Loyal North Lancashire Regiment

DATE OF BRAVERY: 25 SEPTEMBER 1915
GAZETTED: 30 MARCH 1916

Henry Kenny was born in Hackney, north-east London, on 27 July 1888 and won his VC for bravery at the Battle of Loos, the first major assault by the British Army on the Western Front. This battle was fought by the British 1st and 4th Corps in support of the campaign orchestrated by General Joseph Joffre, the French commander-in-chief, in Champagne. It became infamous for the heavy casualties suffered by poorly trained British troops and for their use of poison gas against the Germans, and confirmed – at a terrible cost – the assessment of Secretary of State for War Lord Kitchener: 'the German lines in France may be looked on as a fortress that cannot be carried by assault'.

On the very first day of the battle, Kenny went out into the open on six occasions in order to carry back wounded men. This was despite heavy shell, rifle and machine-gun fire. On his last rescue mission of the day he was wounded in the neck as he handed the injured soldier over the parapet, but he survived both the battle and the war to enjoy a long life, dying in Chertsey, Surrey, at the age of ninety.

PRIVATE GEORGE STANLEY PEACHMENT

Army: 2nd Battalion, the King's Royal Rifle Corps

DATE OF BRAVERY: 25 SEPTEMBER 1915
GAZETTED: 18 NOVEMBER 1915

George Peachment, one of the youngest men ever to receive the VC, was born in Bury, Lancashire on 5 May 1897. He enlisted in his home town in 1915 and went to France later the same year.

The Battle of Loos began in earnest at 6.30 a.m. on 25 September 1915, although there had already been the typical four-day artillery barrage of the German front line to 'soften up' the enemy. However, when the British used poison gas, things did not go to plan. Men of the 2nd Battalion King's Royal Rifles and 1st Battalion Loyal North Lancs were forced to go 'over the top' because they were choking and coughing on their own gas, which had drifted back into the British front lines after the canisters had been fired at the German positions. Thereafter, two enemy machine-guns which had escaped damage during the artillery bombardment took a terrible toll on the advancing British soldiers. A few Tommies managed to reach the barbed-wire defences but they were cut down by heavy fire. Unsurprisingly, the attack faltered and soldiers took cover in shell holes and natural hollows. At 7.30 a.m., those who had survived began to struggle back to their trenches.

Peachment did not return, due to his bravery in going to the aid of his commanding officer. The *London Gazette* detailed the baby-faced private's courage:

> During very heavy fighting, when our frontline was com-
> pelled to retire in order to reorganise, Private Peachment,
> seeing his Company Commander, Capt. Dubs, lying

wounded, crawled to assist him. The enemy's fire was intense, but . . . Private Peachment never thought of saving himself. He knelt in the open by his officer and tried to help him, but while doing this he was first wounded by a bomb and a minute later mortally wounded by a rifle bullet. He was one of the youngest men in his battalion, and gave this splendid example of courage and self-sacrifice.

Dubs survived his injuries and wrote an affectionate and moving letter to Peachment's mother:

I cannot tell you how sorry I am that your brave son was killed, but I hope it may be some little consolation to you to know how bravely he behaved and how he met his end . . . When we reached the [barbed] wire we found it absolutely untouched by our artillery fire and an almost impassable obstacle as a result. However we had to push on, and I gave the order to try to get through and over it. Your son followed me over the wire and advanced with me about 20 yards through it till we were only about 15 yards from the German trench. None of the other men of the line were able to get as far and he was the only man with me. As a matter of fact I had not noticed your son was with me, but at this point a bomb hit me in the eye, blowing it and part of my face away. I fell to the ground, but on sitting up, found your son kneeling beside me. The German fire was at this time very intense, but your son was perfectly cool. He asked me for my field dressing and started bandaging my head quite oblivious to the fire. His first thought was to help me, and though there was a shell hole nearby where he might have got cover, he never thought of doing so. Of course the Germans were bound to see us sitting up, and one of them threw a bomb which hit your son in the chest while at the same time I received a bullet also in the chest. Your son was beyond feeling any pain, though still alive. I tried to drag him into the shell hole and at the same time keep him from moving, but at that moment a bullet hit him in the head and killed him. After his first wound he was bound to die, in fact he was already, immediately after he received it, unconscious to any pain. I lay beside him there all day, and eventually we were both picked up in the late afternoon when the trench was taken by a flank attack.

I can't tell you how much I admired your son's bravery and pluck. He lost his life in trying to help me and no man could have been braver than he was . . . I have recommended him for the VC and have heard that the Commanding Officer has seen the recommendation. If he gets it, it is sad to think he is not in this world to receive all the congratulations he would get, but perhaps it may be a comfort to you . . . Your son died the finest death that man can die, he showed the greatest gallantry a man can show; and I hope these facts may help you in your sad loss, together with the fact that he was spared all pain and suffering.

CORPORAL ALFRED GEORGE DRAKE

Army: 8th Battalion, the Rifle Brigade (Prince Consort's Own)

DATE OF BRAVERY: 23 NOVEMBER 1915
GAZETTED: 22 JANUARY 1916

Alfred Drake was born in Mile End, London, on 10 December 1893 and won his VC near La Brique, France, at the age of twenty-one. The *London Gazette* reported:

He [Drake] was one of a patrol of four which was reconnoitring towards the German lines. The patrol was discovered when close to the enemy, who opened heavy fire with rifles and a machine gun, wounding the officer and one man. The latter was carried back by the last remaining man. Corpl. Drake remained with his officer, and was last seen kneeling beside him and bandaging his wounds, regardless of the enemy's fire. Later a rescue party, crawling near the German lines, found the officer and corporal – the former unconscious, but alive and bandaged; Corpl. Drake beside him dead and riddled with bullets. He had given his life and saved his officer.

TEMPORARY MAJOR STEWART WALKER LOUDOUN-SHAND

Army: 10th Battalion, the Yorkshire Regiment (Alexandra, Princess of Wales's Own)

DATE OF BRAVERY: 1 JULY 1916
GAZETTED: 9 SEPTEMBER 1916

Stewart Loudoun-Shand was born in Ceylon on 8 October 1879 and educated at Dulwich College, south-east London. In his late teens, he started a career in banking in Ceylon, but when the Boer War broke out in 1899 he wanted to see action and joined the Pembrokeshire Yeomanry. He served throughout the South African conflict, then returned to Ceylon and accepted a mercantile appointment in Port Elizabeth. However, the outbreak of the Great War tempted him away again. He returned to Britain, joined the Yorkshire Regiment, and was given command of a company.

He won his VC on 1 July 1916, the first day of the Battle of the Somme. The *London Gazette* reported:

When his company attempted to climb over the parapet to attack the enemy's trenches, they were met by very fierce machine-gun fire, which temporarily stopped their progress. Major Loudoun-Shand immediately leapt on the parapet, helped the men over it, and encouraged them in every way until he fell mortally wounded. Even then he insisted on being propped up in the trench, and went on encouraging the non-commissioned officers and men until he died.

SERGEANT ALBERT GILL

Army: 1st Battalion, the King's Royal Rifle Corps

DATE OF BRAVERY: 27 JULY 1916
GAZETTED: 26 OCTOBER 1916

Albert Gill was born in Birmingham on 8 September 1879 and won his VC at the age of thirty-six during the Battle of the Somme. The *London Gazette* described the circumstances:

At Delville Wood, France, the enemy made a very strong counter-attack on the right flank of the battalion, and rushed the bombing post, after killing all the bombers. Sergt. Gill rallied the remnants of his platoon, none of whom were skilled bombers, and reorganised his defences, a most difficult and dangerous task, the trench being very shallow and much damaged. Soon afterwards the enemy nearly surrounded his men by creeping up through the thick undergrowth, and commencing sniping at about 20 yards' range. Although it was almost certain death, Sergt. Gill stood boldly up in order to direct the fire of his men. He was killed almost at once, but not before he had shown his men where the enemy were, and thus enabled them to hold up their advance. By his supreme devotion to duty and self-sacrifice he saved a very dangerous situation.

Gill is buried at Delville Wood Cemetery, Longueval. His widow, Rosetta, received Albert's posthumous VC from George V at Buckingham Palace on 29 November 1916.

†CAPTAIN NOEL GODFREY CHAVASSE

Army: Royal Army Medical Corps, attached to 1/10th Battalion, the King's (Liverpool Scottish) Regiment

DATE OF BRAVERY: VC – 9/10 AUGUST 1916; BAR – 31 JULY–2 AUGUST 1917
GAZETTED: VC – 26 OCTOBER 1916; BAR – 14 SEPTEMBER 1917

Noel Chavasse, one of just three men to have won the VC and bar, was born in the vicarage at St Peter le Bailey, Oxford, on 9 November 1884. When his father became the Bishop of Liverpool in 1900, Chavasse was educated at Liverpool College School, and in 1908 he graduated with a first in philosophy from Trinity College, Oxford. While at university, he was a talented sportsman, earning blues for athletics and lacrosse. After qualifying as a doctor in 1912, he became house physician at the Royal Southern Hospital, Liverpool. The following year, he became house surgeon at the same hospital.

Once the war broke out, he served with the Royal Army Medical Corps in France and Belgium, where he was attached to the 10th King's (Liverpool Scottish). This battalion saw action in June 1915 at Hooge, near Ypres, when Chavasse continually went into no man's land for nearly forty-eight hours until he was satisfied that there were no more wounded men who needed treatment. He won the Military Cross for his efforts. Shortly afterwards, he asked one of his sisters to buy 1,000 pairs of socks and other comforts out of his own money for the battalion.

On 27 July 1916, the battalion was moved to trenches in front of Guillemont. Although unable to reconnoitre the enemy positions, they still attacked at 4.20 a.m. on 9 August. A few hours later, they had sustained 189 casualties out of 600 men. Chavasse attended to the wounded all day under heavy fire, frequently in view of the enemy. During the night, he searched for injured men directly in front of the enemy lines. The next day, he recruited a stretcher-bearer and, under heavy shell fire, carried a critically injured man 500 yards to safety. On the return journey, Chavasse was wounded but it did not stop him from further sterling deeds that night. Helped by twenty volunteers, he rescued three wounded men from a shell-hole just thirty-six yards from the enemy trenches. He also buried the bodies of two officers and collected numerous identity discs from dead soldiers. It was estimated that during those two days, Chavasse saved the lives of some twenty seriously wounded men as well as treating countless 'ordinary' cases that passed through his hands.

Almost a year later, the battalion moved to trenches near Wieltje, to the north-east of Ypres. Preparations were made for what was to be the third Battle of Ypres – an attempt to recapture the Passchendaele Ridge. The new offensive began on 31 July and the Liverpool Scottish, poorly protected against the enemy's mustard gas, lost 2 officers and 141 other ranks. On the first evening of the battle, Chavasse was wounded in the skull. He had his injury bandaged but refused to be evacuated. Time and again, under heavy fire and in appalling weather, he went into no man's land to search for and attend to the wounded. With virtually no food, in great pain and desperately weary, he certainly saved numerous lives. In the early hours of 2 August, he was finally taking a rest at his aid post when it was struck by a shell. Everyone in the post was either killed or wounded. Chavasse himself suffered at least six injuries but he crawled for half a mile to get help for the others. He was taken through Ypres to the 46th Field Ambulance and then on to the 32nd Casualty Clearing Station, but his face was unrecognisable and he had a serious wound to the abdomen. After an operation on the latter injury, he found the strength to dictate a letter to his fiancée (and cousin), Gladys Chavasse, in which he explained why he had carried on working in spite of his injuries. He insisted 'duty called and duty must be obeyed'. He died at 2 p.m. on 4 August.

The bar to his VC was gazetted on 14 September 1917 and the decoration was presented to his next of kin. The citation praised Noel Chavasse, VC and Bar, MC, for 'his extraordinary energy and inspiring example'. He was the only man to win a VC and bar in the Great War, and has at least twelve memorials dedicated to his memory – more than any other VC holder in the world.

LANCE CORPORAL THOMAS BRYAN

Army: 25th (Service) Battalion, the Northumberland Fusiliers

DATE OF BRAVERY: 9 APRIL 1917
GAZETTED: 8 JUNE 1917

Thomas Bryan was born in Stourbridge, Worcestershire, on 21 January 1882 and worked as a miner in Castleford, Yorkshire, before enlisting in the Northumberland Fusiliers. His moment of glory on the battlefield came on the first day of the Arras Offensive when he took part in an attack on the German positions on the southern slopes of the Vimy Ridge. He was a member of the 34th Division, operating to the right of the Canadian forces, who were attacking the main ridge.

Early in the battle, the 34th Division was held up by a well-placed machine-gun, which from a distance of 300 yards was mowing down British soldiers as they came over the ridge. In no time, there was a huge pile of dead and wounded bodies in front of the British trenches. Bryan identified the problem and decided to tackle it. The *London Gazette* recorded how he succeeded in doing so:

> Although wounded, this Non-Commissioned Officer went forward alone with a view to silencing a machine-gun which was inflicting much damage. He worked up most skilfully along a communication trench, approached the gun from behind, disabled it and killed two of the team as they were abandoning the gun. As the machine-gun had been a serious obstacle in the advance to the second objective [taking the Vimy Ridge], the results obtained by Lance Corporal Bryan's gallant action were far-reaching.

George V presented Bryan with his VC at St James' Park, Newcastle, on 17 June 1917. After the war, Bryan returned to the pits in Castleford and later in Doncaster. He died on 13 October 1945.

SERGEANT (LATER CAPTAIN) HARRY CATOR

Army: 7th Battalion, the East Surrey Regiment
DATE OF BRAVERY: 9 APRIL 1917
GAZETTED: 8 JUNE 1917

Harry Cator was born in Drayton, Norfolk, on 24 January 1894 and before the war worked on the Midland and Great Northern Railway. He enlisted in the Army on 3 September 1914, the day after marrying his girlfriend, and landed at Boulogne on 2 June 1915. Over the next year, the East Surreys were part of the 37th Brigade, 12th Division, which took part in some of the heaviest fighting of the war. Cator won the

Military Medal for his bravery on 23 August 1916 when he rescued a number of wounded soldiers from no man's land after the attack on Ovillers, during the Battle of the Somme.

However, on 9 April 1917, he showed still greater courage on the first day of the Scarpe Battle, near Arras. As it advanced, his platoon suffered heavy losses as a result of enemy machine-gun fire from 'Hangest Trench', near the Arras–Feuchy road, and Cator decided he had to do something to stop the slaughter of his comrades. He and another soldier advanced across open ground and headed for the machine-gun post at one end of the trench through a hail of bullets. The other man was soon killed, but Cator continued forward, picking up a Lewis gun and some ammunition as he went. When he was close enough, he stopped, took aim with the Lewis gun, and killed the machine-gun team. He then single-handedly held on to that end of the trench, which enabled a bomb squad to take the rest of it, capturing a hundred prisoners and four more machine-guns.

Three days after his fearless action, Cator was badly wounded by a bursting shell which fractured his jaw. While he was recovering in hospital in Bristol he was told he had won the VC, and he received the medal from George V at Buckingham Palace on 21 July 1917. He became a civil servant after being discharged from the Army in 1919, and during the Second World War he was a captain and quartermaster in the Norfolk Home Guard. Later, he served as commandant of Cranwick prisoner-of-war camp in Norfolk. He died in Norwich on 7 April 1966.

ACTING CAPTAIN ARTHUR HENDERSON

*Army: 4th Battalion, the Argyll and Sutherland Highlanders
(Princess Louise's), attached to 2nd Battalion*

DATE OF BRAVERY: 23 APRIL 1917
GAZETTED: 5 JULY 1917

Arthur Henderson was born in Paisley on 6 May 1893 and enlisted in the Argyll and Sutherland Highlanders in August 1914. He took part in the Battle of the Somme as an acting captain and commanded A Company of his battalion in the second Battle of the Scarpe. He and his company were ordered to attack part of the Hindenburg Line, near Fontaine-les-Croisilles, on 23 April 1917.

The offensive began at 4.45 a.m. with an attack by two companies of Argyll and Sutherland Highlanders flanked by one company from the Middlesex Regiment and one from the 4th Suffolk Regiment. By 6.30 a.m., Henderson's company had achieved its objective. However, four hours later, the Germans counter-attacked and drove back the Suffolks on Henderson's right, which in turn meant that the Highlanders and the Middlesex Regiment were isolated. Henderson personally led a bayonet charge against a 'large body' of the enemy, even though his company was being attacked from the front and the rear.

The next morning, it became apparent that A Company and a platoon from B Company had held their position in spite of being isolated and up against a far larger enemy force, which by then had withdrawn. However, Henderson, who had been wounded during the attack the previous day, was shot and killed as he tended to his injured men that morning. His father received his VC on his behalf from George V at Buckingham Palace on 21 July 1917.

MICHAEL ASHCROFT

CORPORAL EDWARD FOSTER

Army: 13th Battalion, the East Surrey Regiment

DATE OF BRAVERY: 24 APRIL 1917
GAZETTED: 27 JUNE 1917

Edward Foster was born in Streatham, south London, on 4 February 1886 and became a dustman after leaving school. He joined the East Surreys shortly after the outbreak of war, and – at 6 feet 2 inches tall and 20 stones – rapidly became an instantly recognisable member of the regiment. Typically for the Army at the time, he was given the nickname 'Tiny'. He won his VC for bravery at Villers Plouich, France, as the *London Gazette* reported:

> During an attack the advance was held up in a portion of a village by two enemy machine guns which were entrenched and strongly covered by wire entanglements. Corporal Foster, who was in charge of two Lewis guns, succeeded in entering the trench and engaging the enemy guns. One of the Lewis guns was lost, but Corporal Foster, with reckless courage, rushed forward and bombed the enemy, thereby recovering the gun. Then getting his two guns into action, he killed the enemy gun team and captured their guns, thereby enabling the advance to continue successfully.

After the war, Wandsworth Borough Council re-employed their hero dustman but, as a mark of respect, promoted him to 'Dusting Inspector'. Foster, who was described as 'a big man with a big heart' and 'most modest and unassuming', died suddenly on 22 January 1946, just before his sixtieth birthday.

SECOND LIEUTENANT FRANK BERNARD WEARNE

Army: 10th Battalion, the Essex Regiment, attached to 11th Battalion

DATE OF BRAVERY: 28 JUNE 1917
GAZETTED: 2 AUGUST 1917

Frank Wearne was born in Kensington, west London, on 1 March 1894 and was educated at Bromsgrove School, Worcestershire, and Corpus Christi, Oxford. He enlisted in September 1914, received his commission six months later and then was attached to the 10th (Service) Battalion, Essex Regiment, with whom he sailed for France in July 1915. The following May, the 10th Essex moved into billets at Franvillers, near Amiens. The next month, Wearne pulled off a coup by capturing a German soldier – the first to fall to the 10th Essex – during a night patrol.

On 3 July, just after the beginning of the Battle of the Somme, Wearne was seriously wounded in the ear and was evacuated to England. He eventually recovered but never returned to the 10th Essex, instead serving with the 11th. He returned to France in May 1917 and joined C Company in the Loos Salient. The next month he was given orders to lead a raiding party, and early on the evening of 28 June it assembled in a large dugout. Once it left that trench the fighting was fierce, as the *London Gazette* recorded:

> [Wearne] gained his objective in the face of much opposition and by his magnificent example and daring was able to maintain this position for a considerable time, according to instructions. During this period 2nd Lieutenant Wearne and his small party were repeatedly counter-attacked. Grasping the fact that if the left flank was lost his men would have to give way, 2nd Lieutenant

Wearne, at a moment when the enemy's attack was being heavily pressed and when matters were most critical, leapt on the parapet, and followed by his left Section, ran along the top of the trench, firing and throwing bombs. His unexpected daring threw the enemy off his guard and back in disorder. Whilst on the top of the trench 2nd Lieutenant Wearne was severely wounded, but refused to leave his men. Afterwards he remained in the trench, directing operations, consolidating his position and encouraging all ranks. Just before the order to withdraw was given, the gallant officer was again severely hit for the second time, and while being carried away was mortally wounded. By his tenacity in remaining at his post and his magnificent fighting spirit, he was enabled to hold on to the flank.

Colonel Spring, the 11th Essex's commanding officer, recommended Wearne for his VC on account of his 'superb courage, leadership and self-sacrifice'. The decoration was presented to Wearne's father by George V at Buckingham Palace on 20 October 1917.

TEMPORARY CAPTAIN HAROLD ACKROYD

Army: Royal Army Medical Corps, attached to 6th Battalion, the Royal Berkshire Regiment (Princess Charlotte of Wales's)

DATE OF BRAVERY: 31 JULY/1 AUGUST 1917
GAZETTED: 6 SEPTEMBER 1917

Harold Ackroyd was born in Southport, Lancashire, on 18 July 1877, and forty years later he was fearless in his determination to help wounded soldiers at Ypres, Belgium. The *London Gazette* described his astonishing courage in the heat of battle:

During recent operations Capt. Ackroyd displayed the greatest gallantry and devotion to duty. Utterly regardless of danger, he worked continuously for many hours up and down in front of the line tending the wounded and saving the lives of officers and men. In doing so he had to move across the open under heavy machine-gun, rifle and shellfire. He carried a wounded officer to a place of safety under very heavy fire. On another occasion he went some way in front of our advanced line and brought in a wounded man under continuous sniping and machine-gun fire. His heroism was the means of saving many lives, and provided a magnificent example of courage, cheerfulness and determination to the fighting men in whose midst he was carrying out his splendid work.

After two days of unstinting bravery that earned him the VC, Ackroyd emerged uninjured. However, he was killed on the same battlefield just ten days later, before he knew of the award.

PRIVATE (LATER FLIGHT SERGEANT) GEORGE IMBACH McINTOSH

Army: 1/6th Battalion, the Gordon Highlanders/RAF

DATE OF BRAVERY: 31 JULY 1917
GAZETTED: 6 SEPTEMBER 1917

George McIntosh was born in Buckie, Scotland, on 24 April 1897 and enlisted in the Gordon Highlanders in 1913. He disembarked at Le Havre in November 1914, and over the next two and a half years was present at most of the major engagements fought by his battalion.

On 30 July 1917, the 1/6th Gordons – as part of the 152nd Brigade, 51st Highland Division – moved into the line for the assault on Pilckem Ridge, near Ypres. At 3.50 a.m. the next day, a barrage of eighteen-pounder shrapnel burst on the German front line, then continued for the next six to eight minutes while the infantry crossed no man's land. By 4.40 a.m., the first objective had been achieved and the main German observation posts overlooking the Ypres salient were in British hands.

It was just about possible to ford the Steenbeck River, which was some fifteen feet wide but thick with mud because its drainage had been damaged by shelling. At about 7 a.m., the 1/6th Gordons, who had been held in reserve up to that point, approached the river and began wading through the muddy water. They quickly came under heavy fire from an enemy emplacement beyond the opposite bank and the advance was threatened, but that was the cue for McIntosh to spring into action. He decided, without orders, to cross the Steenbeck alone. The *London Gazette* described what happened next:

> Private McIntosh immediately rushed forward under heavy fire, and reaching the emplacement, he threw a Mills grenade into it, killing two of the enemy and wounding a third. Subsequently entering the dug-out he found two light machine-guns, which he carried back with him. His quick grasp of the situation and the utter fearlessness and rapidity with which he acted undoubtedly saved many of his comrades, and enabled the consolidation to proceed unhindered by machine-gun fire. Throughout the day the cheerfulness and courage of Private McIntosh was indomitable, and to his fine example in a great measure was due the success which attended his company.

McIntosh survived the First World War and, on the outbreak of the Second, tried to rejoin his old regiment. He was too old to be accepted as an infantryman, but he managed to enlist instead in the RAF, in which he served as ground crew. He ended the war in 1945 as a flight sergeant, then returned to his pre-war job as a caretaker at Buckie High School, where he remained until retirement. He had the freedom of Buckie conferred on him in December 1955 and died in Aberdeen five years later.

SERGEANT JOSEPH LISTER

Army: 1st Battalion, the Lancashire Fusiliers

DATE OF BRAVERY: 9 OCTOBER 1917
GAZETTED: 26 NOVEMBER 1917

Joseph Lister was born in Salford, Lancashire, on 19 October 1886. He won his VC at Ypres, as the *London Gazette* recorded:

> When advancing to the first objective, his company came under machine-gun fire from the direction of two 'pill-boxes'. Seeing that the galling fire would hold up our advance and prevent our troops keeping up with the barrage, Sergt. Lister dashed ahead of his men and found a machine-gun firing from a shell-hole in front of the 'pill-box'. He shot two of the enemy gunners, and the remainder surrendered to him. He then went on to the 'pill-box' and shouted to the occupants to surrender. They did so with the exception of one man, whom Sergt. Lister shot dead; whereupon about 100 of the enemy emerged from shell-holes farther to the rear and surrendered. This non-commissioned officer's prompt act of courage enabled our line to advance with hardly a check and to keep up with the barrage, the loss of which might have jeopardised the whole course of the local battle.

Lister died on 19 January 1963 in Stockport, aged seventy-six.

†TEMPORARY LIEUTENANT COLONEL WILFRITH ELSTOB

Army: 16th Battalion, the Manchester Regiment

DATE OF BRAVERY: 21 MARCH 1918
GAZETTED: 9 JUNE 1919

Wilfrith Elstob was born in Chichester, Sussex, on 8 September 1888. He proved himself a formidable soldier during the First World War. Yet, as well as being a tough and brave serviceman, Elstob wrote sensitive, thoughtful letters. In one to his friend Hubert Worthington, dated 6 May 1917, he wrote: 'Hu, I hardly dare mention the losses, for my heart is full and I know how you will feel. On the battlefield as one moved about amongst shells and bullets – Death seemed a very small thing and at times enviable. Here we are English and German – we, or rather those damned Journalists, talk about Hate – it seems to me to disappear on the battlefield. People who have not been there talk a lot of damned nonsense. We are all "blind", as a private soldier on the night after the battle said to me. "We know it is not their quarrel, sir".'

By March 1918, Elstob had already been awarded the Distinguished Service Order (DSO) and the Military Cross (MC). However, it was for his astonishing bravery while commanding the 16th Battalion that he won the VC. On 21 March, the battalion was based in and around a stronghold, which since its capture by the 2nd Manchesters, was known as Manchester Hill. The control of this hill was vitally important – it meant control of the St Quentin-Savy road. A few days earlier, Elstob had addressed his men and, pointing at the blackboard showing various company locations, said: 'This is Battalion HQ. Here we fight and here we die.'

The British knew that there was going to be a massive German attack on its positions. It began at 6.30 a.m. on 21 March with the roar of innumerable heavy guns. A combination of thick fog and smoke from the heavy shelling made it impossible for the battalion to see the Germans advancing. Yet by 8.30 a.m., news came that A Company was virtually surrounded. Minutes later B Company had suffered the same fate. By 11.30 a.m., as the fog lifted, the enemy could be seen advancing in massive numbers. However, using a buried telegraph cable, Elstob sent a message to his Brigade Commander: 'The Manchester Regiment will defend Manchester Hill to the last man.'

The men on the hill soon became surrounded and hopelessly outnumbered. Other than D Company, many of the men were not used to fighting. They were a mixed collection of cooks, signalmen, regimental police and others, but they battled courageously. When the enemy entered the area by a trench leading from the St Quentin-Savy road, Elstob fought ferociously to stop them advancing, killing an entire German bombing party using only his revolver. When the ammunition from this ran out, he threw bombs and fired on the enemy with a rifle. Elstob was wounded but, after having his injury dressed, cheered on his men shouting 'You are doing magnificently, boys! Carry on – keep up a steady fire and they'll think there's a battalion here.'

In the afternoon, Elstob was even more inspirational and utterly fearless. Sergeant Arrundale later recounted seeing him blown five yards by a shell and wounded three times. Yet Elstob told him: 'Arrundale, they can't damn well kill me.' Elstob asked Brigade Headquarters for a reinforcement of twenty men, but they could not be spared. A staff officer at Brigade Headquarters later reported: 'At about 2 p.m. he said that most of his men were killed or wounded, including himself; that they were all getting dead-beat, that the Germans had got into the [Manchester Hill] Redoubt and hand-to-hand fighting was going on. He was still quite cheery. At 3.30 he was spoken to on the telephone and said that very few were left and that the end was nearly come. After that no answer could be got.'

One survivor later recalled Elstob's last words: 'Tell the men not to lose heart. Fight on!' Elstob held his ground firing up the trench towards the enemy when they were only some twenty-five yards away. As the enemy prepared for its final assault, he was called upon to surrender. 'Never!' he replied and moments later he was dead. By 4 p.m., the final members of the 16th, battered and wounded, surrendered. Elstob had been killed, six months before his thirtieth birthday, because he was determined to fulfil his pledge that the Manchesters would fight to the last man to defend Manchester Hill.

TEMPORARY CAPTAIN (LATER BRIGADIER) MANLEY ANGELL JAMES

Army: 8th (Service) Battalion, the Gloucestershire Regiment

DATE OF BRAVERY: 21 MARCH 1918
GAZETTED: 28 JUNE 1918

Manley James was born in Odiham, Hampshire, on 12 July 1896. After leaving school at eighteen, he joined the Gloucestershire Regiment in January 1915 as a second lieutenant. That July, he was posted to the 'Butterfly' Division of the same regiment as a lieutenant but was invalided home after being severely injured in the thigh at La Boiselle on the third day of the Battle of the Somme. In December, he returned to France as a member of Brigade HQ staff. However, he lobbied for a return to active duty and by early 1917 he was back with his regiment at the front. He was wounded by shrapnel in February, mentioned in dispatches in April and promoted to captain in May.

The 8th Battalion saw action at Wytschaete and Messines Ridge. A Company, with James in command, played a key role in the capture of a vital strongpoint at Druids Farm on 9/10 July 1917. A week later, the *London Gazette* announced he had won the Military Cross for his actions that night:

> Previous to our attack he took up a forward position under heavy hostile barrage in order to obtain accurate information as to the progress of our advance. He afterwards went forward and assisted to consolidate, as well as in the capture of a strong point, and having rallied the supports when they were disorganised by hostile fire, he led them to their position. He then made a very daring personal reconnaissance of the whole line under heavy shelling and rifle fire that he might send back a report to his battalion commander, and his total disregard of danger and brilliant initiative throughout the action were largely responsible for its success.

The men of A Company distinguished themselves again in a counter-attack on 27/8 July. As a result of their collective bravery in these two actions, Major General Tom Bridges, commanding 199th Division, awarded the company the Badge of Honour. This decoration, also known as the 'Butterfly Badge', was thereafter worn on the right sleeve by every member of A Company. It was awarded to only one other unit – a section of the Royal Engineers – throughout the Great War.

Unsurprisingly, James was much admired by his men. An anonymous biographical sketch entitled 'Our Captain' appeared in the *Butterfly Bulletin* published 'in the Trenches' in

November 1917: 'The Capt. has established himself firmly in the esteem of all men from the latest recruit to the oldest member of the Company and we all look forward to the time when Capt. James will receive the further honours that we are confident he will gain.'

On 21 March 1918, the first assault of the German Spring Offensive was launched. During this attack – the 'Kaiser Battle' – the 8th Gloucesters were subjected to one of the most intensive bombardments of the war. Along a forty-mile front, a total of 6,473 German guns opened up for several weeks, firing both explosives and gas. In a letter to James's father, the commanding officer of the 8th wrote: 'The battalion fought most gallantly on the 21st and 22nd and your son as usual was untiring. "A" Coy. had lost 75% of their men and were overwhelmed by fresh masses of the enemy. On the 23rd only stragglers came out.'

The survivors were convinced that their captain must be among the dead. One wrote: 'Captn. James said to us few left ["]we are surrounded boys every man for himself[";] he then got on the fire step and started firing at the advancing enemy[,] telling us to run if we could possibly get away . . . After that I saw nothing of the Captain or other officers nor have I seen them since.'

On 25 April 1918, the British Red Cross wrote to James's mother, reporting that two eyewitnesses had seen him dead: 'Capt. James was shot in the head by a bullet and died instantly; I saw it,' said one private; and A Company's sergeant major stated, 'Capt. James was killed in the retreat from Cambrai.' In May, a third report was sent to Mrs James, also indicating her son was dead. However, on 24 May, a telegram was sent to the War Office: 'Manley James Glosters [*sic*] prisoner wounded wiring camp when known.' The next month, the *London Gazette* announced that he had won the VC but had little cast-iron information on his whereabouts or his state of health:

> Capt. James led his company forward with magnificent determination and courage, inflicting severe losses on the enemy and capturing 27 prisoners and two machine-guns. He was wounded, but refused to leave his company, and repulsed three hostile onslaughts the next day. Two days later, although the enemy had broken through on his right flank, he refused to withdraw, and made a most determined stand, inflicting very heavy losses on the enemy and gaining valuable time for the withdrawal of guns. He was ordered by the senior officer to hold on to the spot 'to the last', in order to enable the brigade to be extricated. He then led his company forward in a local counter-attack on his own initiative, and was again wounded. He was last seen working a machine-gun single-handed, after having been wounded a third time. No praise can be too high for the gallant stand made by this company, and Capt. James, by his dauntless courage and magnificent example, undoubtedly enabled the battalion to be withdrawn before being completely cut off.

In fact, after receiving his third wound, James had been taken prisoner on 23 March. He had been moved first by horse ambulance and then by motor ambulance to a field hospital, and spent the rest of the war in various PoW camps. After the Armistice, he was released, arriving home on Christmas Day 1918. He received his VC from George V at Buckingham Palace on 22 February 1919. James, and other heroes like him, found it difficult to get a regular commission into the Army, but he was more persistent than most and was finally commissioned as a lieutenant on 8 December 1920.

During the inter-war years, he served a great deal abroad,

including in Germany and Egypt. By 1942, he was a brigadier in command of 128th Infantry Brigade, which had prepared for desert warfare. In February that year, the 128th joined other Allied forces on the Algerian coast. There followed fierce battles against overwhelming odds and James received the Distinguished Service Order. The *London Gazette* of 21 May 1942 reported:

> He commanded his Brigade, and at times more than his brigade, with considerable success. He stopped the enemy attack on Beja, and the fact that the Hampshires fought so well must be attributed to a great extent to his personal leadership. Personally as brave as a Lion, he was at the same time careful and solicitous about how he committed his troops. His difficulties were not lightened by the fact that all through the campaign he was suffering from ear trouble, from which anyone with less guts would have gone sick at an early stage of the operations.

Naturally, the press hailed James's remarkable double – a VC in the First World War and a DSO in the Second.

After the campaign in North Africa, he fought in Italy. In September 1943, he was wounded near Salerno and was eventually evacuated in a hospital ship to Egypt to recover. The next year, he trained troops for the D-Day landings. From 1945 to 1948, he commanded the British Air Force of Occupation in Germany. In 1948, he was appointed director of Ground Defence at the Air Ministry. He retired in 1951 and was made an MBE in 1958. Brigadier Manley James, VC, DSO, MBE, MC, died at his home in Bristol on 23 September 1975, aged seventy-nine.

LIEUTENANT (LATER MAJOR) ALLAN EBENEEZER KER

Army: 3rd Battalion, the Gordon Highlanders, attached to 61st Battalion, Machine-Gun Corps

DATE OF BRAVERY: 21 MARCH 1918
GAZETTED: 4 SEPTEMBER 1919

Allan Ker was born in Edinburgh on 5 March 1883 and educated at Edinburgh Academy and Edinburgh University. He was commissioned into the Gordon Highlanders on 11 June 1915 but from 22 August 1916 was attached to the Machine-Gun Corps, travelling to France with the 61st Battalion.

He won his VC near St Quentin when, after a heavy bombardment, the Germans penetrated the British line, and the flank of the 61st Division became exposed. The *London Gazette* takes up the story:

> Lieutenant Ker with one Vickers gun succeeded in engaging the enemy's infantry, approaching under cover of dead ground, and held up the attack, inflicting many casualties. He then sent back word to his Battalion Headquarters that he had determined to stop with his Sergeant and several men who had been badly wounded and fight until a counter-attack could be launched to relieve him. Just as ammunition failed his party were attacked from behind by the enemy with bombs, machine-guns and with the bayonet. Several bayonet attacks were delivered, but each time they were repulsed by Lieutenant Ker and his companions with their revolvers, the Vickers gun having by this time been destroyed. The wounded were collected into a small shelter, and it was decided to defend them to the last and to hold up the enemy as long as possible. In one of the

many hand-to-hand encounters a German rifle and bayonet and a small supply of ammunition was secured, and subsequently used with good effect against the enemy. Although Lieutenant Ker was very exhausted from want of food and gas poisoning and from the supreme exertions he had made during ten hours of the most severe bombardment, fighting and attending to the wounded, he refused to surrender until all his ammunition was exhausted and his position was rushed by large numbers of the enemy. His behaviour throughout the day was absolutely cool and fearless, and by his determination he was materially instrumental in engaging and holding up for three hours more than 500 of the enemy.

During the Second World War, Ker was employed – with the rank of major – by the Department of the Chief of the Imperial General Staff at the War Office. He died in London on 12 September 1958.

SECOND LIEUTENANT BERNARD MATTHEW CASSIDY

Army: 2nd Battalion, the Lancashire Fusiliers

DATE OF BRAVERY: 28 MARCH 1918
GAZETTED: 3 MAY 1918

Bernard Cassidy was born in London on 17 August 1892 and won his VC at Arras, France. The *London Gazette* described the heroism he displayed on 28 March 1918:

At a time when the flank of the division was in danger, Lieut. Cassidy was in command of the left company of his battalion, which was in close support. He was given orders prior to the attack that he must hold on to the position to the last. He most nobly carried this out to the letter. The enemy came on in overwhelming numbers and endeavoured to turn the flank. He, however, continually rallied his men under a terrific bombardment. The enemy were several times cleared out of the trench by his personal leadership. His company was eventually surrounded but Lieut. Cassidy still fought on, encouraging and exhorting his men until eventually killed. By his most gallant conduct the whole line was held up to this point, and the left flank was undoubtedly saved from what might have been a disaster.

ACTING CORPORAL (LATER COMPANY QUARTERMASTER-SERGEANT) ALEXANDER PICTON BRERETON

Canadian Expeditionary Force: 8th Battalion, Manitoba Regiment

DATE OF BRAVERY: 9 AUGUST 1918
GAZETTED: 27 SEPTEMBER 1918

Alexander Brereton was born in Manitoba, Canada, on 13 November 1892. One of six children, he was educated at Hamiota and joined the Army on 31 January 1916. He won his VC during the final stages of the First World War – the day after the Allies launched their Hundred Days' Offensive, during which they gradually gained control.

Brereton's platoon was ambushed on 9 August 1918 east of Amiens, France. Machine gunners threatened to wipe out the entire platoon, which was highly exposed, but, as the *London Gazette* of 27 September 1918 explained, Brereton then went into action:

> This gallant NCO at once appreciated the critical situation, and realised that unless something was done at once his platoon would be annihilated.

On his own initiative, without a moment's delay and alone, he sprang forward and reached one of the hostile machine-gun posts, where he shot the man operating the machine-gun and bayoneted the next man who attempted to operate it, whereupon nine others surrendered to him. Corpl. Brereton's action was a splendid example of resource and bravery, and not only undoubtedly saved many of his comrades' lives, but also inspired his platoon to charge and capture the five remaining posts.

LANCE SERGEANT (LATER LIEUTENANT) EDWARD BENN SMITH

Army: 1/5th Battalion, the Lancashire Fusiliers
DATE OF BRAVERY: 21–23 AUGUST 1918
GAZETTED: 22 OCTOBER 1918

Edward Smith was born in Maryport, Cumberland, on 10 November 1898 and enlisted in July 1917. He arrived in France on 10 December and joined his regiment, the 1/5th Lancashire Fusiliers. He won the Distinguished Conduct Medal (DCM) and the VC for his actions in two battles in August 1918.

His DCM for courage during the Battle of Amiens was announced in the *London Gazette* of 30 October 1918:

> Whilst returning from the enemy line with a patrol he noticed a party of about forty of the enemy coming to take up night outpost dispositions. Though they were ten times the strength of his patrol, he waited for them and attacked them, inflicting heavy casualties and scattering them. He then most skilfully withdrew his patrol and brought it back without casualties. He showed the greatest enterprise and marked ability to command.

On 20 August 1918, Smith's battalion assembled west of the Beaumont Hamel–Puisieux-au-Mont road in preparation for the attack by the British 3rd and 4th Armies. Then, at 4.45 the following morning, the 1/5th advanced in heavy mist and under an intense barrage. Shortly after 7 a.m., at 'Beauregard Dovecote', Smith performed the first of a number of brave acts that won him the VC. The *London Gazette* reported:

> Sergeant Smith, while in command of a platoon, personally took a machine-gun post, rushing the garrison with his rifle and bayonet. The enemy, on seeing him advance, scattered to throw hand grenades at him. Regardless of all danger, and almost without halting in the rush on the post, this NCO shot and killed at least six of the enemy. Later, seeing another platoon requiring assistance, he led his men to them, took command of the situation and captured the objective. During the enemy counter-attack on the following day he led a section forward and restored a portion of the line. His personal bravery, skill and initiative were outstanding, and his conduct throughout exemplified magnificent courage and skill and was an inspiring example to all.

Smith received his VC from George V at Buckingham Palace on 9 November 1918. He continued in the Army after the war, serving in Malaya, Shanghai and Tientsin. On the outbreak of the Second World War, he re-enlisted on a short service commission as lieutenant and quartermaster. He accompanied the British Expeditionary Force to France and died from gunshot wounds to the head on 12 January 1940, aged forty-one.

ACTING LIEUTENANT COLONEL RICHARD ANNESLEY WEST

Army: North Irish Horse, attached North Somerset Yeomanry, seconded to 6th Battalion, Tank Corps

DATE OF BRAVERY: 21 AUGUST AND
   2 SEPTEMBER 1918
GAZETTED: 3 OCTOBER 1918

Richard West, who received four bravery awards in the course of the First World War, was born in Cheltenham on 26 September 1878. He served in the Boer War, ending up as a lieutenant in Kitchener's Fighting Scouts, and continued his military career in South Africa long after the war was over. At the outbreak of the Great War, he joined the North Irish Horse, Cavalry Special Reserve and became a lieutenant on 11 August 1914 and a captain on 18 November 1915. Shortly before the latter promotion, he had been attached to the North Somerset Yeomanry with the temporary rank of major.

On New Year's Day 1918, the *London Gazette* announced that he had won the Distinguished Service Order (DSO):

> On 11 April, 1917, at Monchy-le-Preux, his squadron was sent forward to reinforce the right flank of the Brigade under very heavy shell and machine-gun fire. By his excellent example, rapid grasp of the situation and skilful disposition of his squadron he did much to avert an impending German counter-attack. He had shown great ability in command of a squadron since July, 1915.

He became an acting major in the Tank Corps on 18 January 1918 and an acting lieutenant colonel on 22 August, in command of the 6th Light Tank Battalion. While with the Tank Corps, he won his second bravery medal, the Military

Cross (MC), which was announced in the *Gazette* in November 1918:

> During the advance on 8 Aug., at Guillencourt, in command of a company of Light Tanks, he displayed magnificent leadership and personal bravery. He was able to point out many targets to his Tanks that they would not otherwise have seen. During the day he had two horses shot under him, while he and his orderly between them killed five of the enemy and took seven prisoners. On the 10th he rendered great services to the Cavalry by personally reconnoitring the ground in front of Le Quesnoy, and later in the day, under very heavy machine-gun fire, rallied and organised the crew of Tanks that had been ditched, withdrawing them after dark.

Less than two weeks after the action at Guillencourt, West earned a bar for his DSO. This was gazetted on 7 November 1918:

> For conspicuous gallantry near Courcelles on 21 Aug. 1918. In consequence of this action being fought in a thick mist, this officer decided to accompany the attack to assist in maintaining direction and cohesion. This he did mounted, until his horse was shot under him, then on foot until the final objective was reached. During the advance, in addition to directing his Tanks, he rallied and led forward small bodies of Infantry lost in the mist, showing throughout a fine example of leadership and a total disregard of personal safety, and materially contributed to the success of the operations. Major West was in command of the battalion most of the time, his Commanding Officer having been killed early in the action. The consistent gallantry displayed

by this officer throughout the operations since 8 Aug. has been remarkable.

Partly because of his actions on 21 August, but even more for his heroism on 2 September, West also won the VC. The *Gazette* announced:

> On a subsequent occasion, it was intended that a battalion of Light Tanks, under the command of this officer, should exploit the initial Infantry and Heavy Tank attack. He therefore went forward in order to keep in touch with the progress of the battle, and arrived at the front line when the enemy were in process of delivering a local counter-attack. The Infantry Battalion had suffered heavy officer casualties, and its flanks were exposed. Realising that there was a danger of this battalion giving way, he at once rode out in front of them under extremely heavy machine-gun and rifle fire and rallied the men. In spite of the fact that the enemy were close upon him, he took charge of the situation and detailed non-commissioned officers to replace officer casualties. He then rode up and down in front of them in face of certain death, encouraging the men and calling to them: 'Stick it, men; show them fight, and for God's sake put up a good fight.' He fell riddled by machine-gun bullets. The magnificent bravery of this very gallant officer at the critical moment inspired the infantry to redoubled efforts, and the hostile attack was defeated.

As well as winning the VC, DSO (with bar) and MC, West was mentioned three times in dispatches during the Great War. His VC was bought privately by the trust for a sum significantly higher than the 'record' auction price at that time.

SERGEANT SAMUEL FORSYTH

New Zealand Expeditionary Force: New Zealand Engineers, attached to 2nd Battalion, Auckland Infantry Regiment

DATE OF BRAVERY: 24 AUGUST 1918
GAZETTED: 22 OCTOBER 1918

Samuel Forsyth was born in Wellington, New Zealand, on 3 April 1891 and won his VC at Grevillers, France, during a heated battle in which his regiment had been on the attack. The *London Gazette* reported:

> On nearing the objective, his company came under heavy machine-gun fire. Through Sergt. Forsyth's dashing leadership and total disregard of danger, three machine-gun positions were rushed, and the crews taken prisoner before they could inflict many casualties on our troops. During subsequent advance his company came under heavy fire from several machine-guns, two of which he located by a daring reconnaissance. In his endeavour to get support from a Tank, he was wounded, but after having the wound bandaged, he again got in touch with the Tank, which, in the face of very heavy fire from machine-guns and anti-Tank guns, he endeavoured to lead with magnificent coolness to a favourable position. The Tank, however, was put out of action. Sergt. Forsyth then organised the Tank crew and several of his men into a section, and led them to a position where the machine-guns could be outflanked. Always under heavy fire, he directed them into positions which brought about a retirement of the enemy machine-guns and enabled the advance to continue. The gallant NCO was at that moment killed by a sniper. From the commencement of the attack, until the time of his death Sergt. Forsyth's courage and coolness, combined with great power of initiative,

proved an invaluable incentive to all who were with him, and he undoubtedly saved many casualties among his comrades.

COMPANY SERGEANT MAJOR MARTIN DOYLE

Army: 1st Battalion, the Royal Munster Fusiliers

DATE OF BRAVERY: 2 SEPTEMBER 1918
GAZETTED: 31 JANUARY 1919

Martin Doyle, a prisoner of war who regained his freedom and went on to win a VC in the same conflict, was born at New Ross, County Wexford on 25 October 1891. In 1909, he joined the Royal Irish Regiment and he was serving in India at the outbreak of the First World War, whereupon he was recalled home with his regiment. He travelled to France in December 1914 and was later attached to the Royal Munster Fusiliers.

He was awarded the Military Medal in March 1918 for capturing a large barn occupied by a German gun crew. He later said of the attack: 'We had to cross about 1,000 yards of open country, exposed to terrible shell and machine-gun fire. The casualties were very heavy. I called for volunteers and went over the top with my bayonet at the charge, but when I reached the barn I was alone. I bayoneted the two Germans that I found there, seized their machine-gun and took possession of the barn.'

Shortly afterwards, he was captured by the Germans and badly treated; but after a successful Allied counter-attack, he regained his freedom. He was then promoted to acting company sergeant major and in that role became one of twenty-nine Irishmen to win the VC during the Great War. The *London Gazette* reported that he had taken command of his company because of officer casualties at Riencourt:

Observing that some of our men were surrounded by the enemy, he led a party to their assistance, and by skilled leadership worked his way along the trenches, killed several of the enemy and extricated the party, carrying back, under heavy fire, a wounded officer to a place of safety.

Later, seeing a tank in difficulties, he rushed forward under intense fire, routed the enemy who were attempting to get into it, and prevented the advance of another enemy party collecting for a further attack on the tank. An enemy machine-gun now opened on the tank at close range, rendering it impossible to get the wounded away, whereupon CSM Doyle, with great gallantry, rushed forward, and, singlehanded, silenced the machine-gun, capturing it with three prisoners. He then carried a wounded man to safety under very heavy fire. Later in the day, when the enemy counter-attacked his position, he showed great power of command, driving back the enemy and capturing many prisoners. Throughout the whole of these operations CSM Doyle set the very highest example to all ranks by his courage and total disregard of danger.

Doyle left the British Army in July 1919 and joined the Irish 'Free State Army' in February 1922. He served during the Civil War and was wounded, but then re-enlisted into the peacetime army in May 1924 before retiring in 1939. He died in Dublin the following year.

PRIVATE (LATER CORPORAL) JACK HARVEY

Army: 1/22nd (County of London) Battalion, the London Regiment (the Queen's)

DATE OF BRAVERY: 2 SEPTEMBER 1918
GAZETTED: 15 NOVEMBER 1918

Jack Harvey was born in Peckham, south London, on 24 August 1891 and joined the Army on 26 November 1914. He served with distinction throughout the war and was present at many of the major battles, but he won his VC very near the end of the conflict, on 2 September 1918, near Peronne, France. The *London Gazette* reported:

> The advance of his company was held up by intense machine-gun fire; this man at once dashed forward a distance of fifty yards alone through our barrage and in the face of heavy enemy fire, and rushed a machine-gun post, shooting two of the team and bayoneting another. He then destroyed the gun, and continued to work his way along the enemy trench, and going forward alone for about two hundred yards, single-handed rushed an enemy dug-out, which contained thirty-seven Germans, and compelled them to surrender. By these two acts of great gallantry he saved the company heavy casualties, and enabled the whole of the attacking line to advance. Throughout the entire operation he showed the most magnificent courage and determination, and by the splendid example he set to all ranks materially assisted in the success of the operation.

Harvey died in Redhill, Surrey, on 15 August 1940, just before his forty-ninth birthday.

SERGEANT LAURENCE CALVERT

Army: 5th Battalion, the King's Own Yorkshire Light Infantry

DATE OF BRAVERY: 12 SEPTEMBER 1918
GAZETTED: 15 NOVEMBER 1918

Laurence Calvert was born in Leeds on 16 February 1892 and was educated locally before joining the Territorials on 17 April 1914. He was awarded the Military Medal for bravery during the attack on Vaulxcourt, France, on 2 September 1918, and won the VC just ten days later at Havrincourt, when heavy machine-gun fire was severely hindering an operation. The *London Gazette* detailed his bravery on the latter occasion: 'Alone and single-handed Sergt. Calvert, rushing forward against the machine-gun team, bayoneted three and shot four. His valour and determination in capturing single-handed two machine-guns and killing the crews thereof enabled the ultimate objective to be won. His personal gallantry inspired all ranks.'

He was also made a Chevalier de l'Ordre de Leopold II (of Belgium) for his fighting record during the final months of the war. He died in Dagenham, Essex, on 7 July 1964.

LANCE CORPORAL (LATER CORPORAL) ALFRED WILCOX

Army: 2/4th Battalion, the Oxfordshire and Buckinghamshire Light Infantry

DATE OF BRAVERY: 12 SEPTEMBER 1918
GAZETTED: 15 NOVEMBER 1918

Alfred Wilcox was born in Aston, Birmingham, on 16 December 1884 and was educated locally at Burlington Street School. Before the Great War, he was a part-time soldier, joining the Royal Warwickshire Volunteer Battalion in 1905 and completing four years' service. When work took him to Liverpool, he did another three years' part-time service. He became a full-time soldier in the Royal Buckinghamshire Hussars on 25 March 1915. However, he was soon dismounted – changed from a cavalry to a foot soldier – and switched to the Oxfordshire and Buckinghamshire Light Infantry. He went to France in December 1917 and was promoted to lance corporal in April 1918.

He won his VC near Laventie, France, and later described the events of the day:

> I was in charge of the leading section; my duty was to cut through the wire and locate the posts. Having got to the wire and successfully cut it, I went back for my section which I had left in a shell hole 100 yards to the rear, only to find all but one wounded. That one I told to follow me. Getting through the gap I had already cut, and making my way in the trench the enemy was holding, I got into it, and, bombing my way, captured my first gun. Being quite safe from the enemy fire, I still proceeded up the trench, capturing a second gun after a hand-to-hand struggle, in which I bayoneted my man; then bombing a third post, killing five. My own rifle by this time being clogged with mud, I had to resort to German stick bombs [grenades], which accounted for a fourth post with its gun. I carried on, driving the remainder of the post right away, leaving behind about twelve dead in all and four guns (one light, three heavy). I then returned to the guns. Finding I could not remove the latter three, I put them out of action, and had to withdraw owing to lack of support and no firearms, my own gun having been dumped for free use of German stick bombs.

Wilcox was wounded on 2 November 1918 but recovered and was discharged from the Army on 2 May 1919. He later returned to the Midlands and died in Birmingham on 30 March 1951.

TEMPORARY SECOND LIEUTENANT (LATER CAPTAIN) WILLIAM ALLISON WHITE

Army: 4th Battalion, King's Own Royal Lancaster Regiment; and 38th Battalion, Machine-Gun Corps

DATE OF BRAVERY: 18 SEPTEMBER 1918
GAZETTED: 15 NOVEMBER 1918

William White was born in Mitcham, Surrey, on 19 October 1894 and joined the Territorial Army as a private in February 1910. After completing his tour of duty as a machine-gun sergeant in February 1916, he was discharged. However, he immediately joined the Machine-Gun Corps as a staff sergeant instructor, and was commissioned a second lieutenant on 26 June 1918.

He won the VC for his bravery during an attack at Gouzeaucourt, France. The *London Gazette* reported:

> When the advance of the infantry was being delayed by an enemy machine-gun, he rushed the gun position single handed, shot the three gunners and captured the gun. Later, in similar circumstances, he attacked a gun accompanied by two men, but both the latter were immediately shot down. He went on alone to the gun position and bayoneted or shot the team of five men and captured the gun. On a third occasion, when the advance was held up by hostile fire from an enemy position, he collected a small party and rushed the position, inflicting heavy losses on the garrison.

Subsequently, in consolidating the position by the skilful use of captured enemy and his own machine-guns, he inflicted severe casualties on the enemy. His example of fearless and unhesitating devotion to duty under circumstances of great personal danger greatly inspired the neighbouring troops, and his action had a marked effect on the operations.

White received his VC from George V at Buckingham Palace on 27 March 1919. He died in Wellington, Shropshire, on 13 September 1974.

TEMPORARY LIEUTENANT ROBERT VAUGHAN GORLE
Army: A Battery, 50th Brigade, Royal Field Artillery
DATE OF BRAVERY: 1 OCTOBER 1918
GAZETTED: 14 DECEMBER 1918

Robert Gorle was born in Southsea on 6 May 1896, the son of Major Harry Gorle, DSO. He was educated at Malvern College and Rugby, and before the Great War was working as a farmer in the Transvaal, South Africa. He won his VC for bravery displayed at Ledeghem, Belgium, when he was in command of an eighteen-pounder gun, working closely with the infantry. The *London Gazette* reported:

He brought his gun into action in the most exposed positions on four separate occasions, and disposed of enemy machine-guns by firing over open sights under direct machine-gun fire at 500 to 600 yards' range. Later, seeing the infantry were being driven back by intense hostile fire, he, without hesitation, galloped his gun in front of the leading infantry, and on two occasions knocked out enemy machine-guns which were causing the trouble. His disregard of personal safety and dash were a magnificent example to the wavering line, which rallied and retook the northern end of the village.

After the war, Gorle returned to farming in southern Africa. He died in Durban on 9 January 1937.

LIEUTENANT WALLACE LLOYD ALGIE

Canadian Expeditionary Force: 20th Battalion, 1st Central Ontario Regiment

DATE OF BRAVERY: 11 OCTOBER 1918
GAZETTED: 21 JANUARY 1919

Wallace Algie was born in Alton, Ontario, on 10 June 1891 and was working as a banker until he enlisted in Toronto in April 1916. By autumn 1918, he was serving with the Central Ontario Regiment, which was supporting the British 3rd and 4th Armies in their offensive. At this point in the war, German resistance was crumbling along much of the Western Front, and on 9 October Cambrai fell to the Canadians. They then tried to consolidate their gains over the next few days, which was when Algie won his VC. The *London Gazette* reported:

> For most conspicuous bravery and self-sacrifice on 11th October, 1918, north-east of Cambrai, when with attacking troops which came under heavy enfilade machine-gun fire from a neighbouring village. Rushing forward with nine volunteers, he shot the crew of an enemy machine-gun, and, turning it on the enemy, enabled the party to reach the village. He then rushed another machine-gun, killed the crew, captured an officer and 10 enemy, and thereby cleared

the end of the village. Lt. Algie, having established his party, went back for reinforcements but was killed when leading them forward. His valour and personal initiative in the face of intense fire saved many lives and enabled the position to be held.

CORPORAL FRANK LESTER

Army: 10th Battalion, the Lancashire Fusiliers
DATE OF BRAVERY: 12 OCTOBER 1918
GAZETTED: 14 DECEMBER 1918

Frank Lester was born on 18 February 1896 in Huyton, near Liverpool. After leaving school, he worked as a joiner and then in his family's market-garden business in Irby, on the Wirral. He was the organist at the local chapel before enlisting in the 10th South Lancashire Regiment on 30 March 1916.

Initially, he worked as a training instructor at Prees Hill in Shropshire and Kimmel Park in north Wales. He was promoted to sergeant instructor before being transferred to the Lancashire Fusiliers at his own request. In early 1918, he was sent to France, which meant that he was obliged to revert to the rank of private (this was standard after a move of this nature). After a huge German offensive, he was reportedly one of only thirty men from a force of a thousand to answer a roll-call, all of the others having been killed or wounded. In March, he himself was wounded and sent home. After recuperating, he resumed training and was promoted to corporal. In September, he was sent back to France to rejoin his regiment. Then, in the dying days of the war, he won the VC, as the *London Gazette* announced:

> For most conspicuous bravery and self-sacrifice during the clearing of the village of Neuville . . . when, with a party of

about seven men under an officer, he was the first to enter a house from the back door, and shot two Germans as they attempted to get out by the front door. A minute later a fall of masonry blocked the door by which the party had entered. The only exit into the street was under fire at point-blank range. The street also was swept by the fire of machine-guns at close range. Observing that an enemy sniper was causing heavy casualties to a party in the house across the street, Private Lester exclaimed, 'I'll settle him,' and, dashing out into the street, shot the sniper at close quarters, falling mortally wounded at the same instant. This gallant man well knew it was certain death to go into the street, and the party opposite was faced with the alternative of crossing the fireswept street or staying where it was and being shot one by one. To save their lives he sacrificed his own.

PRIVATE MARTIN MOFFAT

Army: 2nd Battalion, Prince of Wales's Leinster Regiment
DATE OF BRAVERY: 14 OCTOBER 1918
GAZETTED: 26 DECEMBER 1918

Martin Moffat was born in Sligo, Ireland, on 15 April 1884. He joined the 6th Battalion, Connaught Rangers, and served with them in France from December 1915. In early 1918, he was transferred to the Leinster Regiment, and by mid-October, he and his new comrades were involved in fierce fighting near Ledeghem, Belgium.

The Battle of Courtrai started early on the morning of 14 October. The Allied offensive went well and the 88th Brigade, led by the Leinster Battalion, crossed the Menin–Roulers railway and had cleared Ledeghem by about 9 a.m. However, they then met heavy enemy resistance at a fortified farmhouse.

It was here that Moffat won his VC, as the *London Gazette* reported: 'Rushing to the house through a hail of bullets, Private Moffat threw bombs, and then working towards the back of the house, rushed the door single handed, killing two and capturing 30 of the enemy. He displayed the greatest valour and initiative throughout.'

Moffat's actions cleared the way for the rest of the battalion to advance. He took charge of his own prisoners and, supported by other men, then took them to the assistant provost marshal, from whom he demanded a receipt for their safe delivery. He was back at the front line later that morning. He drowned while swimming near Sligo on 5 January 1946, aged sixty-one.

SERGEANT HORACE AUGUSTUS CURTIS

Army: 2nd Battalion, the Royal Dublin Fusiliers

DATE OF BRAVERY: 18 OCTOBER 1918
GAZETTED: 6 JANUARY 1919

Horace Curtis was born in St Anthony-in-Roseland, Cornwall, on 7 March 1891. The *London Gazette* reported his bravery in a battle east of Le Cateau in the final weeks of the Great War:

> his platoon came unexpectedly under intense machine-gun fire. Realising that the attack would fail unless the enemy guns were silenced, Sergeant Curtis, without hesitation, rushed forward through our own barrage and the enemy fire, and killed and wounded the two teams of two of the guns, whereupon the remaining four guns surrendered. Then turning his attention to a train-load of reinforcements, he succeeded in capturing over 100 enemy before his

comrades joined him. His valour and disregard of danger inspired all.

Curtis died in Redruth, Cornwall, on 11 July 1968.

PRIVATE (LATER LANCE CORPORAL) ALFRED ROBERT WILKINSON

Army: 1/5th Battalion, the Manchester Regiment

DATE OF BRAVERY: 20 OCTOBER 1918
GAZETTED: 6 JANUARY 1919

Alfred Wilkinson was born in Leigh, Lancashire, on 5 December 1896 and was educated at local schools in the town. He worked as a factory worker at the Mather Lane Spinning Company before the war and enlisted in the Royal Scots Greys in December 1914. However, he transferred the following year to the Seaforth Highlanders and, finally, to the 1/5th Manchester Regiment.

Unconfirmed reports suggest that he showed great bravery while serving with the Seaforths at the beginning of the Battle of the Somme. It appears he was acting as a 'runner' – carrying a message by motorcycle from one area of the battlefield to another – when the last coach of a hospital train was hit by a bomb from a German plane just as it passed him. Wilkinson himself was hit in the face by shrapnel from the explosion, and consequently had to have fourteen teeth extracted. In spite of this injury, he remained on the scene and came across an Australian soldier, a dispatch rider, who had been seriously wounded. Wilkinson apparently not only carried the Australian back to a casualty clearing station but donated his own blood for a life-saving transfusion.

It will probably never be established for certain whether that tale is true, but it is certainly in keeping with the courage that

Wilkinson displayed when winning his VC later in the war, during the attack on Marou. The *London Gazette* reported:

> four runners in succession having been killed in an endeavour to deliver a message to the supporting company, Private Wilkinson volunteered for the duty. He succeeded in delivering the message, though the journey involved exposure to extremely heavy machine-gun and shell fire for 600 yards. He showed magnificent courage and complete indifference to danger, thinking only of the needs of his company, and entirely disregarding any consideration for personal safety. Throughout the remainder of the day Private Wilkinson continued to do splendid work.

By the time his VC was gazetted, Wilkinson's family already knew of the award because he had told them of it the previous December: 'Dear Mother – I have got some good news for you this time. It is quite true about my decoration. I have been awarded the VC. I feel too glad to write now, as I have just had it [the riband] pinned on my breast by my officer. He is more proud of me than I am, nearly.' In addition to the VC, which Wilkinson formally received from George V at Buckingham Palace in February 1919, he was accorded a civic reception at Leigh. There he was presented with fifty pounds by the directors of the Mather Lane Spinning Company and with a gold watch from the St Joseph's Boys' and Young Men's Society (of which he had been a member). A further £442 10s 6d had been raised by public subscription.

After the outbreak of the Second World War, he joined the Home Guard and was appointed a special constable. However, on 18 October 1940, he died, aged just forty-three, as a result of gas poisoning at Bickershaw Colliery, where he had been working.

PRIVATE FRANCIS GEORGE MILES

Army: 1/5th Battalion, the Gloucestershire Regiment

DATE OF BRAVERY: 23 OCTOBER 1918
GAZETTED: 6 JANUARY 1919

Francis Miles was born in Clearwell, Gloucestershire, on 9 July 1896 and before the war was employed by the Princess Royal Colliery Company in the Forest of Dean. In December 1914, he enlisted with the 9th Gloucesters, and he crossed to France the following September. However, a poisoned foot meant he was unable to travel on to Salonika with the rest of his battalion. When he recovered, he was attached to the 8th Gloucesters and also to the Royal Engineers, where his mining skills stood him in good stead. In July 1917, he was wounded when a mine exploded but again he recovered and was subsequently sent to Italy to join the 5th Gloucesters. He remained there until his regiment reinforced the 25th Division in France in August 1918.

He won the VC for his actions during an advance at Bois de l'Eveque. On 23 October 1918 his company had been held up by a line of enemy machine-guns in a sunken road. The *London Gazette* reported what happened next:

> Private Miles alone, and on his own initiative, went forward under exceptionally heavy fire, located a machine-gun, shot the gunner, and put the gun out of action. Observing another gun nearby, he again advanced alone, shot the gunner, rushed the gun, and captured the team of eight. Finally, he stood up and beckoned to his company who, acting on his signals, were enabled to work round the rear of the line and to capture 16 machine-guns, one officer and 50 other ranks. It was due to the courage, initiative and entire disregard of personal safety shown by this very gallant

soldier that the company was enabled to advance at a time when any delay would have jeopardised seriously the whole operation.

Miles returned to the Forest of Dean after the war and his home village presented him with a gold watch. He joined the Territorial Army (Monmouth Regiment) in the 1920s before re-enlisting with the Gloucesters at the start of the Second World War. He was finally discharged in June 1940 with the testimonial: 'A man of excellent character clean and willing who deserves well of his country.' He died on 8 November 1961 and remains the only private from the Gloucesters ever to win the VC.

SERGEANT JAMES CLARKE

Army: 15th Battalion, the Lancashire Fusiliers

DATE OF BRAVERY: 2 NOVEMBER 1918
GAZETTED: 6 JANUARY 1919

James Clarke, who won his VC just nine days before the end of the Great War, was born in Winsford, Cheshire, on 6 April 1894. He joined the 15th (1st Salford Pals) Battalion, Lancashire Fusiliers, in 1915 and travelled with them to France in November of that year. He then served throughout the remainder of the war, taking part in some of the fiercest fighting on the Western Front.

By the end of October 1918, it had become imperative to control all the ground to the west of the Sambre–Oise canal in France. The most stategically important feature close to the canal was the Happegarbes Spur, and the 15th Battalion was entrusted with its capture. They moved into the line, west of the spur, on 30 October. Three days later, while in charge of a platoon, Clarke won his VC, as the *London Gazette* reported:

He led his men forward with great determination, and on being held up by heavy machine-gun fire, rushed forward through a thick, strongly-held ridge, captured in succession four machine-guns, and single-handed bayoneted the crews. Later he led the remnants of his platoon to the capture of three machine-guns and many prisoners. In the later stages of the attack on the same day, when his platoon was held up by enemy machine-guns, he successfully led a Tank against them over very exposed ground. Continuing the attack on 3 Nov., after capturing many prisoners and gaining his objective, he organised his line most skilfully and held up the enemy. On 4 Nov., in the attack in the Oise–Sambre Canal, under heavy fire from the canal bank, he rushed forward with a Lewis-gun team in the face of an intense barrage, brought the gun into action, and effectively silenced the enemy's fire, thus enabling his company to advance and gain their objectives. Throughout the whole of these operations Sergt. Clarke acted with magnificent bravery and total disregard of personal safety, and by his gallantry and high sense of duty set an inspiring example to all ranks.

By dusk on 4 November, 15th Battalion, with two companies of the King's Own Yorkshire Light Infantry, had achieved its objective. The Happegarbes Spur had been cleared of enemy troops and the west bank of the canal was secure. Within a week, the war was over.

Clarke died in Rochdale, Lancashire, on 16 June 1947.

Gallipoli

In early 1915, the war on the Western Front was not going well for the Allies: fighting was bogged down, casualties were high and all the signs were that it would not be the short conflict that most had predicted. Winston Churchill, the Secretary of State for War, and others thought it would be advantageous to open a second front in the East. This, it was thought, would distract the Germans on the Western Front, possibly knock Turkey out of the war, and enable the Allies to prop up Russia. It was therefore decided to land an expeditionary force on the Gallipoli peninsula in the Dardanelles.

CORPORAL (LATER SERGEANT) JOHN ELISHA GRIMSHAW

Army: 1st Battalion, the Lancashire Fusiliers

DATE OF BRAVERY: 25 APRIL 1915
GAZETTED: 15 MARCH 1917

SERGEANT ALFRED JOSEPH RICHARDS

Army: 1st Battalion, the Lancashire Fusiliers

DATE OF BRAVERY: 25 APRIL 1915
GAZETTED: 24 AUGUST 1915

John Grimshaw, one of the famous 'Six Before Breakfast' winners of the VC, was born in Abram, Lancashire, on 20 January 1893. He was nineteen when he joined the Lancashire Fusiliers, two years before the outbreak of the First World War. When war was declared, Grimshaw was in India with the rest of the 1st Battalion, but shortly thereafter they were sent to Gallipoli.

Alfred Richards, another of the 'Six Before Breakfast' club, was born in Plymouth on 25 August 1880. He gave his trade as 'musician' when, aged fourteen, he enlisted in the Lancashire Fusiliers (his father's old regiment) as a bandboy. He was appointed a full drummer when serving in Ireland near the end of the century and was promoted to lance corporal in Crete in 1899. Over the next seven years, he served in Malta, Gibraltar and Egypt before returning to England. After just two months as a civilian, though, he re-enlisted, rejoining his old battalion in India, where they stayed until the posting to the Dardanelles.

The Lancashire Fusiliers were chosen to land on and take control of a small, sandy cove – codenamed W Beach – between Cape Helles and Tekke Burnu. It was so well defended that the Turks may have regarded it as impregnable to an attack from open boats. Nevertheless, it was decided to launch an offensive at 6 a.m. on 25 April 1915. The defenders knew exactly when it was coming, because, as was customary throughout the First World War, the attack was preceded by a sustained bombardment by heavy guns which ceased just before the assault began. As a result, there was no element of surprise to aid the British troops in the biggest amphibious landing of the war.

Captain Willis, who led C Company during the attack, was one of several survivors to record the events of the day:

> Not a sign of life was to be seen on the Peninsula in front of us. It might have been a deserted land we were nearing in our little boats. Then crack! . . . The signal for the massacre had been given; rapid fire, machine-guns and deadly accurate sniping opened from the cliffs above, and soon the casualties included the rest of the crew and many men.

The timing of the ambush was perfect; we were completely exposed and helpless in our slow-moving boats, just target practice for the concealed Turks, and within a few minutes only half of the thirty men in my boat were left alive. We were now 100 yards from the shore, and I gave the order 'overboard'. We scrambled out into some four feet of water and some of the boats with their cargo of dead and wounded floated away on the currents still under fire from the snipers. With this unpromising start the advance began. Many were hit in the sea, and no response was possible, for the enemy was in trenches well above our heads.

We toiled through the water towards the sandy beach, but here another trap was awaiting us, for the Turks had cunningly concealed a trip wire just below the surface of the water and on the beach itself were a number of land mines, and a deep belt of rusty wire extended across the landing place. Machine-guns, hidden in caves at the end of the amphitheatre of cliffs, enfiladed this.

Our wretched men were ordered to wait behind this wire for the wire-cutters to cut a pathway through. They were shot in helpless batches while they waited, and could not even use their rifles in retaliation since the sand and the sea had clogged their action. One Turkish sniper in particular took a heavy toll at very close range until I forced open the bolt of a rifle with the heel of my boot and closed his career with the first shot, but the heap of empty cartridges round him testified to the damage he had done. Safety lay in movement, and isolated parties scrambled through the wire to cover. Among them was Sergeant Richards with a leg horribly twisted, but he managed somehow to get through.

Captain Clayton, who was killed in action six weeks later, also described desperate scenes:

There was tremendously strong barbed wire where my boat was landed. Men were being hit in the boats as they splashed ashore. I got up to my waist in water, tripped over a rock and went under, got up and made for the shore and lay down by the barbed wire. There was a man there before me shouting for wire-cutters. I got mine out, but could not make the slightest impression. The front of the wire was by now a thick mass of men, the majority of whom never moved again. The noise was ghastly and the sights horrible. I eventually crawled through the wire with great difficulty, as my pack kept catching on the wire, and got under a small mound which actually gave us protection. The weight of our packs tired us, so that we could only gasp for breath. After a little time we fixed bayonets and started up the cliffs right and left. On the right several were blown up by a mine [this later proved to be 'friendly fire' – a British naval shell]. When we started up the cliff, the enemy went, but when we got to the top they were ready and poured shots on us.

The *London Gazette* reported that the Fusiliers

were met by a very deadly fire from hidden machine-guns which caused a great number of casualties. The survivors, however, rushed up to and cut the wire entanglements, not withstanding the terrific fire from the enemy, and after overcoming supreme difficulties, the cliffs were gained and the position maintained. Amongst the very gallant officers and men engaged in this most hazardous undertaking, Capt. Willis, Sergt. Richards and Private Keneally have been selected by their comrades as having performed the most signal acts of bravery.

The Lancashire Fusiliers had started the day with 27 officers and 1,002 other men. Twenty-four hours later a head count revealed just 16 officers and 304 men.

John Grimshaw was not gazetted until almost two years after the landing and received his VC only because of pressure from his comrades, who felt he had been hard done-by. Initially, he had received the Distinguished Conduct Medal and was more than content with that, unaware that his fellow-Fusiliers were campaigning for the decoration to be 'upgraded'. Indeed, when a journalist from the *Daily Dispatch* told him of his VC, he replied, 'Whose leg are you pulling?' and needed a great deal of convincing that it was true. The people of Abram were so proud of his achievement that they presented him with a gold watch and chain to go along with the medal. By that time, he was living and working in Hull as a musketry instructor, having been invalided out of the Fusiliers with severe frostbite. He died in Isleworth, London, on 20 July 1980, aged eighty-seven.

Richards, who had been shot, was evacuated to Egypt, where surgeons amputated his right leg just above the knee. He then returned to England and was discharged on 31 July 1915. His discharge papers read: 'no longer fit for war service (but fit for civil employment)'. When he was given his decoration, he was known as the 'Lonely VC' because he had no family and was living alone at the Princess Christian Soldiers' and Sailors' Home in Woking. However, in September 1916 he married Dora Coombes, who had nursed him during the previous year. His disability did not prevent him joining the Home Guard during the Second World War, when he served as a provost sergeant in London. He died in Southfields, London, on 21 May 1953.

CORPORAL (LATER STAFF SERGEANT) WILLIAM COSGROVE

Army: 1st Battalion, the Royal Munster Fusiliers

DATE OF BRAVERY: 26 APRIL 1915
GAZETTED: 23 AUGUST 1915

William Cosgrove was born at Ballinookera, near Aghada, Co Cork, on 1 October 1888. He was one of five sons of a local farmer, Michael Cosgrove, and his wife, Mary. Cosgrove attended a local school before becoming an apprentice butcher at Whitegate, on the edge of Cork harbour.

Cosgrove enlisted into the Royal Munster Fusiliers in 1910. He served with his regiment in India and Burma but, after the outbreak of the First World War, was sent with his battalion to the Dardanelles. On 25 April, the troops began landing at V beach near Cape Helles, Gallipoli, in the face of a murderous enemy fire. Cosgrove, then twenty-six, a mountain of a man standing six foot six tall and weighing sixteen stone, won his VC the next day. The man known affectionately as the 'East Cork Giant' led his section in an attack on the Turkish positions. When they were stopped by six foot posts and thick barbed wire, Cosgrove used his great strength to help his men break through. The *London Gazette* of 23 August 1915 recorded: 'Corporal Cosgrove on this occasion pulled down the posts of the enemy's high wire entanglement single-handed, notwithstanding a terrific fire from front and flanks, thereby greatly contributing to the successful clearing of the heights.'

Cosgrove later described how he shouted to his men: 'Pull them [the posts up]. Put your arms around them and pull them out of the ground.' Cosgrove recalled: 'I dashed at the first one: heaved and strained, and then it came out in my arms . . . as you'd lift a child. I believe there was wild cheering when they saw what I was at, but I only heard the screech of the bullets and saw dust rising all around from where they hit. I could not tell how many I pulled up. I did my best.'

Late in the fighting that day, Cosgrove was seriously wounded by machine-gun bullets but fought on. He later said: 'One of the bullets struck me in the side, and passed clean through me.' Cosgrove subsequently underwent two operations at Malta hospital and eventually made a partial recovery. However, his injuries left him with recurring health problems and he died at Millbank Hospital, London, on 14 July 1936.

†LANCE CORPORAL (LATER CAPTAIN) ALBERT JACKA

Australian Imperial Force: 14th Battalion (Victoria)

DATE OF BRAVERY: 19/20 MAY 1915
GAZETTED: 24 JULY 1915

Bert Jacka was born on a dairy farm in Geelong, Victoria, Australia, on 10 January 1893. On 7 August 1914, he joined the 14th Australian Infantry, and the following year he took part in the historic landings at Gallipoli on 25 April. His VC was won for actions at 'Courtney's Post', where some of the severely depleted 14th Battalion had been sent to support those Anzacs, who were under relentless attack from the Turks.

At 3.30 a.m. on 20 May, a party of Turks crept up to the trench occupied by Jacka and his comrades and threw in eight bombs. Three men were killed and all of the rest, with the exception of Jacka, were injured. The Turks then jumped into the trench and most of the remaining Australians fled. Jacka, though, kept up a relentless fire on the enemy and thereby prevented their advance. After a quarter of an hour, he was asked if he would charge the Turks if some men could be found to back him up. 'Yes, two or three,' he replied. With three volunteers, and leading from the front, Jacka launched his counter-attack on the mouth of the communication trench. However, the soldier who followed him was shot three times and the charge was abandoned. Instead, Jacka asked one of the other volunteers to keep up a steady fire while he went along several trenches, crossed no man's land and then ambushed the Turks from the rear. He shot five Turks and bayoneted two others. 'Well, I managed to get the beggars,' he said the next morning. Another of the volunteers had killed two more Turks as they tried to escape. A dangerous and daring action had been a total success.

Jacka was promoted to sergeant and then company sergeant major while still in the Dardanelles, and after the evacuation from Gallipoli he went to Egypt, where he became a second lieutenant in March 1916. He served on the Western Front from 7 July 1916 and won the Military Cross (MC) for actions at Pozieres on 5 August of that year. He and fourteen other men from the 14th Battalion were sent to relieve the Anzacs, who were holding an advanced trench under heavy German bombardment. Early in the morning, the Germans attacked and swept through the Anzac ranks. By now, only seven Australians were uninjured and Jacka himself had been slightly wounded. As the Germans began to round up Anzac prisoners and wounded, Jacka told the seven fit men to attach their bayonets, saying: 'If we stay here they are bound to capture us and I would sooner be dead than a prisoner. The supports cannot be long in coming. Let's go for them.' With these words ringing in their ears, the men advanced at scores of Germans, shooting their rifles from the hip. In fierce hand-to-hand fighting, Jacka was wounded for a second time and the Germans started to encircle the Australian troops. However, support arrived in the nick of time. Many Germans were shot, fifty were taken prisoner and the Australian prisoners were freed. One stretcher-bearer, who had seen the ferocious fight, said: 'I don't know who I've got, but the bravest man in the Aussie Army is on that stretcher just ahead. It's Bert Jacka, and I wouldn't give a gyppo piaster [a derogatory reference to a small denomination Egyptian coin] for him. He is knocked about dreadfully.' Bill Jacka, who visited his brother at the regimental aid post, left the ward thinking: 'By Jove, you've had it . . . I won't be seeing you again.' But Bert survived.

Having been evacuated to Britain, Jacka received his belated VC from the Prince of Wales (George V was ill). But he was disappointed and angry that he had not instead been given a bar to his VC for his actions at Pozieres, which he felt were six times more demanding than the heroics he had performed at Gallipoli. After flirting with joining the Flying Corps, he returned to his battalion and won a bar to his MC for several one-man patrols at Bullecourt, where he personally guided the British tanks into position. Jacka, who was promoted to captain in December 1916, was finally removed from the war by a mustard-gas attack on 15 May 1918 at Villers Bretonneux, which led to him twice undergoing surgery to save his life.

Jacka's VC was the first awarded to a soldier from the Commonwealth forces during the Great War and earned him £500 put up by a Melbourne businessman for being the first Australian to win the VC. He enjoyed the recognition, but not the publicity that went with it. When asked about the inspiration for his carefully planned attack at Gallipoli, he was often dismissive, saying: 'I think I lost my nut.' He never fully recovered from his war injuries, although he lived long enough to be elected Mayor of St Kilda. However, he collapsed at a council meeting and died on 17 January 1932, aged thirty-nine.

The Middle East

The Middle East theatre of the war was fought between the Allied Powers, mainly forces from Britain and the Russian Empire, versus the Central Powers, mostly forces from the Ottoman Empire. The Ottoman Empire, in military terms, was a weak link for the Central Powers. Its army was large but often ineffective and it would probably have been defeated in mid-1915 without being propped up by Germany.

The Ottoman Empire's entry into the Great War on 29 October 1914 – the result of a secret pact with Germany – saw a number of campaigns in the Middle East. These included the Caucasus Campaign, the Dardanelles Campaign (known in Australia and New Zealand as the Gallipoli Campaign), the Mesopotamian Campaign, the Sinai and Palestine Campaigns, and the Arabia and Southern Arabia Campaigns. The Allied Powers gradually assumed control in these areas as the war progressed.

NAIK (LATER JEMADAR) SHAHAMAD KHAN

Indian Army: 89th Punjab Regiment

DATE OF BRAVERY: 12/13 APRIL 1916
GAZETTED: 26 SEPTEMBER 1916

Shahamad Khan was born on 1 July 1879 in the village of Takhti, near Rawalpindi, India. He joined the Army on 1 December 1904 and served in many theatres during the Great War, including Egypt, the Dardanelles, France and Mesopotamia. It was near Beit Ayeesa, Mesopotamia, that he won his VC on 12/13 April 1916. The *London Gazette* described his bravery that day:

He was in charge of a machine-gun section in an exposed position in front of and covering a gap in our new line within 150 yards of the enemy's entrenched position. He beat off three counter-attacks, and worked his gun single-handed after all his men, except two belt-fillers, had become casualties. For three hours he held the gap under very heavy fire while it was being made secure. When his gun was knocked out by hostile fire he and his two belt-fillers held their ground with rifles till ordered to withdraw. With three men sent to assist him he then brought back his gun, ammunition and one severely wounded man unable to walk. Finally he himself returned and removed all remaining arms and equipment except two shovels. But for his gallantry and determination our line must have been penetrated by the enemy.

Khan survived the war and died in his home village on 28 July 1947. The VC that was purchased privately by the trust in 1999 is an official replacement: the location of the original is not known.

PRIVATE (LATER SERGEANT) JOHN READITT

Army: 6th Battalion, the South Lancashire Regiment (the Prince of Wales's Volunteers)

DATE OF BRAVERY: 25 FEBRUARY 1917
GAZETTED: 5 JULY 1917

John Readitt was born in Clayton Bridge, Manchester, on 19 January 1897. He enlisted in April 1915, eight months after war had been declared, at the age of just eighteen. Soon he was sailing for the Dardanelles, and in November 1915 he entered the Balkan theatre of war. At some point that winter he was stricken with severe frostbite. In February 1916, his battalion moved to Egypt and four months later to Mesopotamia, to prepare for the relief of the British garrison at Kut-el-Amara, which was besieged by the Turkish Army fighting with the Central Powers.

By the end of the year, the army of British and Indian forces was ready to retake Kut, but first it had to dislodge the enemy from strongholds near the Rivers Tigris and Hai. Despite heavy rain hampering progress, the British trenches gradually crept forward, and by February 1917 the main concentration of Turkish troops was in retreat along the Tigris towards Baghdad. On 24 February, Kut was evacuated by the retreating Turks but the next day the British launched a major offensive.

This allowed the 6th Battalion in general and John Readitt in particular to make their marks. During fierce fighting, the battalion captured a crucial watercourse despite the loss of twenty-one men killed and fifty-eight wounded. The *London Gazette* described Readitt's pivotal role in this action:

> Five times he went forward in the face of very heavy machine-gun fire at very close range, being the sole survivor on each occasion. These advances drove back the enemy machine-guns, and about 300 yards of watercourse was made good in an hour. After his Officer had been killed, Private Readitt, on his own initiative, organised and made several more advances. On reaching the enemy barricade he was forced by a counter-attack to retire, giving ground slowly and continuing to throw bombs. On supports reaching him, he held a forward bend by bombing until the position was consolidated. The action of this gallant soldier saved the left flank and enabled his Battalion to maintain its position.

An account in *Empire News* of 8 July 1917 said: 'The Turkish commander, whom we captured later in the day, said he had never seen anything finer than the way that stripling (Readitt is only 20 years of age) had stood up to a whole army.' Readitt later became a sergeant but was taken ill at Kut and discharged on 18 July 1919. He received his VC from George V at Buckingham Palace on 26 November that year.

After the war, he took over his father's shoe-repair business and lived modestly, rarely wishing to discuss his VC. He died on 9 June 1964.

RESSAIDAR BADLU SINGH

Indian Army: 14th Lancers (the Scinde Horse), attached to 29th Lancers (Deccan Horse)

DATE OF BRAVERY: 23 SEPTEMBER 1918
GAZETTED: 27 NOVEMBER 1918

Badlu Singh was born in Dhakla village in the Punjab, India, in 1876. At nineteen, he joined the 14th (Murray's) Jat Lancers and by 1915 had risen to the rank of Jemadar. In September of that year, he was posted to the North-West Frontier, but in May 1916 he was transferred to France. He saw continuous service on the Western Front until March 1918, when the 14th Lancers arrived in Egypt in support of the 29th (Deccan) Lancers. By this time, Singh had been promoted to Ressaidar.

On 23 September 1918, his regiment formed part of the advanced guard of the 12th Cavalry Brigade in the Jordan Valley. Their task was to block the escape route of the Turkish 7th and 8th Armies. However, the advance of the regiment was halted by a large force of Turks and several machine-guns, which prompted Captain Jackson to take D Company on a wide outflanking move to attack the enemy's rear. Singh then spotted the enemy machine-gun posts that had been firing on his comrades.

The *London Gazette* takes up the story:

> On nearing the [enemy] position Ressaidar Badlu Singh realised that the squadron was suffering casualties from a small hill on the left front occupied by machine-guns and 200 infantry. Without the slightest hesitation he collected six other ranks and with the greatest dash and entire disregard of danger charged and captured the position, thereby saving very heavy casualties to the squadron. He was mortally wounded on the very top of the hill when capturing one of the machine-guns single-handed, but all the machine-guns and infantry had surrendered to him before he died. His valour and initiative were of the highest order.

The forty-two-year-old Singh left a widow, two sons and a daughter.

Southern Europe

Austria-Hungary, Germany and the Ottoman Empire – the Central Powers – were also involved in heavy fighting in southern Europe. They had hoped to count on the support of Italy, but this did not happen: Italy declared war on Austria-Hungary, which it considered an aggressor, in May 1915. Fifteen months later, Italy declared war against Germany. Italy won sporadic military victories yet, by the autumn of 1917, it was on the retreat. Later, however, it reorganised, held the Piave River and throughout 1918 prevented the Austrians breaking through the line.

There was also fierce fighting in the Balkans from early in the

Great War. In 1914, the Austrians had initial successes in Serbia before the invaders were expelled by the end of the year. In 1915, after Bulgaria was persuaded by the Austrians to join the attack, the Serbian army was again overwhelmed. By 1918, the Bulgarians were trying to hold this front line on their own, but they failed and signed an armistice in September 1918.

PRIVATE HUBERT WILLIAM LEWIS
Army: 11th Battalion, the Welch Regiment
DATE OF BRAVERY: 22/23 OCTOBER 1916
GAZETTED: 15 DECEMBER 1916

Hubert 'Stokey' Lewis was born in Milford Haven, Pembrokeshire, on 1 May 1896. After attending the National School in Milford, he started work in the town's fish market, but in early autumn 1914 he attended a recruiting meeting. He appears to have been caught up in the wave of patriotism that was sweeping the country and enlisted. On 5 September, he and seventy-five other volunteers from the town left for an adventure with (Lord) Kitchener's New Army. Lewis was one of forty-six men to be sent to Maindy Barracks, Cardiff, the depot of the Welch Regiment. There he joined the 11th Battalion, otherwise known as the Cardiff Commercial Battalion or the 'Cardiff Pals'.

After training, he departed for France on 4 September 1915. By this point, Bulgaria had joined the war on Germany's side, opening a new front, and Lewis's battalion was one of those detailed to leave the Western Front for Greece. There they joined General Sir Bryan Mahon's Expeditionary Force and dug in around Salonika as they waited for an offensive by German and Bulgarian forces. However, eventually the British decided to attack first, and on 17 October 1916 Lieutenant Colonel H.F. Wingate, the battalion's commanding officer, was ordered to mount a raid on the German trenches situated on the heights of Dorsale.

Lewis, a small but strong man, was a member of D Party, one of the four raiding parties. Bad weather delayed the assault but finally, at 9 p.m. on 22 October, it began. As D Party rushed forward to reach the starting point for their final assault, they were spotted by a German sentry and the air became alive with red flares and machine-gun and rifle fire. Over the next forty minutes – and only 300 yards from their 'starting point' – D Party was subjected to an intense shelling from the enemy. Lewis was hit in the arm but saw that others were more badly injured and therefore declined medical attention. Then, in a lull in the bombardment, Captain Guthrie Morgan, commander of the raiding party, charged across 120 yards of wire entanglements with 150 men, including the wounded Lewis. As they reached the enemy trenches, there was fierce hand-to-hand combat and the British seized control. This led to a German counter-attack and Lewis was wounded for a second time, but again he refused medical treatment. Instead, he headed down a seemingly empty trench and was confronted by three German soldiers, but he launched a ferocious bayonet assault on the men and they quickly surrendered. However, the Germans then started another counter-attack and the signal to withdraw was given. As the men of D Party made the two-hour descent, Lewis saw a comrade fall. Despite his own two wounds, Lewis carried the other man down the hillside, dodging shells and shrapnel as they went. At 4.30 a.m., he put down the wounded man, walked away and collapsed with exhaustion.

The announcement that Lewis had received the VC was greeted with great excitement in south Wales. He returned home a hero in January 1917, and at a press conference in the Grand Hotel, Cardiff, won over those present with his modesty.

'I joined the Welch Regiment as a raw recruit, and I am proud of the fact that I have not disgraced the honour and proud record of the Regiment,' he said. He even pointed out an inaccuracy in the *London Gazette*'s citation, denying he had been wounded three times: 'I can only remember being wounded twice.' After a jubilant homecoming in Milford, he received his VC from George V at Buckingham Palace on 5 February 1917, but he was back serving on the Balkan Front within ten days.

On 19 June 1918, he once more distinguished himself on the battlefield, again near Salonika, when he was part of an attacking force which was repulsed by heavy fire and gas. Seeing his commander, Captain Morgan, collapse, Lewis went to his aid. Despite being affected by gas himself and having to fight off the attention of several Bulgarians, he picked up Morgan and carried him to safety. After the war was over, Morgan wrote to Lewis, thanking him for his actions: 'It is impossible for me to express how grateful I am to you for saving my life. You certainly deserve a bar to your Victoria Cross.'

However, the bar was never forthcoming and Lewis returned to live simply in Milford, first running his own fish business and later, when that venture failed, working in an ice factory. During the Second World War, he was a member of the Home Guard. He died in Milford on 22 February 1977, aged eighty.

TEMPORARY LIEUTENANT JOHN SCOTT YOULL

Army: 1st Battalion, the Northumberland Fusiliers, attached to 11th (Service) Battalion

DATE OF BRAVERY: 15 JUNE 1918
GAZETTED: 25 JULY 1918

Jack Youll was born in the mining village of Thornley, County Durham, on 6 June 1897, left school at fifteen and became an apprentice electrician at Thornley Colliery. On reaching military age, he volunteered and became a sapper in the Durham Territorials. After training in England, he was sent to France and made such a favourable impression that he was recommended for a commission. In June 1917, he returned to Britain to find he was now a second lieutenant in the Northumberland Fusiliers. Back in France a few months later, he was mentioned in dispatches for his brave role in fierce fighting at Polygon Wood. After the Allied retreat in Italy in October 1917, Youll and his battalion were transferred to that front, and while there he became the first officer with the Northumberland Fusiliers to win the VC since the Battle of Lucknow more than half a century earlier.

On 15 June 1918, the Austrian 11th Army started the Battle of Asiago, or what the British knew as the Battle of Piave. Its artillery attack included gas, shrapnel, high explosive and even armour-piercing shells, fired from every calibre of gun. The British sector of the front was held by the 23rd Division (New Army), which included the 11th Northumberland Fusiliers. The Austrian infantry assault, of four and a half regiments, was formidable, and by 8 a.m. it had broken through the British line. This prompted the 11th Northumberlands to form a defensive flank, while at the same time sending out patrols to gather information that would enable them to keep the Austrians at a distance.

Youll was the leader of one of these patrols, and won his VC for bravery under a fierce barrage. The *London Gazette* described his courage that day:

> Sending his men back to safety, he remained to observe the situation. Unable subsequently to rejoin his Company, 2nd Lieutenant Youll reported to a neighbouring unit, and when the enemy attacked he maintained his position with several

men of different units until the troops on his left had given way and an enemy machine-gun had opened fire from behind him. He rushed the gun, and having himself killed most of the team, opened fire on the enemy with the captured gun, inflicting heavy casualties. Then, finding that the enemy had gained a footing in a portion of the front line, he organised and carried out with a few men three separate counter-attacks. On each occasion he drove back the enemy, but was unable to maintain his position by reason of reverse fire. Throughout the fighting his complete disregard of personal safety and very gallant leading set a magnificent example to all.

Due to the arrival of Allied reinforcements later in the day, the Austrian offensive was rebuffed, although the 11th Northumberlands suffered casualties amounting to a fifth of its strength.

The news of Youll's VC (as well as the Italian bravery award the Al Valore Militare) caused great excitement in Thornley, where a house-to-house collection was made for 'Our VC'. He was publicly honoured at the Thornley Hippodrome on his return home on leave and was given many gifts, including a gold watch and chain, and a silver cigarette case. Youll, a slim, modest man with boyish looks, told cheering locals: 'There are two kinds of honour – the seen and the unseen.' Shortly after he returned to the Italian Front, a local paper quoted a soldier on leave as saying: 'He is one of the lads. And if anybody ever deserved the VC it is 2nd Lieutenant Youll.'

On 27 October 1918 – a fortnight before the Armistice – Youll, still only twenty-one, was struck by a shell and killed in the major British assault on the Piave River. His final words to his adjutant, Lieutenant Cowling, were: 'It's all right, Cowling, we got them stone cold.'

SERGEANT WILLIAM McNALLY

Army: 8th (Service) Battalion, the Yorkshire Regiment (Alexandra, Princess of Wales's Own)

DATE OF BRAVERY: 27 AND 29 OCTOBER 1918
GAZETTED: 14 DECEMBER 1918

William McNally was born in Murton, near Seaham, County Durham, on 16 December 1894. He won his VC at the end of the Great War for bravery at Piave, Italy, when his company was under heavy machine-gun fire from a building on one of its flanks. The *London Gazette* announced:

> Utterly regardless of personal safety, he rushed the machine-gun post single-handed, killing the team and capturing the gun. Later, at Vazzola, on October 29th, 1918, when his company, having crossed the Monticano River, came under heavy rifle fire and machine-gun fire, Sergeant McNally immediately directed the fire of his platoon against the danger point, while he himself crept to the rear of the enemy position. Realising that a frontal attack would mean heavy losses, he, unaided, rushed the position, killing or putting to flight the garrison and capturing the machine-gun. On the same day, when holding a newly captured ditch, he was strongly counter-attacked from both flanks. By his coolness and skill in controlling the fire of his party he frustrated the attack, inflicting heavy casualties on the enemy. Throughout the whole operations his innumerable acts of gallantry set a high example to his men, and his leading was beyond all praise.

Before winning his VC, McNally had previously been awarded the Military Medal (MM) for his bravery on the Somme on

10 July 1916, and also a bar to his MM for his courage at Passchendaele.

McNally died in his home village on 5 January 1976.

Subadar Major Ishar Singh was one of just a handful of men who won the VC between the two world wars. Singh's was awarded for great gallantry on India's North-West Frontier in April 1921. He was the first Sikh to win the decoration and received his VC from the Prince of Wales at Rawalpindi in March 1922.

Winning the only double VC awarded to a fighting soldier, Second Lieutenant Charles Upham, 2nd New Zealand Expeditionary Force, received his first VC for his outstanding leadership and courage on Crete in 1941 (his citation *right*). Surviving the action despite severe wounds, he was awarded his second VC for bravery in the Western Desert a year later. *Below*, receiving the medal from General Sir Claude Auchinleck.

ALEXANDER TURNBULL LIBRARY N.Z

Captain (later Lieutenant Colonel) Eric Wilson holds the virtually unique distinction of being gazetted for a posthumous VC when he was not actually dead. He won his VC in Somaliland in August 1940 but was believed killed during the action; only later did it emerge that he had been wounded and taken prisoner-of-war.

Flying Officer Leslie Manser won his VC, but gave his life in so doing, for saving the lives of his crew when their plane was badly damaged during Operation Millennium, the huge 1,000-bomber night-raid on Cologne in 1942.

Unique in the annals of the Victoria Cross, Flying Officer Lloyd Trigg received his posthumous award solely on evidence presented by the enemy. After sighting a surfaced U-boat in the Atlantic, Trigg attacked and sank it even though his own aircraft was hit and seriously damaged. Crashing into the sea, Trigg and his crew were all killed but his VC was granted on the basis of statements taken from the U-boat's officers.

Two celebrated airmen – Group Captain Leonard Cheshire *(left)* and Sergeant Norman Jackson *(right)*. Jackson won his VC for an extraordinary exploit in 1944 when he climbed out onto the wing of his aircraft when it was travelling at 200 m.p.h. at 20,000 feet in order to extinguish an engine fire.

Another flying hero, Canadian Pilot Officer Andrew Mynarski *(third from right)* sacrificed his life to save that of a comrade in a blazing aircraft over Cambrai.

Naik (later Havildar) Agansing Rai was a Gurkha serving in the Indian Army during the campaign in Burma in June 1944, when his actions so demoralized an enemy force that they fled before him. His other medals include the Burma Star, the Queen Elizabeth Silver Jubilee Medal and the 20 Years' Long Service Medal.

After his Company Commander was wounded, Captain John Randle took charge of the company during the bitter fighting around Kohima, India, in May 1944. He led a successful attack against a strong enemy machine-gun post but was mortally wounded in the assault.

Leading Seaman James 'Mick' Magennis (left) volunteered for the Submarine Service in 1942 and trained for 'special and hazardous duties' in midget submarines – or X-craft. On 31 July 1945, he assisted Lieutenant Ian Fraser (right), in command of HM Midget Submarine XE. 3, in a daring attack on the Japanese cruiser Takao anchored in the Johore Straits, Singapore. They both survived and were awarded the VC for their actions.

Despite the length of the campaign and the number of men under arms, only four VCs were awarded for actions during the Korean War. One of them, perhaps the most colourful, was won by Private 'Bill' Speakman, Black Watch, who, on his own initiative, collected together six men when his unit was in danger of being overrun by the enemy and led a series of charges that saved the situation.

Lance-Corporal Rambahadur Limbu, 10th Gurkha Rifles, was awarded his VC for gallantry in action against insurgents in Sarawak, Malaysia in November 1965.

Warrant Officer Keith Payne was one of four Australian Army personnel who received the VC for their gallantry during the Vietnam War in the late 1960s. Payne's outstanding courage and leadership resulted in saving the lives of many soldiers under his command during a dangerous patrol.

A sergeant in the Parachute Regiment, Ian McKay received his posthumous VC for action in the Falklands War. Pinned down by heavy fire, McKay single-handedly charged the enemy position, thereby allowing his comrades to get safely away, but was himself killed at the moment of victory.

THAMES TELEVISION

Two of the twelve living recipients: Lieutenant Colonel Eric Wilson, who won his VC in Somaliland in 1940, pictured alongside Private Johnson Beharry. Beharry was awarded his medal for action in Iraq in 2004 and is the most recent recruit to the illustrious gallery of heroes who have been awarded the VC over the past one hundred and fifty years.

HRH The Prince of Wales, the President of the Victoria Cross and George Cross Association, meeting Private Johnson Beharry at the Service of Remembrance in 2005.

GETTY IMAGES

I was delighted to meet the Queen at Windsor Castle during the VC 150th anniversary celebrations in 2006 because I know she shares my enthusiasm for the medal.

7

THE FIRST WORLD WAR –
THE ROYAL NAVY

The Royal Navy is the oldest of the British armed services and it is therefore the most senior. From the late seventeenth century to the Great War and beyond, it was the most powerful navy in the world. This meant that during the First World War, enemy countries were reluctant to take on the Royal Navy in a head-to-head battle – and were even more circumspect about any attempt to invade Britain. The Royal Navy sought to blockade the enemy's ports, thereby strangling its trade, as well as keeping its fleet in harbour, out of harm's way. If enemy ships did get out to sea, the aim was to destroy them.

The Royal Navy played a vital role in the war. It kept the United Kingdom supplied with food, raw materials and arms and, despite set-backs, defeated the German campaigns of unrestricted submarine warfare. It was heavily committed in the Dardanelles Campaign against the Ottoman Empire. Furthermore, the Royal Navy fought several battles against the enemy, notably the Battle of Heligoland Bight, the Battle of Coronel, the Battle of the Falkland Islands, the Battle of Dogger Bank and the Battle of Jutland. This latter battle, in the North Sea in 1916, was the best known naval confrontation of the war but was largely indecisive.

MIDSHIPMAN (LATER CAPTAIN) WILFRED ST AUBYN MALLESON

Royal Navy

DATE OF BRAVERY: 25 APRIL 1915
GAZETTED: 16 AUGUST 1915

ABLE SEAMAN WILLIAM CHARLES WILLIAMS

Royal Navy

DATE OF BRAVERY: 25 APRIL 1915
GAZETTED: 16 AUGUST 1915

Wilfred Malleson was born in Kirkee, India, on 17 September 1896, joined the Royal Navy as a cadet in 1912 and was made midshipman on 7 August 1914. He served on *Cornwallis* in the Mediterranean and from 1915 on HMS *River Clyde*.

William Williams was born in Stanton Lacy, Shropshire, on 15 September 1880 and joined the Royal Navy when he was just fifteen. In 1900, he was commended for his bravery by his commanding officer, Captain Percy Scott, when a member of HMS *Terrible*'s naval brigade, which saw action from 1899 to 1900 in Natal during the Boer War and in China during the Boxer Rebellion. On completion of his regular service with the Navy in 1910, Williams joined *Vernon* as a member of the Royal Fleet Reserve; but when the First World War broke out he was recalled to active service on HMS *Hussar*, a torpedo boat converted for use as the communications yacht of the commander-in-chief of the Mediterranean Fleet.

In February 1915, *Hussar* was commanded by Captain Edwin Unwin, a former Merchant Service officer. He was tasked with transforming the Aegean harbour of Mudros into an efficient base for the naval and military forces committed to the forthcoming landings on the Gallipoli peninsula. The British had expected V Beach to be well defended by the Turks, so it was vital that as many troops as possible were landed quickly. The tactic was for open boats, each containing some 300 troops, to be towed by trawlers and steam-driven hoppers (barges) to the shore before the towing craft turned around to bring in a second wave of troops. The commanding officer knew that there would not be sufficient men on the beach for roughly the first hour, so he suggested putting 2,000 troops on board the *River Clyde* and grounding her as close as possible to V Beach. His idea was that these troops would provide immediate support for the open boats and that they could reach the beach over the carefully positioned hoppers and specially built gangways.

On the morning of the landings – 25 April – everything initially went smoothly, but not for long. By 6.25 a.m., the British force was under a heavy assault from two companies of Turks armed with a pom-pom gun and four machine-guns. Furthermore, the bridge that was meant to enable troops to reach the shore was incomplete, so those moving along it were shot down, while those leaping from the open boats were caught on wire entanglements and drowned. In short, it was chaos, and the British force suffered terrible casualties.

Commander Unwin and William Williams dived into the sea under heavy fire, secured a rope to some drifting lighters (barges used to carry cargo to and from ships moored in open water), then hauled them towards a spit of rock that gave direct access to the shore. But the rope was too short to reach the rocks, so Unwin and Williams held the lighters in position for over an hour in chest-deep water, still under sustained fire from the Turks. This enabled a small number of men to reach the shelter of a sandy bank on the beach. Eventually, a shell exploded near the two men in the water and Williams was killed, but by then some extra rope had been found and the lighters were secured to the rocks. Troops began to pour over the bridge, but again they encountered heavy casualties.

After Williams had been killed, Unwin, who was utterly exhausted, returned to the *River Clyde*. However, ignoring doctor's orders, he soon returned to work in the lighters and was wounded three times. Midshipman George Drewry toiled alongside him, despite sustaining a serious head wound. When Drewry finally grew too exhausted to carry on, Midshipman Wilfred Malleson took over from him. He was shot but still made two unsuccessful attempts to resecure the line to the rocks after it had worked loose. Seaman George Samson also distinguished himself with great courage throughout the day until he was felled by machine-gun fire. Yet all four men – Unwin, Drewry, Malleson and Samson – survived to receive their VCs. At 9 a.m., after more than 1,000 casualties had been sustained, the operation was finally called off.

Malleson was promoted to acting sub-lieutenant on 15 May 1916 and joined the battleship *Lord Nelson*, on which his brother Rupert was already serving. He was then promoted to lieutenant on 30 March 1918, two months after he had been presented with his VC by George V at Buckingham Palace. As a captain, he came out of retirement and served during the Second World War. Thereafter, he lived quietly in Cornwall and died in Truro at the age of seventy-eight.

As well as being the Royal Navy's first posthumous VC, Williams was the first from that service to win the decoration for more than thirty years. His father was presented with the medal by George V at Buckingham Palace on 16 November 1916. Williams was fondly remembered in his home town of Chepstow, where a memorial painting of the *River Clyde* was placed in the parish church. And Edwin Unwin was never in any doubt that Williams's courage surpassed both his own and that of the other three *River Clyde* VCs, often referring to the able seaman as 'the bravest sailor I ever met'.

†FIRST-CLASS BOY JOHN TRAVERS CORNWELL

Royal Navy

DATE OF BRAVERY: 31 MAY 1916
GAZETTED: 15 SEPTEMBER 1916

Jack Cornwell, the boy sailor who was hailed as a hero, was born at Leyton, east London, on 8 January 1900. He yearned to be a sailor when he left school, but his parents, desperate not to lose him, persuaded him to become a tea boy on a Brooke-Bond van instead. However, when the Great War broke out, he was given the chance to join the Navy and went for preliminary training at Devonport from 27 July 1915. Thereafter, he became a first-class boy on HMS *Chester*, part of Admiral Beatty's North Sea Squadron.

The following year, Beatty came up against the German High Seas Fleet near Jutland. During the fighting on 31 May, Cornwell was seriously injured, but he remained standing alone, awaiting orders, at an exposed post until the action was over. By then, dead and wounded crew lay all around him. Jack himself died two days later in Grimsby. Initially, he went to a pauper's grave, but when news of his bravery spread, the public demanded a more fitting send-off, and he was reinterred after an impressive funeral. A few months later, his father died from bronchial catarrh while on active service with the Royal Defence Corps and was placed in the same grave as his son.

Jack's mother learned of her son's bravery in a letter from the *Chester*'s captain.

I know you would wish to hear of the splendid fortitude and courage shown by your son during the action of 31 May. His devotion to duty was an example for us all. The wounds which resulted in his death within a short time were received in the first few minutes of the action. He remained steady at his most exposed post at the gun, waiting for orders. His gun would not bear on the enemy; all but two of the ten crew were killed or wounded, and he was the only one who was in such an exposed position. But he felt he might be needed, and, indeed, he might have been; so he stayed there, standing and waiting, under heavy fire, with just his own brave heart and God's help to support him. I cannot express to you my admiration of the son you have lost from this world. No other comfort would I attempt to give to the mother of so brave a lad, but to assure her of what he was, and what he did, and what an example he gave. I hope to place in the boys' mess a plate with his name on and the date and the words: 'Faithful unto Death'. I hope some day you may be able to come and see it there. I have not failed to bring his name prominently before my Admiral.

After the war ended, the *Daily Telegraph* of 26 November 1919 said of Jack Cornwell: 'The story was in the minds of the whole Empire how a boy showed what a boy could do in the way of making history, and giving an example of how English boys should live and how English boys should die.'

PETTY OFFICER (LATER CHIEF PETTY OFFICER) ERNEST HERBERT PITCHER

Royal Navy

DATE OF BRAVERY: 8 AUGUST 1917
GAZETTED: 2 NOVEMBER 1917

Ernest Pitcher was born in Mullion, Cornwall, on 31 December 1888, the son of a coastguard. He joined the Royal Navy at the age of fourteen and by August 1914 was serving on the super-Dreadnought *King George V.* The following year, he volunteered for service in the expanding Q-ship fleet, at one stage Britain's 'answer' to German U-boats, which had caused terrible damage to the Allies' merchant fleets in the early stages of the war. After the U-boats had proved their supremacy at sea, a pattern had emerged whereby a U-boat, to preserve costly torpedoes and allow it to plunder its target's valuables, would surface close to a merchant ship and accept the soft target's 'surrender'. The merchant crew would then leave their ship to the German submariners, who would take any valuables that took their fancy before scuttling it. The Q-ship, a gunship disguised to look like a merchant ship, was devised to combat this practice. As soon as the U-boat surfaced to collect its booty, the gunship would blow it out of the water. Pitcher served on the ex-collier *Loderer*, also known as HMS *Farnborough*, or *Q.5.*

Loderer, which had been built in 1904, was fitted out at the naval dockyard in Devonport with the typical devices of a Q-ship: five twelve-pounder guns variously concealed by a 'steering house' aft, hinged flaps on the main deck and dummy cabins on the upper deck; two six-pounder guns hidden at either end of the bridge; and a Maxim gun in a dummy hencoop amidships. There were eleven officers and fifty-six men on board, with Pitcher one of the few regular Royal Navy ratings. *Loderer* was commissioned under her original name on 21 October 1915 but was renamed *Farnborough* after the Admiralty received an anonymous tip-off that her new role as U-boat bait had been leaked to the Germans.

On 22 March 1916, *Farnborough* made the fourth Q-ship U-boat 'kill' of the war when she sank Kapitan-Leutnant Guntzel's *U.68* with all hands. This success led to the Q-ship's captain, Lieutenant Commander Gordon Campbell, being promoted to commander. On 17 February 1917, to the west of Ireland, *Farnborough* accounted for her second kill, *U.83*, which was sunk with the loss of all hands bar an officer and one seaman.

The following month, Pitcher and most of the rest of *Q.5*'s crew elected to follow Commander Campbell to his next Q-ship: another former collier which was renamed *Pargust*. She had improved equipment and armaments, including a four-inch gun, and went to sea in May, but she was torpedoed a month later by Kapitan-Leutnant Rose's *UC.29*. The decoy 'panic party' left the ship and when the U-boat surfaced the remaining crew fired thirty-eight shells at it, causing it to blow up and sink. *Pargust*, which had been damaged in the attack, was towed into a nearby port the next day but her crew survived the attack. Under the thirteenth rule of the VC Royal Warrant, an officer and a rating were each given a medal on behalf of the whole crew, while Commander Campbell received a bar to the Distinguished Service Order he had won for his second kill. Pitcher was awarded one of eight Distinguished Service Medals.

Most of *Pargust*'s crew now followed Campbell on to *Dunraven*. At 10.58 a.m. on 8 August 1917, their new ship, disguised as a British merchant vessel, was zigzagging some 130 miles off Ushant when a U-boat was sighted on the horizon. *Dunraven* maintained her course as the U-boat,

*UC.*71, closed. At 11.17, the enemy submarine dived, then resurfaced 5,000 yards away on the starboard quarter. The U-boat opened fire at 11.43 and Commander Campbell, acting in the manner of a panicking merchant captain, sent out a distress signal giving the ship's position. He also fired off some token rounds from the ship's little two-and-a-half-pounder gun, as if it were the only weapon he possessed. The U-boat closed again and, when a torpedo almost hit *Dunraven*, the crew generated a cloud of steam to simulate boiler trouble. At the same time, Campbell dispatched a 'panic party' to make it look as if the ship was being abandoned. The submarine now scored three quick hits on *Dunraven*'s poop. The first detonated a depth charge which wounded three men and cut communications between Pitcher, the captain of the four-inch gun crew, and the bridge. However, Pitcher's team decided not to move, since leaving the ship would have given the game away. It was imperative that the Germans had to remain convinced that the ship had already been abandoned. The second and third shells started a major fire which meant Pitcher and several others were now concealed on a 'red-hot deck'. They lifted boxes of cordite off the deck and on to their knees in a bid to stop them exploding, but still they did not flee. At that point, *UC.*71 was obscured by black smoke from *Dunraven*'s stern, which presented Campbell with a dilemma. He knew an explosion on his own vessel was inevitable, but if he delayed in giving the order to abandon ship he might get a clear shot at the submarine. He later wrote: 'To cold-blood-edly leave the gun's crew to their fate seemed awful, and the names of each of them flashed through my mind, but our duty was to sink the submarine. By losing a few men we might save thousands not only of lives but of ships and tons of the nation's requirements. I decided to wait.'

The explosion on *Dunraven* came at 12.58 p.m., before the

U-boat could be fired upon. It blew out the stern of the ship and propelled the four-inch gun and its crew into the air. The gun landed on the well-deck and one man was thrown into the sea, while Pitcher and another crewman landed on mock railway trucks made of wood and canvas, which cushioned their falls and saved their lives.

As *UC.71* crash-dived, two shots were fired at her but without any telling effect. Pitcher and the other wounded men were now removed to the cabins, where they stayed for the rest of the action with 'shells exploding all around them'. As Campbell was preparing a torpedo attack, *Dunraven* was shelled abaft the engine room. Then the U-boat resurfaced and for twenty minutes torpedoed the Q-ship until diving again at 2.50 p.m. Campbell responded by firing two torpedoes. Both missed but, fortunately for *Dunraven*'s crew, the U-boat had now exhausted its own supply of torpedoes and fled the scene. A British destroyer, *Christopher*, towed the battered Q-ship towards Plymouth but, as the weather deteriorated, she sank at 3 a.m. Many bravery awards were made to the crew of the *Dunraven*, with the VC assigned specifically to Pitcher's gun crew going to him after a ballot to see who should receive it.

This action involving *Dunraven* was a turning point. Three weeks later it was agreed that there was a stalemate in this form of warfare and the Q-service was wound down. Pitcher received the gun crew's VC from George V at Buckingham Palace on 5 December 1917, as well as the French Medaille Militaire and the Croix de Guerre. On 1 August 1920, he was promoted to chief petty officer; and seven years later he retired from the Royal Navy after a quarter of a century's service. He then worked in Swanage as a woodwork teacher in a boys' preparatory school. For a time, he also ran a pub, the Royal Oak in Herston. However, he rejoined the Royal Navy on 5 August 1940, and served on shore for five years at Poole,

Portland and Yeovilton. He died in 1946 at the Royal Naval Auxiliary Hospital in Sherborne, Dorset.

LIEUTENANT COMMANDER GEORGE NICHOLSON BRADFORD

Royal Navy

DATE OF BRAVERY: 22/23 APRIL 1918
GAZETTED: 17 MARCH 1919

George Bradford was born in Darlington on 23 April 1887 and was educated at the local grammar school, the Royal Naval School in Eltham, south-east London, and Eastman's School in Southsea, near Portsmouth. He joined *Britannia* in 1902 and was renowned as a fine athlete and boxer, becoming Navy officers' welterweight champion and twice appearing in the finals of the Army and Navy Officers' championships.

On the night of 22 April 1918, Bradford was in command of the naval storming party aboard *Iris II* – an ex-Mersey ferry – at Zeebrugge, Belgium. The aim was to block the harbour and prevent German U-boats entering and exiting. The *London Gazette* described the commander's heroism that night:

> When *Iris II* proceeded alongside the Mole [the harbour wall at Zeebrugge] great difficulty was experienced in placing the parapet anchors owing to the motion of the ship. An attempt was made to land the scaling ladders before the ship was secured. Lieutenant Claude E.K. Hawkings managed to get one ladder in position and actually reached the parapet, the ladder being crushed to pieces just as he stepped off it. This very gallant young officer was last seen defending himself with his revolver. He was killed on the parapet. Though securing the ship was not part of his duties, Lieut.-Commander Bradford climbed up

the derrick [a small crane used to load and unload cargo] which carried a large parapet anchor and was rigged out over the port side; during this climb the ship was surging up and down and the derrick crashing on the Mole. Waiting his opportunity, he jumped with the parapet anchor on to the Mole and placed it in position. Immediately after hooking on the parapet anchor, Lieut.-Commander Bradford was riddled with bullets from machine-gun fire and fell into the sea between the Mole and the ship. Attempts to recover his body failed. Lieut.-Commander Bradford's action was one of absolute self-sacrifice. Without a moment's hesitation he went to certain death, realising that in such action lay the only possible chance of securing *Iris II* and enabling her storming parties to land.

Bradford's body was found and buried a few days later by the Germans. He had been killed on his thirty-first birthday.

His mother received his posthumous VC from George V on 3 April 1919 at Buckingham Palace. It was the second time she had attended such a ceremony on behalf of one of her four sons. Lieutenant Roland Bradford, of the 9th Battalion, Durham Light Infantry, had won the VC for his bravery on 1 October 1916 at Eaucourt L'Abbaye, France. He survived that battle but died in Cambrai, France, on 30 November 1917. A third son, James, won the Military Cross – also when serving with the Durham Light Infantry. He was killed in the Battle of Arras in May 1917. Her eldest son, Thomas, who won the Distinguished Service Order, survived the war. Mrs Bradford placed 'In Memoriam' notices in *The Times* on the anniversaries of her three sons' deaths every year until her own death in 1951.

LIEUTENANT (LATER LIEUTENANT COMMANDER) PERCY THOMPSON DEAN

Royal Naval Volunteer Reserve

DATE OF BRAVERY: 22/23 APRIL 1918
GAZETTED: 23 JULY 1918

Percy Dean was born in Blackburn on 20 July 1877. He attended King Edward's School, Bromsgrove, then joined the family businesses: slate trading and cotton spinning. In 1913, he became a town councillor and three years later he joined the Royal Naval Volunteer Reserve (RNVR) as a sub-lieutenant. The following year, he was promoted to lieutenant. He won his VC at Zeebrugge at the age of forty.

At the time, he was commanding Motor Launch (ML) 282, which was supporting three blockships, the old light cruisers *Thetis*, *Intrepid* and *Iphigenia*, in their mission. The *London Gazette* reported:

> Lieutenant Dean handled his boat in a most magnificent and heroic manner when embarking the officers and men from the blockships at Zeebrugge. He followed the blockships in and closed the *Intrepid* and *Iphigenia* under a constant and deadly fire from machine and heavy guns at point blank range, embarking over 100 officers and men. This completed he was proceeding out of the canal, when he heard that an officer was in the water. He returned, rescued him, and then proceeded, handling his boat throughout as calmly as if engaged in a practice manoeuvre. Three men were shot down at his side whilst he conned his ship [directed it by giving instructions to the helmsman]. On clearing the entrance to the canal the steering gear broke down. He manoeuvred his boat by the engines, and avoided

> complete destruction by steering so close in under the Mole that the guns in the batteries could not depress sufficiently to fire on the boat. The whole of this operation was carried out under a constant machine-gun fire at a few yards' range. It was solely due to this officer's courage and daring that ML 282 succeeded in saving so many valuable lives.

Eventually, Dean managed to transfer the men to the destroyer *Warwick*; although hit many times, his own ship did not sink.

As a result of his exploits at Zeebrugge, Dean was promoted in April 1918 to the temporary rank of lieutenant commander RNVR. That December, shortly after the end of the Great War, he was elected as one of two Coalition Unionist MPs for Blackburn and served the constituency until 1922. He is one of the very few holders of the VC to become an MP. He died on 20 March 1939.

LIEUTENANT GEOFFREY HENEAGE DRUMMOND

Royal Naval Volunteer Reserve

DATE OF BRAVERY: 9/10 MAY 1918
GAZETTED: 28 AUGUST 1918

Geoffrey Drummond was born on 25 January 1886 in St James's Place, London, the son of Captain Algernon Drummond of the Rifle Brigade. He was educated at Evelyn's School in Middlesex, Eton College and Christchurch, Oxford. In 1915, he joined the Royal Naval Volunteer Reserve.

On the same night as the raid on Zeebrugge (see previous two entries), the British made a similar attempt to block the harbour at Ostend, Belgium, but the Germans had received word of that raid and it was unsuccessful. The next month, however, the British decided to make a second attempt to blockade Ostend, using *Vindictive* and *Sappho* as blockships. Many of those involved in the first raid took part again.

Again the operation did not go according to plan because the old cruiser *Sappho* suffered engine trouble and had to abandon the mission. Despite thick fog, *Vindictive* continued on and eventually reached the mouth of the harbour. However, a shell hit the ship, killing her captain, Commander A.E. Godsal, and seriously wounding his navigating officer, Lieutenant Sir John Alleyn. Lieutenant V.A.C. Crutchley took command, but *Vindictive* soon ran aground and the order was given to abandon ship.

Motor Launch (ML) 254, under the command of Drummond, had also been hit by a shell as she followed *Vindictive*. The explosion had killed an officer and a sailor, and badly injured Drummond and his coxswain. However, Drummond, who had three separate wounds, was determined to save the crew of *Vindictive*, as the *London Gazette* reported:

> Notwithstanding his wounds, he remained on the bridge, navigated his vessel, which was already seriously damaged by shell fire, into Ostend harbour, placed her alongside *Vindictive*, and took off two officers and 38 men, some of whom were killed and many wounded while embarking. When informed that there was no one alive left on board, he backed his vessel out clear of the piers before sinking exhausted from his wounds. When HMS *Warwick* fell in with ML 254 off Ostend half an hour later the latter was in a sinking condition. It was due to the indomitable courage of this gallant officer [Drummond] that the majority of the crew of the *Vindictive* were rescued.

In *The Victoria Cross at Sea*, John Winton quotes Drummond's own vivid description of the action:

The firing seemed to grow in intensity, machine guns' rattle piercing the deeper roar of the batteries. Star shells, searchlights, the glare of the bombardment gave us plenty of light. One could clearly see figures on the piers, and even the hotel buildings along the shore. But a sea mist had fallen, and actually visibility was so bad that I had to rip open the canvas roof of the bridge and stand on the shelf with my head and shoulders out, and work the telegraphs with my feet. By this time, I was getting rather numb from loss of blood. A machine gun about 20 yards away on the other pier was doing its level best. It gave me two bullets in the right forearm, but they dropped out on the way home, having penetrated only about half an inch; my theory is that, fired point blank, they had not picked up their spin, and so were held up by my duffle coat.

Lieutenant Crutchley was the last to leave *Vindictive* and step aboard ML 254. As the motor launch moved away, the charges on *Vindictive* went off, scuttling the ship and partly blocking the harbour entrance. But that was not the end of the drama. As ML 254 exited the harbour, she passed ML 276, under the command of Lieutenant Roland Bourke, on her way in. (In fact, the two launches collided, but there was no major damage to either of them.) Bourke was already a war hero, having won the Distinguished Service Order for saving the crew from *Brilliant* after the failed Ostend mission the previous month. This time, he excelled himself still further: he stayed for ten minutes under heavy fire to ensure there were no further crew members on board *Vindictive*. Just as he was leaving, he heard cries from the water. Lieutenant Sir John Alleyn and two sailors – all injured – were clinging to an upturned boat. Despite being under a continuous fire, Bourke picked up the three men before heading to safety. Crutchley and Bourke were gazetted for VCs on the same day as Drummond, and they all received their decorations from George V on 11 September 1918.

On the outbreak of the Second World War, Drummond again volunteered for the RNVR, but his age and his health problems counted against him and he was turned down. Two years later, he slipped on some coal, banged his head, and died soon afterwards. He was fifty-five.

TEMPORARY COMMANDER (LATER MAJOR GENERAL) DANIEL MARCUS WILLIAM BEAK

Royal Naval Volunteer Reserve (Drake Battalion, Royal Naval Division)/Army

DATE OF BRAVERY: 21–25 AUGUST AND
  4 SEPTEMBER 1918
GAZETTED: 15 NOVEMBER 1918

Daniel Beak, who received four bravery awards during the last two years of the Great War, was born in Southampton on 27 July 1891. He joined the Royal Naval Volunteer Reserve in 1915 and shortly thereafter served at Gallipoli, where he was present at the evacuation.

The *London Gazette* of 26 January 1917 announced Beak's first decoration, a Military Cross: 'He led his men in the attack with great courage and initiative and materially assisted in the capture of the enemy line. He set a fine example throughout.' On 18 July the same year, it was announced that he had been awarded a bar to that medal: 'For conspicuous gallantry during operations, when he continually dashed forward, under heavy fire, to reorganise the men, and led them on with great bravery through the enemy barrage and machine-gun fire.'

Just over a year later – on 26 July 1918, the *Gazette* announced that he had won the Distinguished Service Order:

> During a night attack by the enemy the right flank of his division was left in a dangerous position. He arranged for a flank to be formed in that direction, and subsequently covered the retirement of two brigades with a composite rear-guard which he organised and commanded. His initiative and presence of mind greatly assisted in extricating these brigades from a very difficult situation. Throughout, the skilful handling of his battalion was particularly noticeable.

In July 1918, the German forces renewed their attack on the French lines over a hundred-mile front in the vicinity of Rheims. To start with, the Germans did well, crossing the River Marne for the first time since 1914. But soon their assault stalled, in part because they came up against the Royal Naval Division, including Beak's Drake Battalion, which had arrived in the Hamel–Aveluy sector in May for a planned Allied offensive. During late August and early September, Beak showed outstanding courage and leadership, surpassing even his earlier exploits. The *London Gazette* later detailed the acts that led to the award of his VC:

> For most conspicuous bravery, courageous leadership and devotion to duty during a prolonged period of operations. He led his men in attack, and, despite heavy machine-gun fire, four enemy positions were captured. His skilful and fearless leadership resulted in the complete success of this operation and enabled other battalions to reach their objectives. Four days later, though dazed by a shell fragment, in the absence of the brigade commander, he

reorganised the whole brigade under extremely heavy gun fire, and led his men with splendid courage to their objective. An attack having been held up, he rushed forward, accompanied by only one runner, and succeeded in breaking up a nest of machine-guns, personally bringing back nine or ten prisoners. His fearless example instilled courage and confidence into his men, who then quickly resumed the advance under his leadership. On a subsequent occasion he displayed great courage and powers of leadership in attack, and his initiative, coupled with the confidence with which he inspired all ranks, not only enabled his own and a neighbouring unit to advance, but contributed very materially to the success of the Naval Division in these operations.

At the end of the war, Beak joined the Royal Scots Fusiliers, and in 1932 he was transferred to the King's Regiment with the rank of major. From 1939 to 1940, he commanded the 1st Battalion, South Lancashire Regiment, then was promoted to brigadier and saw service in France. He was made acting major general in 1941 and became General Officer Commanding at Malta in 1942. Major General Daniel Beak, VC, DSO, MC and Bar, died in Swindon on 3 May 1967.

CHIEF PETTY OFFICER GEORGE PROWSE

Royal Naval Volunteer Reserve (Drake Battalion, Royal Naval Division)

DATE OF BRAVERY: 2 SEPTEMBER 1918
GAZETTED: 30 OCTOBER 1918

George Prowse was born into a mining family near Bath in 1886 and followed his father down the local pit. Later, he worked down mines at Grovesend and Gorseinon in south Wales. He joined the Royal Navy at a recruiting office in Swansea on 26 February 1915 and served in the Royal Naval Division from 1916 onwards, first as a petty officer then, from 28 April 1918, as a chief petty officer. He was twice wounded in battle and was awarded the Distinguished Conduct Medal (DCM) along with his VC. (He was eligible for the former decoration – generally given only to soldiers rather than sailors – because the Royal Naval Division was under Army command at the time.)

In the last month of his life, Prowse was so courageous that he almost seemed to have a death wish. He was serving in the Drake Battalion, part of the 63rd Division, which was advancing on the Hindenburg Line. In late August and early September 1918, Prowse took part in several attacks near Pronville, France, and it was for these that he won his VC. The *London Gazette* recorded:

> For most conspicuous bravery and devotion to duty when, during an advance, a portion of his company became disorganised by heavy machine-gun fire from an enemy strong point. Collecting what men were available, he led them with great coolness and bravery against this strong point, capturing it, together with 28 prisoners and five machine-guns. Later he took a patrol forward in face of much enemy opposition and established it on important high ground. On another occasion he displayed great heroism by attacking single-handed an ammunition limber which was trying to recover ammunition, killing three men who accompanied it and capturing the limber. Two days later he rendered valuable services when covering the advance of his company with a Lewis gun section, and located later on two machine-gun positions in a concrete emplacement, which were

holding up the advance of the battalion on the right. With complete disregard of personal safety he rushed forward with a small party and attacked and captured these posts, killing six enemy and taking thirteen prisoners and two machine-guns. He was the only survivor of this gallant party, but by this daring and heroic action he enabled the battalion on the right to push forward without further machine-gun fire from the village. Throughout the whole operations his magnificent example and leadership were an inspiration to all, and his courage was superb.

Prowse knew he had been proposed for the medal when he wrote one of his last letters to his wife, Sarah: 'To know I have been recommended for such an award is the greatest of honours and you can quite imagine I must have done something very great. You say I shall not half be "swanking" now, but you know there is not very much "swank" attached to me.'

He was killed in action on 27 September 1918, near Arleux, France. His body was never found. His widow received his VC from George V at Buckingham Palace on 17 July 1919.

8

THE FIRST WORLD WAR – THE ROYAL FLYING CORPS/RAF

The Royal Flying Corps (RFC) was created by a Royal Warrant on 13 May 1912 and superseded the Air Battalion of the Royal Engineers. It was initially intended to have separate military and naval branches. Inter-service rivalry meant, however, that the Royal Navy was not keen to have naval aviation under the control of an Army corps so it formed its own Royal Naval Air Service (RNAS). When war broke out in Europe in August 1914, the RFC had fewer than 1,400 men, the majority of whom went to France along with 73 planes and 95 support vehicles and a small number of manned balloons.

When war broke out, the airplane was initially viewed by the military as a vehicle for reconnaissance. In the early stages of the war, enemy pilots who saw each other in the air simply went about their reconnaissance duties. The more aggressive ones, however, were soon taking to the skies with revolvers, grenades, rifles and anything else they could get their hands on to fire at enemy pilots to prevent them completing their task. Soon machine-guns were converted for use in planes too and, even by 1915, the number of aerial combats was escalating rapidly. By 1916, planes became generally more sophisticated and by the Battle of the Somme, the RFC had a marked aerial supremacy. It had 421 aircraft, 14 balloons and four kite-balloon squadrons.

On 1 April 1918, the RFC and RNAS were amalgamated to form a new service, the Royal Air Force (RAF), which was controlled by a new Air Ministry. By August 1918, when the Allies began their push for victory, planes were playing a crucial role in supporting the ground offensive. By 1919, just a year after the end of the war, the RAF had 4,000 combat aircraft and 114,000 personnel.

SECOND LIEUTENANT (PROMOTED POSTHUMOUSLY TO LIEUTENANT) WILLIAM BERNARD RHODES-MOOREHOUSE

Royal Flying Corps: 2 Squadron

DATE OF BRAVERY: 26 APRIL 1915
GAZETTED: 22 MAY 1915

William Rhodes-Moorehouse, the first airman to win a VC, was born in London on 27 April 1887. He probably inherited his taste for adventure from his grandfather, William Barnard Rhodes, who left his native Yorkshire in the 1830s in order to settle in New Zealand, becoming one of the first Englishmen to arrive in that wild and remote country. With the help of his three brothers, he amassed a fortune from farming and other business interests, leaving £750,000 – an enormous sum of money at the time – to his half-Maori daughter, Mary Ann, when he died. She married a New Zealander, Edward Moorehouse, had four children with him, then moved to England to raise their family. Will, their eldest son, a robust boy with fair hair and green eyes, was educated at Harrow, where he developed a taste for speed and an interest in the workings of the internal combustion engine. He went to Trinity College, Cambridge, but neglected his studies for his love of engineering and his passion for racing motorcycles and cars.

By the time he was in his early twenties, he had also become fascinated with the new sport of flying. He paid for flying lessons and was one of the pioneer airmen, attracting large crowds when he flew from Huntingdon airfield at a time when a man in flight was still a sensational spectacle. With a friend, James Radley, he even produced a variation of the Bleriot XI aircraft – the Radley–Moorehouse monoplane. He travelled to the USA in 1911, where he piloted a fifty-horsepower Gnome-engined Bleriot to victory in numerous air-speed contests, thereby earning thousands of dollars in prize money. His US tour ended in San Francisco, where he won the coveted Harbor Prize, worth £1,000. While he was there, he became the first man to fly through the arches of the Golden Gate Bridge. He continued to fly competitively on his return to Britain, ending his peacetime flying career with a record-breaking cross-Channel flight in 1912.

When war was declared, he volunteered for the Royal Flying Corps, and his twenty-five-minute flight from Brooklands aerodrome was his first for two and a half years. There was a shortage of experienced pilots on the Western Front, and on 21 March 1915 Rhodes-Moorehouse joined 2 Squadron at Merville, France. His squadron flew the Farnborough-designed Bleriot-Experimental (BE) 2a and 2b, which were sturdy planes but had a maximum speed of just 70 m.p.h. at ground level. Rhodes-Moorehouse began with some familiarisation sorties, but soon had his baptism of German anti-aircraft fire at 7,500 feet over Lille. His logbook records that the top centre section of his plane was hit by a shell on 29 March. Four days later he wrote to his wife, describing the sound of anti-aircraft fire as 'first a whistle, then a noise like a terrific cough'.

Poor weather meant he had few flights in the first two weeks of April, but from the 16th he was performing numerous highly dangerous missions. During one ninety-five-minute reconnaissance, his plane's wings and bracing wire were hit by shrapnel. His brilliant service did not go unnoticed by his superiors and he was recommended for promotion to full lieutenant.

On 22 April the Germans conducted their first gas attack on Allied troops, and for the next four days they took the initiative in battles in and around St Julien and Ypres. On the 26th, the Royal Flying Corps were ordered to bomb the enemy's railway network to prevent reinforcements reaching the front lines. Rhodes-Moorehouse, who had been due some much-deserved leave, was set to bomb the railway junction at Courtrai – one of three targets for four planes. He took off alone from Merville at 3.05 p.m., having been advised by his flight commander, Maurice Blake, to drop his hundred-pound bomb from just below cloud level. But after making the thirty-two-mile flight, he dropped right down to 300 feet to ensure a direct hit. He was greeted with a volley of rifle and machine-gun fire, and when he was directly over the target a burst of machine-gun fire perforated the plane's fuselage and smashed into his thigh. At the same time, fragments from his own bomb ripped through the wings and tailplane.

Badly wounded and in great pain, Rhodes-Moorehouse had two options: land behind enemy lines, receive urgent medical attention and become a prisoner of war; or try to limp back to his home airbase. It came as no surprise to those who knew him that he chose the latter option. Indeed, he dropped a further 200 feet to gain some extra speed and again encountered heavy fire from the ground. This led to two new wounds to his hand and abdomen. Nevertheless, he steered the plane towards his base, crossing the Allied lines over some Indian troops who looked up in awe and later asked for details of his courageous sortie to be translated into Hindustani. Just three days later, they would read in the *Daily Bulletin Issued to the*

Troops that Rhodes-Moorehouse's mission had been a total success and 'would appear worthy to be ranked among the most heroic stories of the world's history'.

At 4.12 p.m., Blake and a group of 2 Squadron officers were sitting on a river bank listening to the gramophone when they saw Rhodes-Moorehouse's badly damaged plane approaching at a low height. The pilot just cleared a hedge, switched off the engine and made a perfect landing. Blake and another officer lifted him from the battered plane, which boasted ninety-five bullet and shrapnel holes. Rhodes-Moorehouse was taken to a nearby office, where he insisted on filing his report while his wounds were tended. He was then moved to a casualty clearing station in Merville, where it was discovered that a bullet had ripped his stomach to pieces. He was given painkillers, but the doctors decided nothing else could be done for him. The next morning, Blake was told his friend was dying and had asked for him. Rhodes-Moorehouse showed his commanding officer a photograph of his wife and son, and asked Blake to write to them and his mother. He said that if he was awarded a Military Cross, it should go to his wife. After a short doze, he revealed: 'It's strange dying, Blake, old boy – unlike anything one has ever done before, like one's first solo flight.' Just after 1 p.m., he received Holy Communion and a note arrived informing him that he had been recommended for the Distinguished Service Order. At 2.25 p.m., with a recently delivered letter from his wife resting on his pillow, William Rhodes-Moorehouse died. He was twenty-seven.

At home, he was instantly acclaimed as a hero. The *Daily Mail* noted: 'Such endurance is enough to make all of us ashamed of ever again complaining of any pain whatever. He was one of those who have never "done their bit" till they have done the impossible.' A leader in *The Times* said: 'his story is too simple and too splendidly complete in itself to need any artifice of narrative or comment; it speaks to us all'.

Air Vice Marshal Sholto Douglas wrote a letter of condolence to the pilot's widow: 'I do hope such courage will be recognised with a DSO although we all think a VC would be none too great a reward for such pluck and endurance.' It was obviously helpful to have such powerful supporters, but it was Blake's lobbying that secured the VC, and very swiftly: Rhodes-Moorehouse's award was gazetted less than a month after his death. At the time, General Sir John French, the British commander, said the pilot had been responsible for 'the most important bomb dropped during the war so far'.

Before his mission, Rhodes-Moorehouse had written several letters to his family, to be sent to them in the event of his death. One particularly touching one was to his baby son Willie, in which he expressed his love and affection for his wife, with whom he stressed he had never had a 'misunderstanding or quarrel'. He urged his son always to seek the advice of his mother and hoped he would be an engineer and obtain 'a useful knowledge of machinery in all forms'. He also urged him to 'keep up your position as a landowner and a gentleman' (the family had acquired the sixteenth-century Parnham House and its estate near Beaminster, Dorset, before the war). Then, with an affectionate farewell, Will Rhodes-Moorehouse signed what he described as his 'first and last letter' to his son. There was a poignant and astute postscript: 'I am off on a trip from which I don't expect to return but which I hope will shorten the War a bit. I shall probably be blown up by my own bomb or if not killed by rifle fire.'

CAPTAIN JOHN AIDAN LIDDELL

Army/Royal Flying Corps: 3rd Battalion, the Argyll and Sutherland
Highlanders (Princess Louise's) and 7 Squadron

DATE OF BRAVERY: 31 JULY 1915
GAZETTED: 23 AUGUST 1915

Aidan Liddell, one of the first pilots to win a VC, was born in Newcastle-upon-Tyne, on 3 August 1888 and educated at Stonyhurst College, Lancashire, and Balliol, Oxford. He earned the nickname of 'Oozy' at school because he was always messing around with engines and chemicals. At Oxford, he took an honours degree in zoology, the only student to do so that year as it was a new subject.

In 1912, 'not wanting to be a slacker', he joined the Special Reserve of Officers of the 3rd Battalion, Argyll and Sutherland Highlanders. The following year, he took up flying, a pastime that was still in its infancy and was fraught with danger. He was promoted to lieutenant in July 1914 and captain the very next month, when hostilities began. In early September, he was twice given the job of burying the dead, writing in a letter home that life was 'nothing except noise and unpleasant smells and sights and jobs'. Matters did not improve: by mid-November he was noting in his diary that he had gone a month without a bath and seven weeks without a change of socks in the trenches, which had started to 'flow like a river' because of the early winter rains. On 26 November, he reflected: 'It's a war with no glamour or glory . . . modern weapons are too deadly, and the whole art of war has been altered . . . to a very slow and tedious and also gruelling business.' Yet he was a dedicated and brave soldier: one comrade told how Liddell had saved his life by helping him when he was wounded. His battalion was finally relieved on 11 December after he had spent forty-three consecutive days in the line. His efforts had been noted, though, as he was mentioned in dispatches by Sir John French, the British commander. Two weeks later, he was present at the famous unofficial ceasefire on Christmas Day, writing to his old college: 'Most of our men and officers, including myself, went out and met them half-way, where we exchanged smokes, newspapers, and various souvenirs for over an hour.'

In January 1915, while on a week's leave in England, Liddell learned he had been awarded the Military Cross for his work with the Machine-Gun Section. However, after rejoining the battalion, his frail health gave way and he was evacuated to England for a complete rest. After a period of recuperation, he obtained his Royal Aero Club Certificate and transferred to the Royal Flying Corps. Some training at three British air bases followed, then he left for France on 23 July 1915 to join 7 Squadron at St Omer. He flew his first sortie on 29 July and his second, with Second Lieutenant Richard Peck as his observer, two days later.

The men took off in an RE5 plane shortly before midday and arrived over Ostend at 5,000 feet. Heading for Bruges, they were suddenly fired on from above by a German biplane. Peck returned fire with his Lewis gun, but then the RE5 lurched forward and rolled on to its back: one of the bursts of enemy fire had ripped through the side of the rear cockpit. Worse still, a bullet had hit Liddell's right thigh, exposing the bone, and the pilot had fallen unconscious with shock. The plane began to drop to the ground as all loose objects in the cockpit, including weapons and ammunition, whistled past Peck's head.

When the aircraft had fallen 3,000 feet, Liddell regained consciousness and righted it. However, the control wheel was half shot away and the throttle was shattered. Liddell, by now behind enemy lines, could either land and face inevitable imprisonment or try to make it back to the Allied lines. He chose the latter option and scribbled a note to Peck saying that he intended to head for some sands west of Nieuport. Peck, though, pointed to an Allied airfield near Furnes as a better option.

For half an hour, in severe pain from his injury, Liddell flew the plane to safety, holding the broken control wheel in one hand and operating the rudder cables with the other. When they reached La Panne airfield Liddell made his approach on full engine power because of the broken throttle, then switched it off before touchdown. He made a perfect landing, then refused to allow a group of Belgian airmen to move him until a doctor arrived. While he was waiting, he tied a tourniquet to stem the flow of blood and made a makeshift splint, and when he was finally lifted from the battered plane he even managed a smile for a waiting photographer. Later, staff at La Panne hospital battled to save his left leg, but septicaemia set in and it was amputated.

Liddell's courageous deeds were well reported in Britain and he received many distinguished visitors while in hospital. On 3 August – his twenty-seventh birthday – he wrote a typically optimistic letter to his mother, saying he was being 'pampered' and 'everyone seems very pleased with my progress'. He also made light of plunging towards the ground in his plane: 'I was waiting for the bump, when suddenly I thought it might be a good thing to straighten her out and try and recover flying position . . . Poor old Peck must have had a terrible shock, not knowing whether I was dead or not, or whether he was going to hit the ground in the machine, or going to fall out . . . glad I wasn't him really.' He also quoted a letter he had received from a Major Hoare, praising his actions: '"How you managed God only knows: but it was a magnificent effort and the General is giving a detailed report on it today to [Sir John]

French. I cannot express to you the admiration we all have for you for what you did. You have set a standard for pluck and determination which may be equalled, but certainly will not be surpassed, during this War.'"

Unfortunately, Liddell's cheerful optimism was misplaced. The blood poisoning had spread and, as his condition worsened, his mother was given permission to visit him. She managed to see him shortly before he died on 31 August. It was a month to the day after he had been shot but he died in the knowledge that he had won the VC, having been told of the award on 18 August. After his death, the Argylls issued a statement of how he would be missed: 'We all feel as if the light has gone out, the light of our Battalion. You see he was always bright. In snow, in muddy trench, or ante-room, he kept us laughing, and his influence will last . . . from the smallest drummer boy to the Colonel, this Battalion asks only to be given the chance to avenge Aidan's death.' More than a thousand people wrote letters of condolence to his parents, including Prince Alexander of Teck, the younger brother of Queen Mary, who praised Liddell for 'playing the game to the end'. His VC was presented to his father by George V at Buckingham Palace on 16 November 1916.

LIEUTENANT (LATER CAPTAIN) WILLIAM LEEFE ROBINSON

Army/Royal Flying Corps: the Worcestershire Regiment and 39 Squadron

DATE OF BRAVERY: 2/3 SEPTEMBER 1916
GAZETTED: 5 SEPTEMBER 1916

Billy Leefe Robinson was born on his father's coffee estate in Tollideta, South Coorg, India, on 14 July 1895. During his schooling, he was never particularly academic but he was sporty, and he ended up at Sandhurst in August 1914. That December, he was commissioned into the Worcestershire Regiment, and in March the following year he joined the Royal Flying Corps in France as an observer, but he was invalided home after being wounded over Lille. Yet, by September, he had not only recovered but had qualified as a pilot. This led to postings to various Home Defence squadrons. In one letter home, he explained his passion for flying: 'You have no idea how beautiful it is above the clouds. I have been up at about 5 o'clock on a still afternoon – you have no idea how glorious it is to gaze at the earth at 7,000 feet or over – but thrilling as that is, the real beauty comes with the clouds . . . I love flying more and more every day, and the work is even more interesting than it was.'

The Great War was the first conflict for centuries in which the civilians of Britain were in fear of their lives. This was because of the German use of Zeppelins in bombing raids up and down the East Coast. Leefe Robinson had his first chance to shoot down one of the airships in April 1916, but failed to do so. However, on the night of 2/3 September Leefe Robinson would succeed and become a national hero. He took off from Sutton's Farm airfield in Essex in his BE2c 2963 plane at 11.08 p.m. on a routine 'search and find' operation. Leefe Robinson was accompanied by Lieutenant Fred Sowerby, his observer. Their first two hours, flying at 10,000 feet between the airfield and Joyce Green, were uneventful. However, at 1.10 a.m., he caught sight of a Zeppelin in two searchlight beams over Woolwich, south-east London. He set off in pursuit but lost it in the thick cloud.

However, searchlights over Finsbury in north London had also spotted the airship – one of sixteen sent from Germany that night on a mass raid – and anti-aircraft guns opened fire on the Schutte-Lanz SL11. By now, Leefe Robinson was desperately short of fuel but he gave chase and was joined, in another plane, by Lieutenants Mackay and Hunt. Tracer fire from the ground lit up the night sky but the airship unloaded its bombs, which enabled it to gain height. As Leefe Robinson closed in, he emptied two drums of ammunition into the airship, but it flew on unhindered: it seemed impregnable. He broke off but then made another attack from astern, firing his last drum into the airship's twin rudders. First a reddish glow appeared inside the airship, then, moments later, it burst into flames. Thousands of Londoners looked up and cheered as it plunged from the sky.

Leefe Robinson landed back at Sutton's Farm at 2.45 a.m. after a gruelling patrol of three and a half hours. He was lifted shoulder high to the edge of the airfield but, despite being exhausted and numb with cold, was then ordered to write his report. His fitters were alarmed to see that part of the plane's central top wing and machine-gun wire guard had been shot away. After finishing his report, the pilot collapsed on his bed and fell asleep. As he dozed, the ecstatic scenes of 'Zepp Sunday' were already under way all over London.

Leefe Robinson's exploits quickly made the news headlines. For many people, it was the finest moment in the war. Photographs of the heroic pilot appeared in newspapers and magazines and he became an instantly recognised figure all over the country. He also received many honours and rewards, but his most cherished moment came when he was invited to Windsor Castle, where George V presented him with his VC on the very same day that the sixteen crew members from the airship he shot down were buried. His VC had come in near-record speed. He was gazetted just two days after his actions and presented with his decoration a mere three days after that. On the day his award was announced, the *Evening News* had bills all over London proclaiming: 'The Zepp: VC for airman.'

Leefe Robinson was delightfully modest about his courage, telling well-wishers: 'I only did my job.' Yet, as well as being the first airman to bring down a Zeppelin, he was the first man to win a VC in – or at least *over* – the United Kingdom.

In a letter to his parents dated 22 October 1916, Leefe Robinson reflected upon his fame:

> I do really feel ashamed for not writing to you darling old people before, but still, there it is – you know what I am. Busy!! Heavens, for the last seven weeks I have done enough to last anyone a lifetime. It has been a wonderful time for me! I won't say much about 'strafing' the Zepp L21 for two reasons; to begin with most of it is strictly secret and secondly I'm really so tired of the subject and telling people so I will only say a few words about it. When the colossal thing actually burst into flames of course it was a glorious sight – wonderful! It literally lit up all the sky around and me as well of course – I saw my machine as in the fire light – and sat still half dazed staring at the wonderful sight before me, not realising to the least degree the wonderful thing that had happened!
>
> My feelings? Can I describe my feelings? I hardly know how I felt as I watched the huge mass gradually turn on end, and – as it seemed to me – slowly sink, one glowing, blazing mass – I gradually realised what I had done and grew wild with excitement. When I had cooled down a bit, I did what I don't think many people would think I would do, and that was I thanked God with all my heart. You know . . . I am not what is popularly known as a religious person, but on an occasion such as that one must realise a little how one does trust in providence. I felt an overpowering feeling of thankfulness, so was it strange that I should pause and think for a moment after the first 'blast' of

excitement as it were, was over and thank from the bottom of my heart that supreme power that rules and guides our destinies?

. . . As I daresay you have seen in the papers – babies, flowers and hats have been named after me also poems and prose have been dedicated to me – oh, it's too much! I am recognised wherever I go about Town now, whether in uniform or mufti – the city police salute me, the waiters, hall porters and pages of hotels and restaurants bow and scrape – visitors turn round and stare – oh it's too thick!

Leefe Robinson's good looks, fame and riches – including well over £4,000 in donations from well-wishers – also meant he was hotly pursued by many young women.

He was sent to France as a flight commander shortly after winning the VC, and in early 1917, while leading six of the new Bristol fighters, encountered Manfred von Richthofen leading a flight of five Albatros fighters. The short, fierce battle that followed led to four of the Bristols being shot down, including Leefe Robinson's. When he was taken prisoner, the Germans quickly realised who he was and made his life all the harder for it. After trying to escape four times in as many months, he was court-martialled and sentenced to a month in solitary confinement. Later, he was taken to the notorious Holzminden prison camp run by the brutal Karl Niemeyer. There he was one of the youngest and most brutalised prisoners – particularly after he escaped briefly – and his health suffered.

He was returned from captivity on 14 December 1918 but by then was desperately weak. Subsequently he contracted influenza, his health deteriorated and he became delirious, reliving his time in captivity: he imagined that Niemeyer and his sentries, armed with fixed bayonets, were standing by his bed. Several times he shouted that he wanted protection from 'the fiend'. On New Year's Eve, Billy Leefe Robinson – one of the greatest heroes of the war – died, aged twenty-three.

SERGEANT THOMAS MOTTERSHEAD

Royal Flying Corps: 20 Squadron

DATE OF BRAVERY: 7 JANUARY 1917
GAZETTED: 12 FEBRUARY 1917

Thomas Mottershead was born in Widnes on 17 January 1892 and won his VC for his actions near Ploegsteert Wood, Belgium. The *London Gazette* reported:

> For most conspicuous bravery, endurance and skill when, attacked at an altitude of 9,000 feet, the petrol tank was pierced and the machine set on fire. Enveloped in flames, which his observer, Lieut. Gower, was unable to subdue, this very gallant soldier succeeded in bringing his aeroplane back to our lines, and though he made a successful landing, the machine collapsed on touching the ground, pinning him beneath wreckage from which he was subsequently rescued. Though suffering extreme torture from burns, Sergt. Mottershead showed the most conspicuous presence of mind in the careful selection of a landing-place, and his wonderful endurance and fortitude undoubtedly saved the life of his observer. He has since succumbed to his injuries.

Mottershead, who had earlier won the Distinguished Conduct Medal, died five days after his crash landing, just before his twenty-fifth birthday.

MICHAEL ASHCROFT

MAJOR EDWARD MANNOCK

RAF: 85 Squadron

DATE OF BRAVERY: 17 JUNE–22 JULY 1918
GAZETTED: 18 JULY 1919

Edward 'Mick' Mannock was born in Brighton on 24 May 1887, the son of a tough Irishman who, after serving in the Boer War, abandoned his wife and three children. Mannock was twenty-seven and working as a labourer in Turkey when the Great War broke out, and when Turkey entered the war on Germany's side he and some other British workers were imprisoned. In jail, he sang patriotic British songs and received regular beatings from the Turkish guards for his impertinence. When he tried to escape, he was put in solitary confinement and his health deteriorated – he had dysentery and suppurating sores – but eventually the American Consulate secured his release. Back in Britain, in July 1915, he re-enlisted in the Territorial unit of the Royal Army Medical Corps, which he had first joined after leaving school. However, some of the requirements of the job – one of which was a duty to treat enemy prisoners – troubled him. (After his experiences in the Turkish prison, he had no compassion for the Central Powers or their soldiers.) Then, a chance meeting with an old friend led to a discussion about flying. In August 1916, Second Lieutenant Mannock transferred to the Number One School of Military Aeronautics at Reading, where he learned mapping, aircraft rigging and gunnery.

Mannock also showed promise as a pilot, though, and on 1 April 1917 he arrived in France. Four days later, he joined his first operational unit, 40 Squadron at Treizennes. Unfortunately, he created a bad first impression among the squadron as a 'boorish know all', and his first sortie, when he was badly shaken by anti-aircraft fire, reinforced this view. However, opinions soon started to change when, through brilliant flying, he pulled his damaged Nieuport Scout (a single-seater French fighter) out of a 'terminal' dive. On 7 May, he claimed his first success when he and five others shot down a kite balloon – a manned, gas-filled balloon used for reconnaissance – five miles behind German lines. On 25 May and 1 June 1917, he was convinced he had enemy 'kills', but he decided to bide his time until he could make a claim that was unquestionable. He did not have long to wait: the following week he sent an Albatros D.III crashing to earth from 13,000 feet.

On 17 September 1917, the *London Gazette* announced that he had won the Military Cross (MC): 'In the course of many combats he has driven off a large number of enemy machines, and has forced down three balloons, showing a very fine offensive spirit and a great fearlessness in attacking the enemy at close range and low altitudes under heavy fire from the ground.' The very next month, the *Gazette* announced a bar to the medal: 'He has destroyed several hostile machines and driven others down out of control. On one occasion he attacked a formation of five enemy machines single-handed and shot one down out of control. On another occasion, while engaged with an enemy machine, he was attacked by two others, one of which he forced to the ground. He has consistently shown great courage and initiative.' Mannock was becoming a better team player, too: during one sortie he protected a promising young pilot, Lieutenant George McElroy. 'McIrish', as Mannock christened him, went on to become the tenth highest-scoring pilot of the war, with forty-six victories.

Mannock himself had his last day with 40 Squadron on 1 January 1918, when he recorded his twenty-first official kill. He next served with 74 (Service) Squadron, flying to France on 30 March. In May, he was reduced to tears by the death of his protégé, Lieutenant Dolan, his wails of grief continuing long into the night. Afterwards, his comrades noticed a new bloodlust, but he never let it cloud his judgement in the air and his number of kills rapidly escalated. He carried out a series of brilliant manoeuvres against his opponents: one kill was described by Ira Jones, a fellow-pilot, as 'a remarkable exhibition of cruel, calculated Hun-strafing'. But amid all the success he remained a realist, never taking off without his revolver: 'to finish myself off as soon as I see the first sign of flames'.

In May 1918, he learned he had won the Distinguished Service Order. In quick succession, he was then awarded two bars to go along with it, and the second was announced on 3 August 1918 – after his death – in the *London Gazette*:

> This officer has now accounted for 48 enemy machines. His success is due to wonderful shooting and a determination to get to close quarters; to attain this he displays most skilful leadership and unfailing courage. These characteristics were markedly shown on a recent occasion when he attacked six hostile scouts, three of which he brought down. Later on the same day he attacked a two-seater, which crashed into a tree.

On 21 June 1918, Mannock was promoted to major and chosen to succeed Major 'Billy' Bishop in command of 85 Squadron. However, a close friend noticed that his nerves seemed to be frayed as he left Britain for his new posting: 'He was in no condition to return to France, but in those days such things were not taken into consideration.' On 24 July, Mannock told his friend Ira Jones by telephone: 'I've caught up with Bishop's score now – seventy-two [including unofficial kills].' Around 5 a.m. three days later, Mannock, flying with Lieutenant Donald Inglis, made his final kill above Lestremme. Disregarding his own strict rule, he then made a couple of low passes over the wreckage, leading the inexperienced Inglis into a storm of small-gun fire from the German trenches. As they zigzagged away from the scene, Inglis noticed a small bluish flame on his major's engine cowling. Then the left wing of Mannock's plane fell away and he plunged into a death spin. Inglis, showered in petrol from his own punctured fuel tank, made a crash landing shortly afterwards. After being pulled from his battered plane, he announced: 'They killed him, the bastards killed my major. They killed Mick.' Edward Mannock was dead at thirty-one.

It later emerged that his body had been thrown out of the plane – or he had jumped clear. He may well have fulfilled his pledge to shoot himself at the first sign of flames in his plane. He was buried in an unmarked grave by a German soldier, who also returned Mannock's identity discs, notebooks and other personal effects.

After the war, it was decided his courage had not been fully recognised. After much lobbying, largely by those who had served under him, the *London Gazette* announced his VC nearly a year after his death. It recognised fifty official kills but concentrated on his achievements in June and July 1918, concluding: 'This highly distinguished officer, during the whole of his career in the Royal Air Force, was an outstanding example of fearless courage, remarkable skill, devotion to duty, and self-sacrifice, which has never been surpassed.' Corporal Edward Mannock, the recipient's wayward father, was presented with his son's VC by George V the same month.

9

THE SECOND WORLD WAR

The Allied Powers, led by the British Empire, the Commonwealth, the United States and, latterly, the Soviet Union, defeated the Axis Powers of Germany, Italy and Japan. The war was fought in response to the expansionist aggression of Nazi Germany under Adolf Hitler, a racist dictator, and the imperial ambitions of Japan in Asia. It was, by far, the largest and deadliest war in history, culminating with the dropping of two atomic bombs on Japan.

Estimates of casualties vary greatly. But it is likely that around 62 million people, or 2 per cent of the world's population at the time, died in the war. Of these, perhaps 25 million were military and 37 million civilian, with the Allies suffering some 80 per cent of the total casualties. The civilian deaths were the result of disease, starvation, massacres, aerial bombing and genocide (it is estimated that the Holocaust alone accounted for at least nine million people, most of them Jews).

Britain and France had tried to avoid another world war by following a policy of appeasement to placate Hitler: in 1938, Neville Chamberlain, the British Prime Minister, famously returned from Munich with an 'agreement' which partitioned Czechoslovakia, declaring that this guaranteed 'peace in our time'. On 1 September 1939, nine days after signing a secret pact with the Soviet Union, Germany invaded Poland. Two days later, Britain and France declared war on Germany.

During the first six months of 1940, the war spread rapidly. The Soviet Union attacked Finland and occupied Latvia, Lithuania and Estonia, then annexed Bessarabia and Northern Bukovina from Romania. Germany, in turn, invaded Denmark, Norway, Luxembourg, Belgium, the Netherlands and France, and made preparations to invade Britain. In June, Italy declared war on Britain, and later invaded British Somaliland but failed in its attempt to overrun Greece.

In 1941, Germany first invaded Greece then betrayed its partner, the Soviet Union: Operation Barbarossa, the largest invasion in history, began on 22 June. Meanwhile, the war spread to North Africa and the Middle East. America showed its support for the Allies by signing a treaty – the Atlantic Charter – with Britain in August 1941; and on 7 December the Japanese launched a surprise air attack on the US Pacific Fleet in Pearl Harbor, Hawaii. The following day the United States declared war on Japan. On the same day, China officially did the same, while Germany declared war on the United States on 11 December.

During 1942 and 1943, the war was fought in several theatres: Europe, the Soviet Union, the Pacific, North Africa, China and South-east Asia. In January 1944, a Soviet offensive relieved the siege of Leningrad and soon the Allies started to gain ground elsewhere. On 6 June 1944 – 'D Day' – the Allies, mainly forces from Britain, Canada and America, invaded German-held Normandy; by 25 August, Paris had been litberated. By April 1945, the Allies had advanced into Italy, and the Western Axis Powers knew the war was lost. The Allies celebrated VE (Victory in Europe) Day on 8 May, while the Soviets celebrated their Victory Day the following morning.

US President Harry Truman now used a new 'super weapon' to bring the war against Japan to a swift end. On 6 August 1945, a nuclear bomb was dropped on Hiroshima, destroying the city. The United States immediately called upon Japan to surrender but received no response, so, three days later, a second bomb was dropped on

Nagasaki. The Japanese finally surrendered on 15 August (VJ Day), while Japanese troops in China formally surrendered to the Chinese on 9 September. The war was finally over.

The Second World War saw weapons and technology improve rapidly over its six-year duration. This played a crucial role in determining the outcome of the war. Many technologies were used for the first time, including radar, jet engines and electronic computers, as well as nuclear weapons. Aircraft, battleship and tank designs made enormous advances so that planes, boats and vehicles that were cutting edge at the beginning of the conflict had become obsolete by its end. The war also saw a shift of power from the British Empire and Western Europe to two new 'superpowers': the United States and the Soviet Union. And it led to the creation in 1945 of the United Nations, which was intended to prevent another world war and thereby succeed where the League of Nations had failed.

One hundred and eighty-two VCs were awarded during the Second World War, of which the trust now has twenty.

The Army

Britain entered the war – and committed substantial land forces to the Allied effort – after Germany invaded Poland in 1939. A British Expeditionary Force (BEF) was sent to France, but was hastily evacuated as Germany swept through the Low Countries and into France in 1940. Only the Dunkirk evacuation saved the entire BEF from capture. The British Army was largely spared the horrors of trench warfare that had dominated the First World War and, as the global conflict progressed, the Army asserted itself as a formidable fighting force.

The British defeated the Italians and Germans at El Alamein in North Africa, Italy and in the D-Day invasions of Normandy. In the Far East, the Army successfully fought the Japanese in Burma. As the *war progressed, the Army developed its Commando units including the Special Air Service (SAS) and repeatedly proved its worth.*

ACTING CAPTAIN (LATER LIEUTENANT COLONEL) ERIC CHARLES TWELVES WILSON

Army: East Surrey Regiment, attached to Somali Mounted Infantry

DATE OF BRAVERY: 11–15 AUGUST 1940
GAZETTED: 14 OCTOBER 1940

Eric Wilson was born in Sandown on the Isle of Wight on 2 October 1912. In August 1940, he was serving in an isolated corner of Africa, in Somaliland, and was involved in some fierce fighting. Two months later, the *London Gazette* announced that he had been awarded the VC posthumously:

> Captain Wilson was in command of machine-gun posts manned by Somali soldiers in the key position of Observation Hill, a defended post in the defensive organisation of the Tug Argan Gap in British Somaliland. The enemy attacked Observation Hill on 11th August, 1940. Captain Wilson and the Somali soldiers under his command beat off the attack and opened fire on the enemy troops attacking Mill Hill, another post within his range. He inflicted such heavy casualties that the enemy, determined to put his guns out of action, brought up a pack battery to within seven hundred yards, and scored two direct hits through the loopholes of his defences, which, bursting within the post, wounded Captain Wilson severely in the right shoulder and in the left eye, several of his team being also wounded. His guns were blown off their stands but he repaired and replaced them and, regardless of his wounds, carried on, whilst his Somali sergeant was killed

beside him. On 12th and 14th August, the enemy again concentrated field artillery on Captain Wilson's guns, but he continued, with his wounds untended, to man them. On 15th August two of his machine-gun posts were blown to pieces, yet Captain Wilson, now suffering from malaria in addition to his wounds, still kept his own post in action. The enemy finally over-ran the post at 5 p.m. on 15th August when Captain Wilson, fighting to the last, was killed.

Or was he? In fact, Wilson had surrendered when his post was overrun and became a prisoner of war. He was released at the end of the war and, at the time of writing, was still living in Sherborne, Dorset, aged ninety-three.

In 2005, the trust reached an agreement with Eric Wilson and his family whereby it purchased his VC. However, under the conditions of the deal that the trust is more than happy to honour, it will remain with this wonderful, courageous man for the rest of his days.

†SECOND LIEUTENANT (LATER CAPTAIN) CHARLES HAZLITT UPHAM

New Zealand Expeditionary Force: 20th Battalion (the Canterbury Regiment)

DATE OF BRAVERY: VC – 22–30 MAY 1941; BAR – 14/15 JULY 1942
GAZETTED: VC – 14 OCTOBER 1941; BAR – 26 SEPTEMBER 1945

Charles Upham, one of the three men to have won a VC and bar, was born in Christchurch, New Zealand, on 21 September 1908. He began his working life as a sheep farmer after taking a diploma at Canterbury Agricultural College, and at the outbreak of the Second World War, he was working in a government agricultural post.

His wartime exploits were, by any measure, extraordinary. He quickly enlisted in the New Zealand Expeditionary Force (NZEF) and was posted, as a private, to its 20th Infantry Battalion. He turned down the offer of a commission because he did not want to miss seeing action oversees. When he reached the Middle East with the first draft from the NZEF, he was sent to an officer cadet training unit, but he had little respect for the military tactics of some of his superiors and passed out bottom of the class. This was ironic given that he would later become one of his country's most tactically astute, as well as bravest, soldiers.

The German invasion of Greece in April 1941 led to Upham, now a platoon commander and second lieutenant, joining the force sent to repel the invaders. He was one of the 28,000 British, Greek, Australian and New Zealand soldiers put on Crete with orders from Winston Churchill to hold the island at all costs. Whereas most soldiers win the VC for a single, often spontaneous, act of bravery, Upham won his for nine days of skill, leadership and heroism. From 22 to 30 May, he destroyed numerous enemy posts, rescued a wounded man under heavy fire and penetrated deep behind enemy lines. He also personally killed twenty-two German soldiers on the way to leading an isolated platoon out of danger. And he did all this despite suffering from dysentery, being blown over by a mortar shell, being wounded in the shoulder by shrapnel and with a bullet in his foot.

Upham's platoon was particularly noteworthy in counter-attacks on Maleme on 22 May. After a day of heroics, that night Upham took out several machine-gun posts single-handed, not with recklessness but using cool nerve and lightning reflexes to stalk his prey. By day, he used the same stalking skill, armed with a rifle, pistol and grenades, to make himself 'invisible' in the Cretan hillsides until he burst from cover and began shooting. In one incident, he displayed astonishing guile. He was on his way to warn his comrades that they were in danger of being cut off by German soldiers when he was fired on by the enemy. In desperation, he feigned death, lay motionless and waited for two soldiers to approach. With one arm in a sling, he used the crook of a tree to aim his rifle, enabling him to shoot the first man. Then he reloaded with his good hand and shot the second German, who was so close that he fell against the barrel of Upham's gun.

Upham's bravery could not stop the Germans prevailing, though, because they had already seized an important airfield and therefore had vital air support. At the end of May, the British and Commonwealth forces were evacuated from Crete, and Upham returned to the Middle East – to Syria. When his VC was gazetted later in the year, he became genuinely distressed that he had been singled out from his comrades and accepted the award only on the understanding that it was a tribute to the entire platoon. He was presented with his VC by General Sir Claude Auchinleck, Commander-in-Chief, Middle East, in the Western Desert on 7 November 1941. It was widely considered that he had done enough to win the VC at least four times during his nine days of frantic action on Crete. However, his modesty prevented him from wearing the ribbon on his tunic or even giving press interviews. Eventually, he was ordered to do both.

The following year, Upham won his bar for his part in the attack on Ruweisat Ridge, Egypt, where the New Zealand force was stranded after being promised armoured support that never arrived. When his blood was up, Upham was terrifyingly effective. He led his company on a 'savage attack' on German and Italian strongpoints, destroying a tank, several guns and vehicles with his favourite weapon – the hand grenade. While doing this, his arm was shattered by a machine-gun bullet. Yet he still reached a forward position and rescued several men who had been isolated. When he was removed to the regimental first-aid post, he had his wounds dressed but insisted on returning to his men. Despite exhaustion, loss of blood and further injuries from artillery and mortar fire, he fought on until only six men remained. Virtually unable to move through exhaustion and injuries, they were overrun and captured.

For months, Upham was assumed to have been killed. However, in October 1942, it was reported that he was a prisoner of war in Italy. Once he had recovered from his wounds (a process that took several months), he started to live up to his nickname 'Pug' (short for pugnacious). He attempted to escape several times, was branded 'dangerous' by his captors and was ultimately imprisoned in Colditz. He was liberated from that infamous fortress prison in April 1945 by advancing US troops.

When King George VI asked Major General Kippenberger whether Upham deserved a bar to his VC, the distinguished soldier replied: 'In my respectful opinion, sir, Upham has won the VC several times over.' News of the second award was delivered by telegram as Upham was having his portrait painted in a studio in Wellington, New Zealand. He read the telegram, then put it in his pocket and continued posing without saying a word. He is widely acknowledged as the most outstanding soldier of the Second World War, and is the only holder of a VC and bar to have been a combative soldier. The other two, Arthur Martin-Leake and Noel Chavasse, were both medical officers who won their decorations for tending to the wounded.

Later, Upham bought the farm he had always longed for, although he did it with his own money, refusing £10,000 raised for that purpose by the residents of Christchurch. He asked for the money to be used instead to fund a scholarship to educate the children of his country's servicemen. He lived a quiet, unassuming life in sheep country, near Parnassus in the South Island, but reportedly never allowed a German-made car or equipment on to his farm. He died in Christchurch on 21 November 1994.

TEMPORARY LIEUTENANT COLONEL GEOFFREY CHARLES TASKER KEYES

Army: Royal Scots Greys, Royal Armoured Corps and 11th Scottish Commandos

DATE OF BRAVERY: 17/18 NOVEMBER 1941
GAZETTED: 19 JUNE 1942

Geoffrey Keyes, who received his VC for one of the most daring actions of the Second World War, was born in Aberdour, Scotland, on 18 May 1917, the son of Lord Keyes of Zeebrugge and Dover, an Admiral of the Fleet. Keyes Jnr had hoped to follow his father into the Royal Navy but he failed the eyesight test. After being educated at Eton and Sandhurst, he joined his uncle's regiment, the Royal Scots Greys, as a second lieutenant. From October 1937, he served in Palestine but, while on leave in February 1940, he volunteered for special service. As an accomplished skier, he was picked for the Narvik Expeditionary Force two months later, but when the Allies had to retreat from Norway he was evacuated back to England and rejoined his regiment. He then briefly served as liaison officer to the Chasseurs Alpins, and for his work in that role was awarded the French Croix de Guerre.

After his return from Norway, he volunteered to join the newly formed Commando organisation. On 25 July, he received a letter from his father saying: 'I am so pleased you applied for that service – because I was going to apply for you. I am Director of Combined Operations, all Commandos and Independent Companies come under my influence . . . Your loving Daddy.' Keyes was posted to the 11th Scottish Commandos and, after a rigorous training programme, embarked for the Middle East in January 1941.

By the autumn, Keyes had formulated a daring plan and, after much persuasion, won over General Headquarters Cairo to sanction an attempt to destroy the German HQ, 250 miles behind enemy lines at Beda Littoria, Libya. Furthermore, the intention was to capture General Erwin Rommel, commander of the Afrika Korps. The 'Rommel Raid' was timed to coincide with a British offensive on 17/18 November 1941. Colonel Robert Laycock, the officer commanding Middle East Commando operations, had reservations about the mission but decided to accompany the force as an observer. He remained at the landing place throughout.

It is Laycock's own full report – rather than the heavily edited version that appeared in the *London Gazette* – which follows:

> Lt. Col. Geoffrey Keyes, Royal Scots Greys, commanded a detachment of a force which landed by submarine . . . behind the enemy lines to attack Headquarters, Base, Installations and Communications. The original plan, formulated several weeks in advance at 8th Army Head-quarters, included orders for attacks on various separate objectives. Although the whole operation was considered to be of a somewhat desperate nature, it was obvious that certain tasks were more dangerous than others.
>
> Colonel Keyes, who was present at all the meetings and assisted in the planning, deliberately selected for himself

from the outset the command of the detachment detailed to attack what was undoubtedly the most hazardous of these objectives – the residence and Headquarters of the General Officer Commanding the German Forces in North Africa. (When the plan was submitted to me as Commander of the Middle East Commandos, in which capacity I may be regarded as having some experience of this type of warfare, I gave it my considered opinion that the chances of being evacuated after the operation were very slender and that the attack on General Rommel's house in particular appeared to be desperate in the extreme. This attack, even if initially successful, meant almost certain death for those who took part in it. I made these comments in the presence of Colonel Keyes, who begged me not to repeat them lest the operation be cancelled.)

In the execution of the Operation Colonel Keyes led his detachment ashore. The majority of the boats, including his own, were swamped on the passage in to the beach but, whereas his officers and men were able to take advantage of the shelter of a cave in which they lit a fire, warmed themselves and dried their clothing, Colonel Keyes remained throughout the night on the beach to meet any men who managed to get ashore from the second vessel.

Shortly before first light the detachment moved to a Wadi [dry riverbed] in which they remained hidden during the hours of daylight. After dark on the second night, Colonel Keyes set off with his detachment towards the objective, but was deterred by his Arab guide, who refused to accompany the party as soon as the weather deteriorated. Without guides, in dangerous and precipitous country, faced with a climb of over 1,800 ft in pitch darkness and an approach march of 18 miles which they knew must culminate in an attack on the German Headquarters, soaked to the skin by continuous torrential rain and shivering from cold from half a gale of wind, the fast ebbing morale of the detachment was maintained solely by Colonel Keyes' stolid determination and magnetic powers of leadership.

Biding throughout the hours of daylight and moving only during darkness Colonel Keyes had led his detachment to within a few hundred yards of the objectives by 2200 hours on the fourth night ashore. Restricted by the depletion of his detachment through stragglers and through the fact that some of his men had never reached the shore from the submarine Colonel Keyes now found himself forced to modify his original orders in the light of fresh information elicited from neighbouring Arabs.

Having detailed the majority of his men to take up positions so as to prevent enemy interference with his attack on General Rommel's residence, Colonel Keyes was left with only one Officer (Captain Campbell) and one other Rank (Sgt. Terry) with whom to break into the house and deal with the Guards and Headquarters Staff. At zero hours (2359 hrs) having dispatched the covering party to block the approaches to the house and to guard the exits from neighbouring buildings, he himself with Captain Campbell and Sergeant Terry crawled forward past the guards, through the surrounding fence and so up to the house itself.

Colonel Keyes hoped to be able to climb in through a window or enter by the back premises but these proved to be inaccessible. He therefore, without hesitation, boldly led his party up to the front door and, taking advantage of Captain Campbell's excellent German, beat on the door and demanded entrance. As soon as the sentry opened the door Colonel Keyes and Captain Terry set upon him but, as he could not be overpowered immediately, Captain Campbell shot him with his revolver. The noise naturally but unfortunately roused the inmates of the house. Colonel Keyes, appreciating that speed was now of the utmost importance, posted Sgt. Terry at the foot of the stairs to prevent interference from the floor above – a task which he accomplished satisfactorily by firing a burst from his Tommy-gun at anyone who attempted to reach the landing.

Although the lights in the passage were burning, those inside the ground floor rooms were extinguished by the occupants. If the raiding party was to achieve any measure of success these rooms had to be entered. This could be done by stealth which would however have taken time and, had the enemy been bold enough to come out into the passage, they would immediately have appreciated that they were attacked by three individuals only, whom they could easily have overpowered. The only alternative was to attempt to bluff the occupants by dashing into each room in turn with a minimum of delay. This latter course Colonel Keyes unflinchingly adopted although he undoubtedly realised that it was almost certain death for the man who first showed himself silhouetted by the passage lights against a darkened doorway.

Colonel Keyes, who instinctively took the lead, emptied his revolver with great success into the first room and was followed by Captain Campbell who threw in a grenade, but the inevitable result of such daring occurred on his entering the second room of the ground floor. He must have been perfectly aware that it was occupied, since Sgt. Terry, who was a few yards away, reported to me later that he could distinctively hear the occupants breathing and moving about inside. Colonel Keyes was shot almost immediately on flinging open the door and fell back into the passage mortally wounded. On being carried outside by Captain Campbell and Sgt. Terry he died within a few minutes.

It may be added that on several occasions before the expedition sailed I suggested to Colonel Keyes that he should detail a more junior officer to take his place in leading the actual assault on the German Headquarters and that he himself should remain at the Operational Rendezvous. I again made this suggestion to him after he got ashore just prior to his leaving my Headquarters south of Chescem-el-Chelb. On each occasion he flatly declined to consider these suggestions saying that, as Commander of his detachment, it was his privilege to lead his men into any danger that might be encountered – an answer which I consider [was] inspired by the highest traditions of the British Army.

From the first conception of the operation, through the stages in which it was planned, during the weary days spent in waiting for the expedition to sail, and up to the last moment where I saw him 250 miles behind the enemy lines, heading for almost certain death, I was profoundly impressed by his confidence and determination to face unlimited danger. Colonel Keyes' outstanding bravery was not that of the unimaginative bravado who may be capable of spectacular action in moments of excitement but that far more admirable calculated daring of one who knew only too well the odds against him. That he was aware of danger I have no doubt from previously discussing the operation with him and from his description of his former brilliant action at Litani River, but that he could ever allow fear to influence his action for one single second is unthinkable to anyone who knew Colonel Keyes.

Of the entire force, only Laycock and Terry made it back to British lines after thirty-seven days in the desert. The remainder were either taken prisoner or killed. It later transpired that Rommel had never used the building raided by

Keyes. In any event, he had been in Rome at the time. Nevertheless, he heard of the raid and clearly respected Keyes' bravery because he sent his personal chaplain to Libya to conduct the funeral of the commando. Sir Winston Churchill, who comforted Admiral Keyes on the loss of his son, said: 'I would far rather have Geoffrey alive than Rommel dead.'

LIEUTENANT COLONEL AUGUSTUS CHARLES NEWMAN

Army: Essex Regiment, attached to 2 Commando

DATE OF BRAVERY: 27 MARCH 1942
GAZETTED: 19 JUNE 1945

Augustus Newman was born in Buckhurst Hill, Essex, on 19 August 1904. He won his VC during a commando-style attack on St Nazaire in France. The *London Gazette* reported:

On the night of 27th/28th March 1942 Lieutenant-Colonel Newman was in command of the military force detailed to land on enemy occupied territory and destroy the dock installations of the German controlled naval base at St Nazaire. This important base was known to be heavily defended and bomber support had to be abandoned owing to bad weather. The operation was therefore bound to be exceedingly hazardous, but Lieutenant-Colonel Newman, although empowered to call off the assault at any stage, was determined to carry to a successful conclusion the important task which had been assigned to him. Coolly and calmly he stood on the bridge of the leading craft, as the small force steamed up the estuary of the River Loire, although the ships had been caught in the enemy searchlights and a murderous cross fire opened from both banks, causing heavy casualties.

Although Lieutenant-Colonel Newman need not have landed himself, he was one of the first ashore and, during the next five hours of bitter fighting, he personally entered several houses and shot up the occupants and supervised the operations in the town, utterly regardless of his own safety, and he never wavered in his resolution to carry through the operation upon which so much depended. An enemy gun position on the roof of a U-boat pen had been causing heavy casualties to the landing craft and Lieutenant-Colonel Newman directed the fire of a mortar against this position to such effect that the gun was silenced. Still fully exposed, he brought machine-gun fire to bear on an armed trawler in the harbour, compelling it to withdraw and thus preventing many casualties in the main demolition area. Under the brilliant leadership of this officer the troops fought magnificently and held vastly superior enemy forces at bay, until the demolition parties had successfully completed their work of destruction.

By this time however, most of the landing craft had been sunk or set on fire and evacuation by sea was no longer possible. Although the main objective had been achieved, Lieutenant-Colonel Newman nevertheless was now determined to try and fight his way out into the open country and so give all survivors a chance to escape. The only way out of the harbour lay across a narrow iron bridge covered by enemy machine-guns and although severely shaken by a German hand grenade, which had burst at his feet, Lieutenant-Colonel Newman personally led the charge which stormed the position and under his inspiring leadership the small force fought its way through the streets to a point near the open country when, all ammunition expended, he and his men were finally overpowered by the enemy. The outstanding gallantry and devotion to duty of this fearless officer, his brilliant leadership and initiative, were largely responsible for the success of this perilous operation which resulted in heavy damage to the important naval base at St Nazaire.

Newman remained a prisoner until the end of the war. He died in Sandwich, Kent, on 26 April 1972.

SERGEANT (LATER CAPTAIN) QUENTIN GEORGE MURRAY SMYTHE

South African Forces: Royal Natal Carabineers

DATE OF BRAVERY: 5 JUNE 1942
GAZETTED: 11 SEPTEMBER 1942

Quentin Smythe was born in Natal, South Africa, on 6 August 1916 and won his VC in the Western Desert in June 1942. His decoration was announced in the *London Gazette* three months later:

> For conspicuous gallantry in action in the Alem Hamza area on the 5th June, 1942. During the attack on an enemy strong point in which his officer was severely wounded, Sergeant Smythe took command of the platoon although suffering from a shrapnel wound in the forehead. The strong point having been overrun, our troop came under enfilade fire from an enemy machine-gun nest. Realising the threat to his position, Sergeant Smythe himself stalked and destroyed the nest with hand grenades, capturing the crew. Though weak from loss of blood, he continued to lead the advance, and on encountering an anti-tank gun position again attacked it single-handed and captured the crew. He was directly responsible for killing several of the enemy, shooting some and bayoneting another as they withdrew.

After consolidation he received orders for a withdrawal, which he successfully executed, defeating skilfully an enemy attempt at encirclement. Throughout the engagement Sergeant Smythe displayed remarkable disregard for danger, and his leadership and courage were an inspiration to his men.

Smythe died in Doonside, Natal, on 21 October 1997. His VC is an official replacement – one of just three in the trust's collection. It is not known how Smythe came to be separated from the original.

LIEUTENANT ALEC GEORGE HORWOOD

Army: 1/6th Battalion, the Queen's Royal Regiment (West Surrey), attached to 1st Battalion, the Northamptonshire Regiment

DATE OF BRAVERY: 18–20 JANUARY 1944
GAZETTED: 30 MARCH 1944

Alec Horwood, the first British officer to win the VC on the Burma Front, was born in Deptford, south London, on 6 January 1914, the son of George Horwood, a former Mayor of Bermondsey. Between the wars, he worked as a clerk in the offices of Hartley's, the jam manufacturers, and in his spare time was a talented amateur cyclist, captaining Bath Road Cycle Club. He was also a member of the Territorial Army, so was called up when hostilities began and sent to France, serving as a sergeant with the West Surrey Regiment. In May 1940, his battalion clashed with German forces that had advanced into Belgium, and after fierce fighting he was taken prisoner while helping a wounded man. However, in Antwerp, accompanied by another officer from the 1/6th Queen's, he slipped his guards then walked more than 100 miles to

Dunkirk. At one point, he avoided enemy patrols by taking to a rowing boat along the coast. He won the Distinguished Conduct Medal for this remarkable escape.

Horwood was now commissioned and attached to the 1st Battalion of the Northamptonshire Regiment, joining them shortly before their deployment with the 20th Indian Division on the Burma Front. On 20 December 1943, the battalion learned that it had to undertake the capture of a strong Japanese position on the west bank of the River Yu at Kyauchaw. The *London Gazette* described what happened four weeks later:

At Kyauchaw on 18 January 1944, Lieutenant Horwood accompanied the forward company of the Northampton-shire Regiment into action against a Japanese defended locality with his forward mortar observation post. Throughout the day he lay in an exposed position, which had been completely bared of cover by concentrated air bombing, and effectively shot his own mortars and those of a half troop of another unit while the company was manoeuvring to locate the exact position of the enemy bunkers and machine-gun nests. During the whole of this time Lieutenant Horwood was under intense sniper, machine-gun and mortar fire, and at night he came back with the most valuable information about the enemy.

On 19 January he moved forward with another company and established an observation post on a precipitous ridge. From here, while under continual fire from the enemy, he directed accurate mortar fire in support of two attacks which were put in during the day. He also carried out a personal reconnaissance along and about the bare ridge, deliberately drawing the enemy fire so that the fresh company which he had led to the position and which was to carry out an attack might see the enemy positions.

Lieutenant Horwood remained on the ridge during the night of 19–20 January and on the morning of the 20 January shot the mortars again to support a fresh attack by another company put in from the rear of the enemy. He was convinced that the enemy would crack and volunteered to lead the attack planned for that afternoon. He led this attack with such calm, resolute bravery that the enemy were reached and while standing up in the wire, directing and leading the men with complete disregard to the enemy fire which was then at point blank range, he was mortally wounded.

By his fine example of leadership on the 18th, 19th and 20th January when continually under fire, by his personal example to others of reconnoitring, guiding and bringing up ammunition in addition to his duties at the mortar observation post, all of which were carried out under great physical difficulties and in exposed positions, this officer set the highest example of bravery and devotion to duty to which all ranks responded magnificently. The cool calculated actions of this officer coupled with his magnificent bearing and bravery which culminated in his death on the enemy wire, very largely contributed to the ultimate success of the operation which resulted in the capture of the position on the 24 January.

After the award was announced, Horwood's widow told reporters: 'The last letter I had from my husband was on January 10th. He said he would love to be back home again, but would not come back till the job was finished . . . I am so terribly proud of him. He was fearless and I don't feel surprised he won this honour.'

†TEMPORARY CAPTAIN JOHN NEIL RANDLE

Army: 2nd Battalion, the Royal Norfolk Regiment

DATE OF BRAVERY: 4–6 MAY 1944
GAZETTED: 12 DECEMBER 1944

John Randle was born in Benares, India, on 22 December 1917. By 1944, he was serving in India and writing considerate, frequent letters home to his wife, Mavis, who had already been deeply affected by the war: her brother, Flying Officer Leslie Manser, VC (see p. 343), had been shot down and killed over Germany on 30 May 1942.

On 4 May 1944, at Kohima in Assam, a battalion of the Norfolk Regiment attacked the Japanese positions on a nearby ridge. When his commander was seriously wounded, Randle took over the command of his company. Amid fierce fighting, he handled a difficult situation calmly and impressively; and when he was wounded in the knee by shrapnel, he continued to inspire his men with his courage, initiative and masterly leadership. Even when his company had captured its objective and consolidated its position, Randle helped bring in all the wounded men lying outside the perimeter. Although suffering severe pain from his wound, he refused to be evacuated, but rather carried out daring moonlight reconnaissance to enable his company to attack the new enemy defensive position.

At dawn on 6 May, Randle again led his men in an attack. While one platoon succeeded in reaching the crest of a hill held by the Japanese, another ran into stiff machine-gun fire from a bunker. Randle assessed the situation and quickly appreciated the importance of the bunker. It covered not only the rear of his new position but the line of communication to the battalion. In short, he realised that it had to be taken if the operation that day was to succeed. So, with total disregard for his own safety,

Randle charged the machine-gun post alone, armed with a rifle, bayonet and hand grenade. He was sprayed with bullets but, bleeding from the face and body, he managed to throw the grenade through the bunker slit. As a final defiant gesture, he flung his body over the slit to seal the bunker before the grenade exploded. Randle had effectively decided to sacrifice his own life to save the lives of his comrades and to enable them to achieve their objective.

He had been a close friend of Group Captain Leonard Cheshire, VC, who later said it brought tears to his eyes when he read of Randle's courage.

SEPOY (LATER SUBADAR) KAMAL RAM
Indian Army: 8th Punjab Regiment
DATE OF BRAVERY: 12 MAY 1944
GAZETTED: 27 JULY 1944

Kamal Ram was born in Bholunpura village, Rajasthan, India, on 18 December 1924. He won the VC for bravery at the River Gari, Italy, at the age of nineteen. The *London Gazette* described how:

> On 12th May, 1944, after crossing the River Gari overnight, the company advance was held up by heavy machine-gun fire from four posts on the front and flanks. As the capture of the position was essential to secure the bridgehead, the company commander called for a volunteer to get round the rear of the right post and silence it. Volunteering at once and crawling forward through the wire to a flank, Sepoy Kamal Ram attacked the post single-handed and shot the first machine-gunner; a second German tried to seize his weapon but Sepoy Kamal Ram killed him with the bayonet, and then shot a German officer who,

appearing from the trench with his pistol, was about to fire. Sepoy Ram, still alone, at once went on to attack the second machine-gun post, which was continuing to hold up the advance, and, after shooting one machine-gunner, he threw a grenade and the remaining enemy surrendered.

Seeing a Havildar making a reconnaissance for an attack on the third post, Sepoy Kamal Ram joined him, and having first covered his companion, went in and completed the destruction of his post. By his courage, initiative and disregard for personal risk, Sepoy Kamal Ram enabled his company to charge and secure [the] ground . . . His sustained and outstanding bravery unquestionably saved a difficult situation at a critical period of the battle and enabled his battalion to attain the essential part of their objective.

Ram survived the war and is believed to have died in India in 1982.

NAIK (LATER HON CAPTAIN) AGANSING RAI

Indian Army: 2nd Battalion, 5th Royal Gurkha Rifles

DATE OF BRAVERY: 26 JUNE 1944
GAZETTED: 5 OCTOBER 1944

Agansing Rai, whose medal is the only Gurkha VC in the trust's collection, was born in Asmara village in eastern Nepal in 1920. In April 1941, he enlisted in the Gurkhas, and two years later he was promoted to section commander with the rank of naik. He then served with the 17th Indian Division during the Burma Campaign of 1944.

The Japanese Army was on the offensive in March 1944. Its ultimate aim was to seize India, but first it had to combat

General William Slim's 14th Army in Central Burma. Under General Mutaguchi, the Japanese attacked with formidable ferocity, and the British IV Corps, centred on Imphal and Kohima, bore the brunt of the attack. Three of its divisions were besieged, including the 17th Indian, the so-called 'Black Cat' Division. IV Corps had just 50,000 men against 90,000 Japanese, but the British and US air forces controlled the skies and the Japanese had no supply routes, so they had to strike quickly. They were determined to take Imphal, but the Black Cats defended their position heroically, and during the ferocious engagement Rai won his VC. The *London Gazette* reported:

> In Burma on 24th and 25th June, 1944, after fierce fighting, the enemy, with greatly superior forces, had captured two posts known as 'Water Piquet' and 'Mortar Bluff'. These posts were well sighted and were mutually supporting and their possession by the enemy threatened our communications. On the morning of 26th June, 1944, a company of the 5th Royal Gurkha Rifles (Frontier Force) was ordered to recapture these positions.
>
> After a preliminary artillery concentration, the company went in to attack but on reaching a false crest about 80 yards from its objective, it was pinned down by heavy and accurate fire from a machine-gun in 'Mortar Bluff' and a 37-millimetre gun in the jungle, suffering many casualties. Naik Agansing Rai, appreciating that more delay would inevitably result in heavier casualties, at once led his section under withering fire directly at the machine-gun and, firing as he went, charged the position, himself killing three of the crew of four. Inspired by this cool act of bravery the section surged forward across the bullet-swept ground and routed the garrison of 'Mortar Bluff'.

This position was now under intense fire from the 37-millimetre gun in the jungle and from 'Water Piquet'. Naik Agansing Rai at once advanced towards the gun, his section without hesitation following their gallant leader. Intense fire reduced the section to three men before half the distance had been covered. But they pressed on to their objective. Arriving at close range, Naik Agansing Rai killed three of the crew and his men killed the other two. The party then returned to 'Mortar Bluff' where the rest of their platoon were forming for the final assault on 'Water Piquet'. In the subsequent advance, heavy machine-gun fire and showers of grenades from an isolated bunker position caused further casualties. Once more, with indomitable courage, Naik Agansing Rai, covered by his Bren gunner, advanced alone with a grenade in one hand and his Thompson Sub-Machine gun in the other. Through devastating fire he reached the enemy position and with his grenade and bursts from his Thompson Sub-Machine gun killed all four occupants of the bunker.

The enemy, demoralised by this NCO's calm display of courage and complete contempt for danger, now fled before the onslaught on 'Water Piquet' and this position too was captured. Naik Agansing Rai's magnificent display of initiative, outstanding bravery and gallant leadership, so inspired the rest of the Company that, in spite of heavy casualties, the result of this important action was never in doubt.

Soon the Japanese were in a fighting retreat amid the monsoon. Their campaign had been a disaster and 65,000 of their men died through combat, starvation and disease. Plans to invade India were abandoned.

Rai received his VC from the Viceroy, Field Marshal Lord

Wavell, in 1945. He was subsequently promoted to company commander with the rank of subedar; and after Indian independence, he joined the Indian Army and was promoted to havildar. He retired in 1971 with the honorary rank of captain and died in Kathmandu on 27 May 2000, aged eighty.

PRIVATE (LATER CORPORAL) RICHARD HENRY BURTON

Army: 1st Battalion, the Duke of Wellington's (West Riding) Regiment

DATE OF BRAVERY: 8 OCTOBER 1944
GAZETTED: 4 JANUARY 1945

Richard Burton was born in Melton Mowbray, Leicestershire, on 29 January 1923. At fifteen, he left school to pursue a career as a bricklayer, but he joined the Northamptonshire Regiment in early 1942. Soon afterwards, he transferred to the Duke of Wellington's, and sailed with them in early 1943 to French North Africa. After a succession of Allied victories, the Germans withdrew and in June 1944 the Duke's Regiment entered Rome. Four months later, as the Germans continued to retreat north, Burton won his VC, which was announced in the *London Gazette* early the next year:

> In Italy on 8 October 1944, two Companies of the Duke of Wellington's Regiment moved forward to take a strongly held feature 760 metres high. The capture of the feature was vital at this stage of the operations as it dominated all the ground on the main axis of the advance. The assaulting troops made good progress to within 20 yards of the crest when they came under withering fire from Spandaus on the crest. The leading Platoon was held up and the Platoon Commander wounded. The Company Commander took another platoon, of which Private Burton was a runner,

through to assault the crest from which four Spandaus at least were firing. Private Burton rushed forward and, engaging the first Spandau position with his Tommy Gun, killed the crew of three. When the assault was again held up by murderous fire from two more machine-guns Private Burton, again showing complete disregard for his own safety, dashed forward toward the first machine-gun using his Tommy Gun until his ammunition was exhausted. He then picked up a Bren Gun and firing from the hip succeeded in killing or wounding the crews of the two machine-guns. Thanks to his outstanding courage the Company was then able to consolidate on the forward slope of the feature. The enemy immediately counter-attacked fiercely but Private Burton in spite of most of his comrades either being dead or wounded, once again dashed forward on his own initiative and directed such accurate fire with his Bren Gun on the enemy that they retired leaving the feature firmly in our hands. The enemy later counter-attacked again on the adjoining Platoon position and Private Burton, who had placed himself on the flank, brought such accurate fire to bear that the counter-attack also failed to dislodge the Company from its position. Private Burton's magnificent gallantry and total disregard of his own safety during many hours of fierce fighting in mud and continuous rain were an inspiration to all his comrades.

Burton survived the war, moved to Scotland and returned to the building trade until retiring in 1986. He said he was 'slightly embarrassed by the adulation' that he received as a holder of the VC. He died at Kirriemuir, Angus, on 11 July 1993.

ACTING SERGEANT (LATER COMPANY SERGEANT MAJOR) GEORGE HAROLD EARDLEY

Army: 4th Battalion, the King's Shropshire Light Infantry

DATE OF BRAVERY: 16 OCTOBER 1944
GAZETTED: 2 JANUARY 1945

George Eardley was born in Congleton, Cheshire, on 6 May 1912. He won a Military Medal in the summer of 1944 and his VC a few months later. The latter was announced by the *London Gazette* in early 1945:

> In North-West Europe on 16th October, 1944, during an attack on a wooded area east of Overloon, strong opposition was met from well-sited defence positions in orchards. The enemy were paratrooped and well equipped with machine-guns. A platoon of the King's Shropshire Light Infantry was ordered to clear these orchards and so restore the momentum of the advance, but was halted some 80 yards from its objective by automatic fire from enemy machine-gun posts. The fire was so heavy that it appeared impossible for any man to expose himself and remain unscathed. Notwithstanding this, Sergeant Eardley, who had spotted one machine-gun post, moved forward, firing his Sten gun; he killed the officer at the post with a grenade. A second machine-gun post beyond the first immediately opened up, spraying the area with fire. Sergeant Eardley, who was in a most exposed position, at once charged over 30 yards of open ground and silenced both the enemy gunners. The attack was continued by the platoon but was again held up by a third machine-gun post, and a section sent in to dispose of it was beaten back, losing four casualties. Sergeant Eardley, ordering the

section he was with to lie down, then crawled forward alone and silenced the occupants of the post with a grenade. The destruction of these three machine-gun posts single-handed by Sergeant Eardley, carried out under fire so heavy that it daunted those who were with him, enabled his platoon to achieve its objective, and in so doing, ensured the success of the whole attack. His outstanding initiative and magnificent bravery were the admiration of all who saw his gallant action.

Eardley survived the war and died in his home town on 11 September 1991.

SEPOY (LATER HAVILDAR) ALI HAIDAR
Indian Army: 13th Frontier Force Rifles
DATE OF BRAVERY: 9 APRIL 1945
GAZETTED: 3 JULY 1945

Ali Haidar was born in the village of Shahu, Kohat, then in India, on 21 August 1913. He won his VC for bravery in the final weeks of the war in Europe, as the *London Gazette* explained:

In Italy, during the crossing of the River Senio, near Fusignano, in daylight on 9th April, 1945, a Company of the 13th Frontier Force Rifles were ordered to assault the enemy positions strongly dug in on the far bank. These positions had been prepared and improved over many months and were mainly on the steep flood banks, some 25 feet high. Sepoy Ali Haidar was a member of the left-hand Section of the left-hand Platoon. As soon as the Platoon started to cross, it came under heavy and accurate machine-gun fire from two enemy posts strongly dug in about 60 yards away. Sepoy Ali Haidar's Section suffered casualties and only 3 men, including himself, managed to get across. The remainder of the Company was temporarily held up. Without orders, and on his own initiative, Sepoy Ali Haidar, leaving the other two to cover him, charged the nearest post which was about 30 yards away. He threw a grenade and almost at the same time the enemy threw one at him, wounding him severely in the back. In spite of this he kept on and the enemy post was destroyed and four of the enemy surrendered. With utter disregard of his own wounds he continued and charged the next post in which the enemy had one Spandau and three automatics, which were still very active and preventing movement on both banks. He was again wounded, this time in the right leg and right arm.

Although weakened by loss of blood, with great determination Sepoy Ali Haidar crawled closer and in a final effort raised himself from the ground, threw a grenade and charged into the second enemy post. Two enemy were wounded and the remaining two surrendered. Taking advantage of the outstanding success of Sepoy Ali Haidar's dauntless attacks, the rest of the Company charged across the river and carried out their task of making a bridgehead. Sepoy Ali Haidar was picked up and brought back from the second position seriously wounded. The conspicuous gallantry, initiative, and determination combined with a complete disregard for his own life shown by this very brave Sepoy in the face of heavy odds were an example to the whole Company. His heroism had saved an ugly situation which would – but for his personal bravery – have caused the Battalion a large number of casualties at a critical time and seriously delayed the crossing of the river and the building of a bridge. With the rapid advance which it was possible to make the Battalion captured 3 officers and 217 other ranks and gained their objectives.

Haidar died in Kohat, by then a district of Pakistan, on 15 July 1999.

The Royal Navy

The Royal Navy had emerged from the First World War with its reputation as the most formidable navy in the world still intact. During the inter-war years, a series of treaties aimed at preventing a naval arms race saw the Royal Navy lose much of its power and world dominance. By 1938, the supposed restrictions of the treaties were effectively null and void, and the Royal Navy re-armed. Many of the Royal Navy ships appeared dated, but there were exceptions, notably the aircraft carriers Ark Royal *and* Illustrious.

During the Second World War, the Royal Navy played a vital role in guarding shipping lanes and it enabled British forces to fight in remote parts of the world, including north Africa and the Far East. Naval supremacy was also important to the amphibious operations carried out, including the invasions of north Africa, Sicily, Italy and Normandy. The Royal Navy suffered a significant setback in 1941 when the battlecruiser HMS Hood *was sunk by DKM* Bismarck *(though the* Bismarck *was sunk herself just days later). By the end of the war, aircraft carriers had replaced battleships as the dominant weapon in naval warfare.*

MICHAEL ASHCROFT

COMMANDER JOHN WALLACE LINTON

Royal Navy

DATE OF BRAVERY: 3 SEPTEMBER 1939–MARCH 1943

GAZETTED: 25 MAY 1943

John 'Tubby' Linton, one of very few men to receive the VC for consistent bravery over several years rather than for a specific act of courage, was born in Malpas, near Newport, Monmouthshire, on 15 October 1905. He went to Osborne School, Winchester, and then to Dartmouth Naval College. In 1922, he passed out with the second prize in his term for mathematics and five years later he joined the Submarine Service as a sub-lieutenant. Over the next sixteen years (except for a two-year period from 1936 to 1938), he was in submarines continuously. He was a strong man and an accomplished athlete: he played rugby for the Navy, the United Services and Hampshire, and had trials for England. As well as being a fine mathematician, he had an excellent 'periscope eye'. He was one of the Navy's most distinguished submarine commanders of the Second World War and was devoted to his job. During the conflict, he commanded two subs – *Pandora* and *Turbulent* – and was relentlessly aggressive in his pursuit of enemy targets. He invariably attacked from close in, thereby making the task all the more dangerous.

Linton's VC reflected his sustained courage over nearly four years. According to the *London Gazette*:

> From the outbreak of War until HMS *Turbulent*'s last patrol Commander Linton was constantly in command of submarines, and during that time inflicted great damage on the Enemy. He sank one Cruiser, one Destroyer, one U-boat,

28 Supply Ships, some 100,000 tons in all, and destroyed three trains by gun-fire. In his last year, he spent two hundred and fifty-four days at sea, submerged for nearly half the time, and his ship was hunted thirteen times and had two hundred and fifty depth charges aimed at her.

His many and brilliant successes were due to his constant activity and skill, and the daring which never failed him when there was an Enemy to be attacked. On one occasion, for instance, in HMS *Turbulent*, he sighted a convoy of two Merchantmen and two Destroyers in mist and moonlight. He worked round ahead of the convoy and dived to attack it as it passed through the moon's rays. On bringing his sights to bear he found himself right ahead of a Destroyer. Yet he held his course till the Destroyer was almost on top of him, and, when his sights came on the convoy, he fired. His great courage and determination were rewarded. He sank one Merchantman and one Destroyer outright, and set the other Merchantman on fire so that she blew up.

In submarines, as in Bomber Command, the longer men served, the less chance they had of survival. By early 1943, Linton had already received the Distinguished Service Order (DSO) and the Distinguished Service Cross (DSC) for his bravery. At just thirty-seven, he was the oldest submarine commander in the Navy. In February, *Turbulent* sailed for her tenth and Linton's twenty-first patrol in the Tyrrhenian Sea. She was supposed to withdraw on 18 March, and two days later her route home was signalled to her, but there was no reply. By 24 March, it was clear that *Turbulent* and her crew had been lost at sea – almost certainly sunk by a mine off the Italian harbour of Maddalena on 17 March. William Linton, the commander's elder son, went with his mother to collect his father's posthumous VC from George VI on 23 February 1944.

MICHAEL ASHCROFT

LIEUTENANT PETER SCAWEN WATKINSON ROBERTS

Royal Navy

DATE OF BRAVERY: 16 FEBRUARY 1942
GAZETTED: 9 JUNE 1942

Peter Roberts was born in Chesham Bois, Buckinghamshire, on 28 July 1917. In September 1935, he joined the Navy as a 'special entry' cadet. After serving on at least three ships, he joined the submarine service in September 1939, and was promoted to lieutenant two months later. His third posting in the submarine service was on board *Thrasher* as first lieutenant from January 1941. By that stage, he had already been recommended for a Distinguished Service Cross, which he eventually received after he was awarded the VC.

The *London Gazette* described the events that led to him winning the latter decoration:

On February 16th in daylight HM Submarine *Thrasher* attacked and sunk a heavily escorted supply ship. She was at once attacked by depth charges and was bombed by aircraft. The presence of two unexploded bombs in the gun casing was discovered, when after dark the submarine surfaced and began to roll. Lieutenant Roberts and Petty Officer Gould volunteered to remove the bombs, which were of a type unknown to them. The danger in dealing with the second bomb was very great. To reach it they had to go through the casing which was so low they had to lie full length to move in it. Through this narrow space in complete darkness they pushed and dragged the bomb over a distance of some 20 feet until it could be lowered over the side.

Every time the bomb was moved there was a loud twanging noise as of a broken spring, which added nothing to their peace of mind. This deed was the more gallant as HMS *Thrasher*'s presence was known to the enemy, she was close to the enemy coast and in waters where his patrols were known to be active day and night. There was a very great chance and they knew it that the submarine might have to crash-dive while they were in the casing. Had this happened they must have drowned.

After the bombs had been dealt with, Lieutenant H.S. Mackenzie, commanding the submarine, slapped Roberts and Gould on the back and said: 'Come and have a drink, you two. You deserve a double, and you're going to get it.'

Later in 1942, Roberts left *Thrasher* to do a periscope course, which he failed. This was a major setback and meant the end of his time in the submarine service. He therefore took up appointments as an instructor in Portsmouth and Devonport. After the war, he was in the cruiser *Black Prince* in the Pacific from 1945 to 1946. Then he saw active service aboard the frigate *Cardigan Bay* in Korea from 1952 to 1953. He retired from the Navy in 1962 and died in Newton Ferrers, Devon, on 8 December 1979.

ACTING CAPTAIN FREDERICK THORNTON PETERS

Royal Navy

DATE OF BRAVERY: 8 NOVEMBER 1942
GAZETTED: 18 MAY 1943

Frederick 'Fritz' Peters, who won five bravery awards spanning the two world wars, was one of the most decorated Canadians of the Second World War. He was born in Charlottetown, British Columbia, on 17 September 1889, the son of Frederick Peters, the Prime Minister and Attorney General of Prince

Edward Island. In 1905, he joined the Royal Navy and three years later, as a midshipman, helped in the rescue work after the Messina earthquake. Later, he served with distinction as a naval officer during the First World War, winning the Distinguished Service Order (DSO) in 1915 and the Distinguished Service Cross (DSC) in 1918 for his record in the destroyer and torpedo flotillas. He then went on to serve with even more credit during the Second World War, gaining a bar to his DSC in July 1940 for his role as commander of HMS *Thirlmere*.

Thereafter, he enjoyed a fascinating career after being posted to the Directorate of Naval Intelligence. While at this so-called 'School of Spies' he worked with Guy Burgess and Kim Philby at a training centre in Hertfordshire that was geared to developing operations for the special services. In his book *My Silent Way*, Philby mentioned the Canadian: 'He often took Guy and me to dinner at the Hungaria to listen to our views on the new project. He had faraway naval eyes and a gentle smile of great charm.'

One daring mission that the School of Spies devised was to seize a vital point in the well-defended harbour of Oran, Morocco. It was decided that the operation should be carried out by a small Anglo-American force. At the same time, members of the Special Boat Squadron (SBS) were instructed to attack shipping in the harbour with top-secret 'mobile mines'. The force approached the boom of the harbour at 2.50 a.m. on 8 November 1942 with Peters in command of two Royal Navy ships, HMS *Walney* and HMS *Hartland*. The latter was spotted in the enemy's searchlights and came under heavy fire. It hit the jetty and eventually blew up at 10.15 a.m., after most of the crew and assault troops had abandoned ship.

Peters was on board *Walney*, which proceeded into the harbour and released three canoes manned by members of the

SBS. It then rammed an enemy destroyer before being caught in searchlights and pummelled by heavy fire. Undeterred, he steered the ship through the boom and towards the jetty in the face of point-blank fire from the shore batteries, a destroyer and a cruiser. The *Walney* reached the jetty on fire and went down with her colours still flying. Blinded in one eye, Peters was the only survivor of seventeen officers and men on the bridge.

The *London Gazette* gave more details of his heroism when it announced his USA Distinguish Service Cross (Military) – awarded by the Americans and quite different from his earlier DSC and bar from the British – on 19 January 1943:

> Captain Peters . . . remained on the bridge in command of his ship in spite of the fact that the protective armour thereon had been blown in by enemy shell fire and was thereby exposed personally to the withering cross fire from shore defences. He accomplished the berthing of his ship, then went to the forward deck and assisted by one officer secured the forward mooring lines. He then with utter disregard of his own personal safety went to the quarter-deck and assisted in securing the aft mooring lines so that the troops on board could disembark. At that time the engine room was in flames and very shortly thereafter exploded and the ship turned on its side and sank.

Peters won his VC for the same act of bravery on 8 November 1942, which was gazetted on 18 May 1943. Peters was taken prisoner and given medical treatment shortly after the action. Casualties on his ship had been high, with more than 50 per cent killed. *Walney* had destroyed one armed trawler and the SBS teams had damaged a destroyer, but the operation had failed because the harbour was too heavily defended. Yet, days later, Oran was in Allied hands after Operation Torch seized much of the Moroccan coast. Peters was then hailed as a hero by the French civilian population, carried shoulder high through the streets and showered with flowers in a bizarre 'victory parade'. However, in a tragic twist of fate, on 13 November – five days after the bravery that won him the VC and the USA DSC (Military) – he was flying from Gibraltar to England when the plane crashed into the sea off Plymouth, killing all five passengers.

Admiral Sir Andrew Cunningham, the task force commander of Operation Torch, later said that Peters' 'courage and leadership achieved all that could be done against odds that proved overwhelming'. Winston Churchill went further, describing the *Walney*'s attack as 'the finest British naval engagement since Trafalgar'.

LIEUTENANT (LATER LIEUTENANT COMMANDER) IAN EDWARD FRASER

Royal Naval Reserve

DATE OF BRAVERY: 31 JULY 1945
GAZETTED: 13 NOVEMBER 1945

ACTING LEADING SEAMAN JAMES JOSEPH MAGENNIS

Royal Navy

DATE OF BRAVERY: 31 JULY 1945
GAZETTED: 13 NOVEMBER 1945

Ian 'Tich' Fraser, who, along with James Magennis, was awarded the VC for one of the most daring acts of the Second World War, was born in Ealing, London, on 18 December 1920. He joined the Blue Funnel Line as a cadet in 1938 and the following year boarded the battleship *Royal Oak* as a midshipman, Royal Naval Reserve, for what he thought would be four months' training. However, the outbreak of war changed that, and he was sent to serve on the destroyer *Keith*. After serving on several other destroyers, he volunteered for submarines.

James 'Mick' Magennis was born in Belfast on 27 October 1919. He joined the Navy as a boy seaman on 3 June 1935 and served on various warships, including the destroyer *Kandahar*, which was mined off Tripoli in December 1941 when Magennis was on board. The next year, he joined the Submarine Branch, and then volunteered for 'special and hazardous duties' – which he soon learned meant midget submarines, or X-craft.

By the spring of 1945, Fraser was in command of the midget submarine *XE.3*, which had three crew, including Magennis as its diver. Although Fraser was only five foot four tall – hence the nickname – even he was unable to stand up in the submarine. On 30 July, just a week before the atomic bomb was dropped on Hiroshima, he was given the task of sinking the *Takao*, a 10,000-ton Japanese cruiser, in the Johore Straits, Singapore. *XE.3* was towed to the area by a conventional submarine, *Stygian*, and slipped her tow at 11 p.m. for the hazardous forty-mile journey through wrecks, minefields, listening posts and surface patrols. Conditions inside the midget sub were cramped, stuffy and uncomfortable. At 12.30 p.m. the next day, the target was in sight and at 1.52 p.m. Fraser began his attack.

At 3.03 p.m. – on his second attempt – Fraser slid *XE.3* directly under the *Takao*, which was anchored in shallow water with her stern less than 100 yards from the Singapore side of the straits. Magennis slid out of the 'wet and dry' compartment – which could be flooded or pumped to let a diver out or in – and began fixing limpet mines to the cruiser. He had to chip away at barnacles for more than half an hour in order to attach the magnetic explosives. Also, the magnets were inexplicably weak so he had to swim and retrieve them time and again. Eventually, despite a leak from his oxygen line, he attached half a dozen limpets to the hull before returning, exhausted, to the submarine. It was almost impossible for him to close the hatch because his hands had been shredded clearing the barnacles.

Fraser now had to release two side charges, each with two tons of Amatol, a high explosive. The port charge slipped away cleanly but the starboard one stuck to the midget submarine. Furthermore, on a falling tide XE.3 had become wedged beneath *Takao* and would not budge. For more than an hour, Fraser struggled with XE.3's controls to break free but to no avail. It looked as if the midget submarine and her crew would be blown to pieces by her own explosives. They knew they had only six hours before the charges went off. Then, suddenly, the midget submarine shot backwards, out of control, surged towards the surface and caused a big splash just fifty yards from the cruiser. Fortunately, none of the Japanese crew saw it, and XE.3 returned to the bottom. However, the starboard charge was still attached. Knowing that Magennis was exhausted and injured, Fraser volunteered to dive to free it. Magennis, who had already done enough to win a VC, insisted he was the more experienced diver and said: 'I'll be all right as soon as I've got my wind, sir.' A little later, he slipped into the water clutching a large spanner, and after seven minutes of struggle succeeded in releasing the charge. As soon as he was on board again, XE.3 began her journey back at full speed, again negotiating the hazards that had been encountered on her approach. Eventually, she rendezvoused with *Stygian* and was towed to safety. The charges that they laid blew a sixty-by-thirty-foot hole in *Takao*'s hull, although it was later learned that she had only a skeleton crew aboard. Several days later, Fraser and

Magennis were on the base ship *Bonaventure* when the telegraphist received a message saying that the two men had been awarded the VC. Even though it was 1 a.m. when the captain heard the news, he insisted on celebrating. On a warm night off the Australian coast, the crew partied until dawn.

Fraser and Magennis received their VCs from George VI at Buckingham Palace on 11 December 1945. The former was made an officer of the US Legion of Merit in 1945, while the people of Wallasey – the town on the Wirral where he had gone to school – raised more than £300 for him and presented it along with a sword of honour. Later, he admitted: 'A man is trained for the task that might win him the VC. He is not trained to cope with what follows. He is not told how to avoid going under in a flood of public adulation. Three months after I received my VC I refused all further invitations to functions in my honour. All this flattery was becoming dangerous.' He came through those dangerous times, though, and eventually became a JP. He also kept his RNR rank and retired as a lieutenant commander in 1966. At the time of writing, he was still living happily in Wallasey, aged eighty-five.

Magennis's gazetting said that he 'displayed very great courage and devotion to duty and complete disregard for his own safety'. As the only VC winner of the Second World War to hail from Ulster, he earned celebrity status in his home city. The citizens of Belfast organised a 'shilling fund' for their new hero, which raised more than £3,000. However, the money was quickly spent as the Magennises succumbed to the temptations that Fraser had wisely spurned. 'We are simple people,' his wife Edna confessed. 'We were forced into the limelight. We lived beyond our means because it seemed the only thing to do.' Magennis died in Halifax, Yorkshire, on 12 February 1986. He passed away hours before his heroism was honoured on a first-day cover issued by the Royal Navy Philatelic Office.

The RAF

After the end of the First World War, the RAF, which had only been founded in 1918, was significantly cut back. However, shortly before and during the Second World War, it again underwent a massive expansion. Military leaders on both sides could see that bomber aircraft were capable of not just inflicting substantial damage, but also demoralising the inhabitants of the nation that was being targeted.

Fighter planes also came into widespread use and dramatic aerial duels took place between rival 'aces' who, even if highly skilled at their job, had a short life expectancy. A defining period of the RAF's existence came during the Battle of Britain in 1940, when it held off the German Luftwaffe and helped to turn the tide of the war. The largest – and most controversial – effort of the RAF was the strategic bombing campaign against Germany by RAF Bomber Command in the latter stages of the war.

FLIGHT LIEUTENANT (LATER WING COMMANDER) RODERICK ALASTAIR BROOK LEAROYD

RAF: 49 Squadron

DATE OF BRAVERY: 12 AUGUST 1940
GAZETTED: 20 AUGUST 1940

Roderick Learoyd was born in Folkestone, Kent, on 5 February 1913. In the summer of 1940, he was in one of eleven Hampden bomber planes from 49 and 83 Squadrons that were ordered to make low-level bombing attacks on the Dortmund–Ems canal close to Munster. Their target was where the canal crossed the River Ems by means of two aqueducts, a crucial point in the German inland-waterway system. The aim was to paralyse the transport of raw materials to Germany's industrial area. The target had been attacked and slightly damaged earlier, but by the day of Learoyd's mission the Germans had strengthened their defences. This was apparent as soon as the first four planes tried to hit the target: two were destroyed and the other two were badly damaged. However, Learoyd's plane and the six others, including one which was hit, managed to drop their bombs, which caused such extensive damage that barge traffic was still being held up a month later.

Learoyd showed exceptional courage by dropping to a dangerously low level in order to have a better chance of hitting the target. The *London Gazette* declared:

> This officer as first pilot of a Hampden aircraft has repeatedly shown the highest conception of his duty and complete indifference to personal danger in making attacks at the lowest altitudes regardless of opposition. On the night of 12th August, 1940, he was detailed to attack a special objective on the Dortmund–Ems Canal. He had attacked this objective on a previous occasion and was well aware of the risk entailed. To achieve success, it was necessary to approach from a direction well known to the enemy through a lane of especially disposed anti-aircraft defences and in the face of the most intense point-blank fire from guns of all calibres. The reception of the preceding aircraft might well have deterred the stoutest heart, all being hit and two lost.
>
> Flight-Lieutenant Learoyd nevertheless made his attack at one hundred and fifty feet, his aircraft being repeatedly hit and large pieces of the main plane torn away. He was almost blinded by the glare of many searchlights at close range but pressed home his attack with the greatest resolution and skill. He subsequently brought his wrecked aircraft home and as the landing flaps were inoperative and

the undercarriage indicators out of action, waited for dawn in the vicinity of his aerodrome before landing, which he accomplished without causing injury to his crew or further damage to his aircraft. The high courage, skill and determination which this officer has invariably displayed, on many occasions in the face of the enemy, sets an example which is unsurpassed.

Learoyd later gave a speech about the day he won his VC:

Fully alive to the importance of the target, Jerry had concentrated scores of searchlights and anti-aircraft batteries along both banks of the canal. The resultant flak was intense and, as we stooged around, waiting for our turn to go in, I saw one of our bombers hit and catch fire. It climbed to about 1,000 feet, then its nose dropped before finally spinning to the ground in flames. From reports which came through later, we learned that the crew had been taken prisoner.

It was now my turn to come in over the aqueduct and let our bombs go. By this time another of our bombers had been hit and was burning furiously to the ground. In order to obtain the best possible view of the aqueduct, it was necessary to get it as directly as possible between us and the moon. So, coming down to 300 feet at a distance of four or five miles north of the target, I commenced my run in, the aqueduct being clearly silhouetted against the light of the moon. Within a mile of the target I came down to 150 feet. By this time, however, Jerry had got our range to a nicety, and was blazing away with everything he'd got.

The machine was repeatedly hit and . . . I was completely blinded by the glare of the searchlights and had to ask my navigator to guide me in over the target. This he did with the utmost coolness and praiseworthy precision. Then, suddenly, I heard him shout: 'Bomb gone.' The delayed-action bomb was fitted with a parachute which, provided the altitude was sufficiently low, gave us a chance of seeing just where it fell. This is what happened on this occasion. For I heard a sudden triumphant shout from the wireless officer: 'Got it!' The bomb had fallen on the aqueduct, which, as a result of the combined attack, was destroyed, and our object successfully accomplished. Then for home!

Learoyd died in Rustington, Sussex, on 24 January 1994.

FLYING OFFICER LESLIE THOMAS MANSER

RAF Volunteer Reserve: 50 Squadron
DATE OF BRAVERY: 30 MAY 1942
GAZETTED: 23 OCTOBER 1942

Leslie Manser, who won his VC during the famous 1,000-bomber raid on Cologne, was born on 11 May 1922 in New Delhi, while his father was employed in India as an engineer with the Post and Telegraph Department. After the family returned to Britain, they settled in Hertfordshire. After completing his schooling, Manser decided to join the armed forces but he was turned down by both the Army and the Royal Navy. In August 1940, however, he was accepted as a prospective pilot by the RAF. He was commissioned as a pilot officer in May 1941 after completing his training. On 27 August 1941, he was posted to his first operational unit: 50 Squadron (Hampdens) based at Swinderby, Lincolnshire. He also served briefly with 420 Royal Canadian Air Force Squadron (Hampdens) until 2 April 1942, when he rejoined 50 Squadron, by then operating from Skellingthorpe,

Lincolnshire. At the time, the squadron was in the process of converting to the new Manchester heavy bomber. On 8 April, Manser piloted one of the new planes in a leaflet drop over Paris, then flew five further sorties into May. He was a skilled pilot and on 6 May – when still a teenager – he was promoted to flying officer. His first taste of action came two days later when, as a second pilot, he took part in the first 100-plus-aircraft raid on Frankfurt. However, this was small beer compared to what was to come.

In early 1942, Bomber Command had been having a torrid time, with almost 5 per cent of its aircraft lost on major operations and fewer than one bomb in ten falling within five miles of its target. After relatively successful raids against the towns of Rostock and Lubeck in March and April, Air Marshal Sir Arthur Harris, the new head of Bomber Command, had conceived a plan – codenamed 'Operation Millennium' – whereby 1,000 British bombers would attack a German city in a single night. The proposal was approved by Winston Churchill and Sir Charles Portal, a marshal of the RAF. Of course, it involved a massive mobilisation of planes, but by 26 May everything was in place. After three false starts targeting Bremen, Cologne (Germany's third-largest city) was chosen to be bombed. Harris sent a personal message to all of the air crews which ended: 'Let him [Jerry] have it – right on the chin.' The force of over a thousand planes took off from fifty-two airfields, mainly in the east of England on the night of 30 May. Manser was captain and first pilot of one of the new Manchesters.

The *London Gazette* takes up his story:

> As the aircraft was approaching its objective it was caught by searchlights and subjected to intense and accurate anti-aircraft fire. Flying Officer Manser held on his dangerous

course and bombed the target successfully from a height of 7,000 feet.

Then he set course for base. The Manchester had been damaged and was still under heavy fire. Flying Officer Manser took violent evasive action, turning and descending to under 1,000 feet. It was of no avail. The searchlights and flak followed him until the outskirts of the city were passed. The aircraft was hit repeatedly and the rear gunner was wounded. The front cabin filled with smoke, the port engine was overheating badly.

Pilot and crew could all have escaped safely by parachute. Nevertheless, Flying Officer Manser, disregarding the obvious hazards, persisted in his attempt to save the aircraft and crew from falling into enemy hands. He took the aircraft up to 2,000 feet. Then the port engine burst into flames. It was ten minutes before the fire was mastered, but then the engine went out of action for good, part of one wing was burnt and the air-speed of the aircraft became dangerously low.

Despite all the efforts of the pilot and crew, the Manchester began to lose height. At this critical moment, Flying Officer Manser once more disdained the alternative of parachuting to safety with his crew. Instead with grim determination, he set a new course for the nearest base, accepting for himself the prospect of almost certain death in a firm resolve to carry on to the end.

Soon the aircraft became extremely difficult to handle and when a crash was inevitable, Flying Officer Manser ordered the crew to bail out. A sergeant handed him a parachute but he waved it away telling the non-commissioned officer to jump at once as he could only hold the aircraft steady for a few more seconds. While the crew were descending to safety they saw the aircraft still carrying their gallant captain plunge to earth and burst into flames. In pressing home his attack in the face of strong opposition, in striving against heavy odds, to bring back his aircraft and crew and finally, when in extreme peril, thinking only of the safety of his comrades, Flying Officer Manser displayed determination and valour of the highest order.

Manser had sacrificed his own life in the knowledge that to do otherwise would have resulted in the almost certain deaths of his crew. He was just twenty. Of the 1,046 aircraft on the mission, 989 claimed to have reached and attacked their targets. In total, 1,455 tons of bombs were dropped and 600 acres of Cologne were destroyed in a little over an hour and a half. This comprised almost as much devastation as had previously been inflicted on Germany up to that point in the war.

FLYING OFFICER LLOYD ALLAN TRIGG

Royal New Zealand Air Force, serving with 200 Squadron, RAF

DATE OF BRAVERY: 11 AUGUST 1943
GAZETTED: 2 NOVEMBER 1943

Lloyd Trigg, the only recipient of the VC to receive it solely on evidence given by the enemy, was born in Houhora, New Zealand, on 5 June 1914. After university he became a farmer, but prior to the Second World War he joined the North Auckland Rifles, his local Territorial unit. Then, on 15 June 1941, he joined the Royal New Zealand Air Force. He proved to be a reasonable pilot and on 1 October 1942 was promoted to flying officer and sailed for England. However, at the end of November, he was posted to 200 Squadron, which was based at Yundum airstrip at the mouth of the River Gambia in West Africa.

By the end of February 1943, he had completed nearly eighty hours of flying on reconnaissance and escort patrols but had not seen any action. This changed the following month when he attacked a U-boat with depth charges. However, he failed to score a direct hit. Two days later, he attacked another U-boat and this time a depth charge struck the submarine's bow. His 'fantastic determination' in hunting out the enemy led to him being recommended for and awarded the Distinguished Flying Cross. However, he never heard of that decoration because of his even greater heroism five months later. The *London Gazette* takes up the story:

> Flying Officer Trigg has rendered outstanding service on Convoy, Escort and Anti-Submarine Duties. He has completed 46 Operational Sorties and has invariably displayed skill and courage of a very high order. One day in August 1943, Flying Officer Trigg undertook, as Captain and Pilot, a patrol in a Liberator Bomber, although he had not previously made any Operational Sorties in that type of aircraft. After searching for eight hours, the Liberator sighted a surfaced U-Boat. Flying Officer Trigg immediately prepared to attack. During the approach the aircraft received many hits from the submarine's anti-aircraft guns and burst into flames, which quickly enveloped the tail. The moment was critical. Flying Officer Trigg could have broken off the engagement and made a forced landing in the sea, but if he continued the attack the aircraft would present a no-deflection target to deadly anti-aircraft fire and every second spent in the air would increase the extent and intensity of the flames and diminish the chances of survival.
>
> There could have been no hesitation or doubt in his mind. He maintained his course in spite of the already

precarious condition of his aircraft and executed a masterly attack. Skimming over the U-Boat at less than 50 feet, with anti-aircraft fire entering his opened bomb doors, Flying Officer Trigg dropped his bombs in and around the U-Boat, where they exploded with devastating effect. A short distance further on the Liberator dived into the sea with her gallant Captain and crew. The U-Boat sank within 20 minutes and some of her crew were picked up later in a rubber dinghy that had broken loose from the Liberator. The Battle of the Atlantic has yielded many fine stories of air attacks on underwater craft, but Flying Officer Trigg's exploit stands out as an epic of grim determination and high courage. His was the path of duty that leads to glory.

On 12 August a Sunderland from 204 Squadron sighted the dinghy and asked a British ship, HMS *Clarkia*, to pick up the survivors, expecting them to be Trigg and his crew. The Germans were worried that they would be mistreated for being the killers of Trigg and his crew, but in fact they were given all the respect demanded for prisoners of war by international conventions. The combination of this fair treatment and Trigg's bravery led to them making a full report to their captors about what had happened.

This evidence – in particular that of two German officers – gave rise to Trigg's VC. The decoration was presented to his widow in New Zealand on 28 May 1944. At the time, the fact that the VC was awarded on the evidence of U-boat personnel was not stressed, although after the war the honourable behaviour of the German PoWs was acknowledged.

SERGEANT (LATER WARRANT OFFICER) NORMAN CYRIL JACKSON

RAF Volunteer Reserve: 106 Squadron

DATE OF BRAVERY: 26/27 APRIL 1944
GAZETTED: 26 OCTOBER 1945

Norman Jackson, whose VC set the 'world record' when it was sold by auction in 2004, was born in Ealing, west London, on 8 April 1919. He was adopted by the Gunter family and attended the Archdeacon Cambridge Primary School and the local grammar school in Twickenham, where he developed an interest in engineering. After completing his education, he became a fitter and turner. On 20 October 1939, he joined the RAF Volunteer Reserve. Initially, he worked as a fitter in Freetown, Sierra Leone, where he was attached to 95 Squadron, but in January 1941 he had the opportunity to join an air crew. Thereafter, he applied for training as a flight engineer and, in September 1942, he returned to England and spent six months at 27 Officer Training Unit. In July 1943, and by now a sergeant, he joined 106 Squadron at Syerston, Newark, and completed nine sorties before the squadron moved to Metheringham, Lincolnshire, in early November.

By 24 April 1944, Jackson had completed his scheduled tour of thirty operations, mostly over heavily defended German targets. However, before taking some time off with friends he volunteered for one more sortie 'for luck' on the night of 26/7 April. Earlier in the day, he had been told that his wife had just given birth to their first son, and the crew decided to celebrate the news on their return from the mission.

It is an understatement to say that things did not go according to plan. The *London Gazette* announced Jackson's VC – and one of the most remarkable stories of the Second World War – on 26 October 1945:

This airman was the flight engineer in a Lancaster detailed to attack Schweinfurt on the night of 26th April 1944. Bombs were dropped successfully and the aircraft was climbing out of the target area. Suddenly it was attacked by a fighter at about 20,000 feet. The captain took evading action at once, but the enemy secured many hits. A fire started near a petrol tank on the upper surface of the starboard wing, between the fuselage and the inner engine. Sergeant Jackson was thrown to the floor during the engagement. Wounds which he received from shell splinters in the right leg and shoulder were probably sustained at that time. Recovering himself, he remarked that he could deal with the fire on the wing and obtained his captain's permission to try to put out the flames. Pushing a hand fire-extinguisher into the top of his life-saving jacket and clipping on his parachute pack, Sergeant Jackson jettisoned the escape hatch above the pilot's head. He then started to climb out of the cockpit and back along the top of the fuselage to the starboard wing. Before he could leave the fuselage his parachute pack opened and the whole canopy and rigging lines spilled into the cockpit. Undeterred, Sergeant Jackson continued. The pilot, bomb aimer and navigator gathered the parachute together and held on to the rigging lines, paying them out as the airman crawled aft. Eventually he slipped and, falling from the fuselage to the starboard wing, grasped an air intake on the leading edge of the wing. He succeeded in clinging on but lost the extinguisher, which was blown away.

By this time, the fire had spread rapidly and Sergeant Jackson was involved. His face, hands and clothing were severely burnt. Unable to retain his hold, he was swept through the flames and over the trailing edge of the wing, dragging his parachute behind. When last seen it was only partly inflated and was burning in a number of places. Realising the fire could not be controlled, the captain gave the order to abandon aircraft. Four of the remaining members of the crew landed safely. The captain and rear gunner have not been accounted for. Sergeant Jackson was unable to control his descent and landed heavily. He sustained a broken ankle, and his right eye was closed through burns and his hands were useless. These injuries, together with the wounds received earlier, reduced him to a pitiable state. At daybreak he crawled to the nearest village, where he was taken prisoner. He bore the intense pain and discomfort of the journey to Dulag Luft with magnificent fortitude. After 10 months in hospital he made a good recovery, though his hands require further treatment and are of only limited use. This airman's attempt to extinguish the fire and save the aircraft and crew from falling into enemy hands was an act of outstanding gallantry. To venture outside, when travelling at 200 miles an hour, at an incredible height and in intense cold, was an almost incredible feat. Had he succeeded in subduing the flames, there was little or no prospect of his regaining the cockpit. The spilling of his parachute and the risk of grave damage to its canopy reduced his chances of survival to a minimum. By his ready willingness to face these dangers he set an example of self-sacrifice which will ever be remembered.

The morning after he landed, Jackson had staggered to a cottage on the edge of a forest and had been verbally abused by its German occupant before two young girls nursed him. He was then paraded through the nearest town, where he was jeered before being sent to Dulag Luft. While there, he made two escape attempts. In the second, he managed to contact US troops near Munich but was recaptured before he could reach them.

He returned to Britain on VE Day and received his VC at Buckingham Palace from George VI on 13 November 1945. Another receipient that day was Group Captain Leonard Cheshire. Norman Jackson died at Hampton Hill, Middlesex, on 26 March 1994, aged seventy-four.

†WARRANT OFFICER (PROMOTED POSTHUMOUSLY TO PILOT OFFICER) ANDREW CHARLES MYNARSKI

Royal Canadian Air Force: 419 Squadron

DATE OF BRAVERY: 13 JUNE 1944
GAZETTED: 11 OCTOBER 1946

Andy Mynarski, whose story is one of the most remarkable in the VC's history, was born in Winnipeg, Canada, to Polish immigrants on 14 October 1916. At the age of sixteen, because his father had died, he started worked as a chamois cutter for a furrier to help support his family. In 1940, he joined the Royal Winnipeg Rifles, a militia unit, but the following year he enlisted in the Royal Canadian Air Force (RCAF) and, after training in Edmonton, passed out as an air gunner. He was promoted to temporary sergeant in Halifax, shortly before going oversees in January 1942.

Mynarski, who was then promoted to Warrant Officer later in 1942, became mid-upper gunner in a seven-man bombing crew flying AVRO Lancasters that was posted to 419 'Moose' Squadron, flying out of Middleton St George, Yorkshire. The crew were chosen to take part in President Eisenhower's 'Transportation Plan', in which the USAAF and RAF were meant to destroy Western Europe's rail, road and bridge networks in order to prevent the Germans from bringing reinforcements to the Normandy beachheads. They were a closely knit team – at a time when the life expectancy of bomber crews was measured in months – who had flown a dozen sorties together. After every mission, they returned to their British base and asked for a slice of their favourite lemon meringue pie, made by one of the cooks. The gunners, Mynarski and Pat Brophy, who in the plane were isolated from the rest of the crew, had grown particularly close, and the former even bailed the latter out of jail after a scrap. Before going to bed, Mynarski (an NCO) tended to give Brophy (an officer) an exaggerated salute and say: 'Good night, sir!'

On the evening of 12 June 1944, a few days after the D-Day landings, their Lancaster took off on its thirteenth sortie, heading for the railway yard at Cambrai. En route, a German Ju-88 streaked under the Lancaster and opened fire. Three explosions rocked the aircraft and at 12.13 a.m. Captain Art de Breyne gave the signal for the crew to bail out. Just as Mynarski was about to jump to safety, he saw Brophy, the rear gunner, struggling to free himself. As soon as he realised his friend was in difficulty, Mynarski crawled on his hands and knees to the tail of the plane. When the plane had been hit, its hydraulic system had been shattered, locking the turret at such an angle that Brophy was unable to escape. With an axe and his bare hands, Mynarski frantically tried to free Brophy, but by now flames had engulfed the aircraft. 'Go back, Andrew! Get out!' shouted Brophy. Mynarski, seeing he could do no more and obeying what was, after all, an order, crawled back to the escape hatch, stood in his burning clothes, glanced towards his friend, and, as he had done so many times before, saluted and said something. Brophy could not hear the words, but he knew what they had been: 'Good night, sir.'

Brophy was now alone in the plane and hurtling towards what seemed his inevitable demise – especially as there were five tons of explosive barely fifty feet from where he was trapped in the turret. It seemed pointless, but as the plane was about to hit the ground, Brophy instinctively adopted the crash position. However, just before the Lancaster slammed into a field, its port wing hit a large tree. This not only tore off the burning wing but saved Brophy from certain death. 'The resulting whiplash effect on the tail of the aircraft snapped my turret around and the doors flew open, freeing me from my potentially explosive and flaming prison,' Brophy later recalled. 'I came to rest against a small tree about thirty to fifty feet from the remains of the aircraft. That is when I heard two explosions together. Only when I felt solid earth tremble under me did I realise the crash was over, and somehow I was alive.'

Six of the seven crew survived their ordeal and were found by French farmers and then helped by the Resistance. Four made it back to Britain, while the other two, including Brophy, were captured by the Germans and imprisoned until the end of the war. The only member of the crew to perish was Mynarski. He had survived his parachute jump but died shortly afterwards as a result of his serious burns.

It was only on Brophy's release in 1945 that the full story could be told and steps taken to ensure that Mynarski received a posthumous VC for 'valour of the highest order'. He became the first member of the RCAF to receive the award. Brophy wrote an article about his friend in 1965 and concluded it with the words: 'I'll always believe that a divine providence intervened to save me because of what I had seen – so the world might know of a gallant man who laid down his life for a friend.'

FLIGHT LIEUTENANT DAVID SAMUEL ANTHONY LORD

RAF: 271 Squadron

DATE OF BRAVERY: 19 SEPTEMBER 1944
GAZETTED: 13 NOVEMBER 1945

David 'Lumme' Lord was born in Cork, Ireland, on 18 October 1913, the son of a serving warrant officer in the Royal Welch Fusiliers. After the Great War, he went with his parents to India and was educated at Lucknow Convent School, travelling to and from it each day by bullock cart. Later, he went to St Mary's School, Wrexham, and St Mary's College, Aberystwyth. He flirted with careers in the Church and as a journalist, but a fascination with flying led him to enlist in the RAF on 6 August 1936. He was awarded his wings on 5 April 1937 and promoted to sergeant that August, when he received a posting to 31 Squadron in Lahore, India. He later served with distinction in Burma, North Africa and Iraq, taking part in a series of hair-raising missions.

Lord's prowess and skill were recognised in July 1943 with a Distinguished Flying Cross (DFC). His recommendation referred to his 'sticking power and devotion to duty' which was 'more than comparable with the best bombers' efforts'. It also praised his role in the 'evacuation of casualties, women and children in the face of enemy opposition . . . on slow and virtually unarmed' aircraft. Once he had 2,500 hours of flying to his credit his commander rated him an 'exceptional' pilot and an 'above-average navigator'. He received his DFC at Buckingham Palace in 1944 but his parents were unable to take a photograph of him with the medal because he leapt into a taxi and fled, saying he would rather have a tooth pulled. Within weeks of the presentation, he was promoted to flight lieutenant.

That September, Lord took part in the first phase of the 'lift' at Arnhem, Holland, a three-day operation to support ground troops who were fighting a losing battle against the German Army. The *London Gazette* announced the VC he earned on that mission:

> Flight Lieutenant Lord was Pilot and Captain of a Dakota aircraft detailed to drop supplies at Arnhem on the afternoon of 19 September 1944. Our airborne troops had been surrounded and were being pressed into a small area defended by a large number of anti-aircraft guns. Air crews were warned that intense opposition would be met over the dropping zone. To ensure accuracy they were ordered to fly at 900 feet when dropping their containers.
>
> While flying at 1,500 feet near Arnhem the starboard wing of Flight Lieutenant Lord's aircraft was twice hit by anti-aircraft fire. The starboard engine was set on fire. He would have been justified in leaving the main stream of supply aircraft and continuing at the same height or even abandoning his aircraft. But on learning that his crew were uninjured and that the dropping zone would be reached in three minutes he said he would complete his mission, as the troops were in dire need of supplies.
>
> By now the starboard engine was burning furiously. Flight Lieutenant Lord came down to 900 feet, where he was singled out for the concentrated fire of all the anti-aircraft guns. On reaching the dropping zone he kept his aircraft on a straight and level course while supplies were dropped. At the end of the run, he was told that two containers remained.
>
> Although he must have known that the collapse of the starboard wing could not be long delayed, Flight Lieutenant Lord circled, rejoined the stream of aircraft and made a

second run to drop the remaining supplies. These manoeuvres took eight minutes in all, the aircraft being continuously under heavy anti-aircraft fire. His task completed, Flight Lieutenant Lord ordered his crew to abandon the Dakota, making no attempt himself to leave the aircraft, which was down to 500 feet. A few seconds later, the starboard wing collapsed and the aircraft fell in flames. There was only one survivor, who was flung out while assisting other members of the crew to put on their parachutes. By continuing his mission in a damaged and burning aircraft, descending to drop the supplies accurately, returning to the dropping zone a second time and, finally, remaining at the controls to give his crew a chance of escape, Flight Lieutenant Lord displayed supreme valour and self-sacrifice.

Flying Officer Harry King, his navigator, was the sole survivor. His parachute opened at the last moment and he survived a heavy fall to become a prisoner of war. The incident was watched from the ground as warring soldiers stopped fighting to see King hurtle out of the Dakota. He made a report on Lord's courage after being repatriated to England on 13 May 1945. As a result, the commander of 271 Squadron recommended Lord for a posthumous VC, and his parents received the award on 18 December 1945.

10

THE WORLD SINCE 1945

The Korean War

The Korean War was fought primarily between armies from the north and south of that country. It began at the end of June 1950 and ended on 27 July 1953. During those three years, more then two million Koreans died, the majority from the north.

Each side blamed the other for starting the war. The north was led by Kim Il-Sung, a communist, who was helped by China and the USSR. The south, led by Syngman Rhee, was helped by many countries under the banner of the United Nations, particularly the United States.

To this day, there has been no formal end to hostilities as the war ended with a truce rather than a peace treaty. So, in theory, North and South Korea are still at war, and the United States continues to have military bases in the latter.

Only four VCs were awarded for this war.

†PRIVATE (LATER SERGEANT) WILLIAM SPEAKMAN

Army: the Black Watch (Royal Highlanders), attached to 1st Battalion, the King's Own Scottish Borderers

DATE OF BRAVERY: 4 NOVEMBER 1951
GAZETTED: 28 DECEMBER 1951

Bill Speakman was born in Altrincham, Cheshire, on 21 September 1927. While at school, he spent his spare time as a drummer boy; but, being tall, gangly and uncoordinated, he was told he would never make a soldier. Nevertheless, he joined the Army Cadets at fourteen and the Black Watch at seventeen.

He won his VC in Korea when he used his six foot six frame to devastating effect against the enemy on 4 November 1951. The North Koreans had bombarded the King's Own Scottish Borderers with heavy and accurate mortar and shell fire for two hours before advancing with wave after wave of men who engaged in hand-to-hand fighting. Acting on his own initiative, Speakman was determined to repulse the attack, so he recruited six volunteers, grabbed a pile of grenades and led a series of charges against the enemy.

The *London Gazette* takes up the story:

> The force and determination of his charge broke up each successive enemy onslaught and resulted in an ever mounting pile of enemy dead. Having led some ten charges, through withering enemy machine-gun and mortar fire, Private Speakman was eventually severely wounded in the leg. Undaunted by his wounds, he continued to lead charge after charge against the enemy and it was only after a direct order from his superior officer that he agreed to pause for a first field dressing to be applied to his wounds. Having had his wounds bandaged, Private

Speakman immediately rejoined his comrades and led them again and again forward in a series of grenade charges, up to the time of the withdrawal of his Company at 21.00 hours. At the critical moment of the withdrawal, amidst an inferno of enemy machine-gun and mortar fire, as well as grenades, Private Speakman led a final charge to clear the crest of the hill and hold it, whilst the remainder of the Company withdrew. Encouraging his gallant, but now sadly depleted party, he assailed the enemy with showers of grenades and kept them at bay sufficiently long enough for his Company to effect its withdrawal ... Private Speakman's heroism under intense fire throughout the operation and when painfully wounded was beyond praise and is deserving of supreme recognition.

Speakman was labelled the 'Beer Bottle VC' by the press because his comrades insisted that he was so driven that, when he ran out of grenades and ammunition, he hurled bottles at the Chinese. Speakman himself initially insisted the story was fantasy, asking: 'Where would you get bottles from?' Yet, on another occasion, he said: 'It's true, we did run out of ammunition and we were in darkness, so you pick up what you can get your hands on – fallen weapons or stones.'

His decoration was highly acclaimed in Britain and it was the first VC to be presented by Queen Elizabeth II. Speakman, however, was a modest man who preferred to concentrate on his military career rather than court the attention the medal inevitably brought. He later served in Malaya (with the SAS), Borneo and Radfan (then part of the British Protectorate of Dhala; now Yemen). After leaving the Army, he went to South Africa, where he worked on board a passenger ship and as a security officer. At the time of writing, he was still living there, aged seventy-eight.

The Malaysia–Indonesia Confrontation

The Malaysia–Indonesia Confrontation took place between 1963 and 1966. As part of its withdrawal from its South-east Asian colonies, the UK moved to combine its colonies on Borneo with those on the Malay peninsula, to form Malaysia. As a result, in September 1963, the Federation of Malaysia was widely recognised internationally.

However, President Sukarno of Indonesia saw the new country as a thinly disguised attempt to continue colonial rule and suspected Malaysia would be used to destabilise his country. In response, Indonesia launched a series of raids into Malaysia. In 1965, with the raids growing in size, Britain took retaliatory measures, sending forces on missions into Indonesia. Towards the end of the year – following a coup d'état – General Suharto came to power in Indonesia. He formally ended hostilities on 11 August 1966, and Indonesia rejoined the United Nations the following month.

Only one VC was awarded during the campaign.

†LANCE CORPORAL (LATER CAPTAIN) RAM BAHADUR LIMBU

Army: 2nd Battalion, 10th Princess Mary's Gurkha Rifles

DATE OF BRAVERY: 21 NOVEMBER 1965
GAZETTED: 21 APRIL 1966

Ram Bahadur Limbu was born in Chyangthapu village, eastern Nepal, in 1939. On 21 November 1965, he was in Sarawak, Malaysia, with fifteen other Gurkhas when they came across an enemy force in the border area. Limbu's company was half the size of the enemy's, who were holding a strong position on the summit of a jungle-covered hill. The only approach to the enemy position was a knife-edge ridge, only wide enough for three men to advance abreast. Even more daunting, the nearest trench had a sentry manning a machine-gun. Limbu led the attack, creeping forward and hoping to reach the sentry unnoticed. However, when he was just ten yards away, the sentry spotted him and opened fire. The comrade on his right was wounded, but Limbu rushed forward and killed the sentry with his grenade.

By now, the Indonesian force was fully alert to the attack and brought down heavy automatic fire on the three intruders, but they concentrated on the trench, which held only Limbu. However, he was determined to lead from the front, so, with an unflinching disregard for his own life, he raced forwards to a better position. He was trying to indicate by shouting and giving hand signals to his platoon commander exactly where the enemy was positioned, but explosions from grenades and relentless automatic fire made this impossible. Limbu therefore raced forward again. At this moment, though, his two comrades were both seriously wounded. He realised they needed immediate first aid so he crept towards them under sustained machine-gun fire. However, when he got within touching distance, he was driven back by the intensity of the fire. He then realised that his only hope was not to creep but to race forward. By now, some support had arrived, and as he ran into the open to pick up his first comrade, two Gurkha machine-guns opened fire on the Indonesians. Having returned with the first wounded man, he paused momentarily, took a deep breath, then went to fetch his other comarde. For a time, he was pinned down by machine-gun fire, but after a series of positive rushes he reached the second man and carried him back through another hail of enemy bullets. The entire action had taken twenty minutes and Limbu had survived hundreds, if not thousands, of bullets aimed at him. A combination of his bravery, skill and sheer good luck meant he had enjoyed a miraculous escape.

Even now, Limbu's contribution was not over. He seized a machine-gun, gave support to his section, and ultimately killed four of the enemy as they tried to escape across the border. An intense battle had raged for an hour: the enemy had lost twenty-four men while the Gurkhas had three killed and two injured.

Limbu travelled to London to receive his VC from the Queen at Buckingham Palace. While there, he stopped off at the Stock Exchange, where he was recognised. Almost to a man, everyone stopped trading and applauded him for three minutes. The chairman of the Exchange then asked to meet him and Limbu was given another long standing ovation. Never before had one of the world's premier financial markets stood still for so long – and it was solely so those there could pay a unique tribute to an incredibly brave man.

At the time of writing, Limbu was sixty-seven years old and living quietly in Punimaya, Nepal.

The Vietnam War

The Vietnam War was a prolonged conflict lasting almost two decades in which the Democratic Republic of Vietnam (DRVN, or North Vietnam) and its allies fought against the Republic of Vietnam (RVN, or South Vietnam) and its allies.

It was widely regarded as a 'proxy war', one of several that occurred during the Cold War between the United States and its Western allies, on the one hand, and the Soviet Union and/or the People's Republic of China, on the other. These wars took place because the superpowers were unwilling to fight each other directly on account of the unacceptable losses that would occur if nuclear weapons were employed.

North Vietnam was supported by the Soviet Union and the People's Republic of China, while the South's main allies were the United States and South Korea. Australian troops also entered the conflict on the South's side. US combat troops were involved from 1959, but not in large numbers until 1965. They left in 1973, two years before the capitulation of South Vietnam on 30 April 1975. Casualties were heavy on both sides: more than a million servicemen and two million civilians are believed to have perished throughout the course of the war.

†WARRANT OFFICER (CLASS II) KEITH PAYNE

Australian Army: Training Team

DATE OF BRAVERY: 24 MAY 1969
GAZETTED: 19 SEPTEMBER 1969

Keith Payne was born in Ingham, Queensland, on 30 August 1933, and after school became an apprentice cabinet-maker. However, he enlisted in the Australian Army on 13 August 1951, and the following year was posted to the 1st Battalion, the Royal Australian Regiment, serving with them in Korea for eleven months from April 1952. He joined the 3rd Battalion on 17 February 1960, accompanied them to Malaya, and became a sergeant on 1 June 1961. He joined the 5th Battalion in February 1965 and was promoted to temporary warrant officer (class II) on 4 June, then served with an officer training unit and in Papua New Guinea (with the 2nd Pacific Islands Regiment) prior to being appointed to the Training Team in Vietnam on 24 February 1969.

Payne was tasked with reconnoitring enemy filtration routes from Laos to Vietnam, and while carrying out these duties he won the VC. He was commanding the 212th Company of the 1st Mobile Strike Force Battalion when it came under attack from a larger North Vietnamese force using rockets, mortars and machine-guns. While some soldiers faltered from the ferocity of the onslaught, Payne rushed forward, firing an Armalite rifle and hurling grenades at the enemy to keep them at bay. He also inspirationally rallied his men, but in doing so was wounded in the hands, upper arm and hip by five pieces of shrapnel. Despite suffering heavy casualties, he then decided to fight his way back to base, covering his withdrawal with grenades and gunfire. By nightfall, he had succeeded in gathering a small party of his own and another company in a defensive perimeter some 350 yards from their original position.

Payne realised that many men, including his company's wounded, had been cut off and were disorientated by their surroundings. He crawled to one of these displaced groups, having tracked them by observing the fluorescence of their footsteps in rotting vegetation on the ground. Then, over the next three hours, he began an 800-yard traverse of the area by moving around quickly and firing sporadically at the enemy. He eventually located forty men and personally dragged some of the wounded to safety. Fit and able soldiers were instructed to crawl on their stomachs with the wounded on their backs. When he finally returned to the temporary perimeter, he found the position had been abandoned and his comrades had returned to base, but he was undeterred. He led his party – and another group of wounded which they encountered en route – back to the base, where they arrived at 3 a.m.

Payne was evacuated from Vietnam in September 1969, the same month that his VC was gazetted. When he arrived in Brisbane, he was welcomed as a war hero. The US recommended the award of a Silver Star, later upgraded to the Distinguished Service Cross, while the Republic of Vietnam honoured him with its Cross of Gallantry with Bronze Star. He left the Australian Army after over two decades' service on

31 March 1975, and at the time of writing was living in Queensland, aged seventy-three.

The Falklands War

The Falklands War was a short-lived conflict fought between Britain and Argentina in 1982 over sovereignty of the Falkland Islands (or the Islas Malvinas), South Georgia and the South Sandwich Islands. The Falklands comprise two large and many small islands in the South Atlantic Ocean east of Argentina, and their ownership had long been disputed. The war was won by the British after 255 Britons and 649 Argentinians had died in the fighting.

At the time, Argentina was gripped by an economic crisis, and General Leopoldo Galtieri, its military leader, thought he could boost the morale of the nation by taking possession of the Falklands. The conflict was triggered by the occupation of South Georgia by Argentine forces on 19 March 1982, followed by the invasion of the Falklands themselves in early April. War was not declared by either side, and there was no military activity outside the islands: the conflict was considered by Argentina as reoccupation of its own territory and by Britain as violation of a British dependency.

Margaret Thatcher, the British Prime Minister, was determined to reclaim the Falklands with an amphibious assault. However, because of the distance involved, this meant assembling a naval task force – under Rear Admiral John 'Sandy' Woodward. By the end of April, Britain had recaptured South Georgia. On 1 May, bombing raids began over the Falklands themselves, and the following day came the most controversial incident of the war – the sinking of the General Belgrano, *an Argentinian light cruiser, with the loss of 323 lives. Two days later, the British suffered a serious loss when an Exocet missile sank the destroyer HMS* Sheffield. *Nevertheless, on the night* of 21 May, the British made an amphibious landing on beaches around San Carlos Water.

On 27 May, and throughout the next day, the British attacked and eventually gained control of Darwin and Goose Green. Colonel Herbert 'H' Jones died leading his men against the enemy in this assault and was awarded a posthumous VC. By 1 June, with the arrival of 5,000 reinforcements, Britain was planning an offensive against Port Stanley, and ten days later British forces launched a night attack against the heavily defended ring of high ground surrounding the capital. Units of 3 Commando Brigade, supported by naval gunfire from several Royal Navy ships, simultaneously assaulted Mount Harriet, Two Sisters and Mount Longdon. On 14 June the Argentinians surrendered, and 9,800 troops were made prisoners of war.

The Falklands War was one of the few major naval operations to have occurred after the Second World War. It showed the vulnerability of surface ships to anti-ship missiles and reaffirmed the effectiveness of aircraft in naval warfare. Meanwhile, submarines again proved their worth. The importance of special forces units, which destroyed many Argentine aircraft and carried out intelligence-gathering operations, was similarly reaffirmed, as was the usefulness of helicopters in combat and logistic operations.

In addition to 'H' Jones's medal, one more VC was awarded during the conflict, and the trust now possesses it.

SERGEANT IAN JOHN McKAY

Army: 3rd Battalion, the Parachute Regiment

DATE OF BRAVERY: 12 JUNE 1982
GAZETTED: 11 OCTOBER 1982

Ian McKay was born on 7 May 1953 in Wortley, near Sheffield. A talented footballer, he left Rotherham Grammar School with six O levels and turned down an offer to sign for Doncaster

Rovers. Instead, he became a boy soldier and made his first tour of Northern Ireland when he was just seventeen. By the time the Falklands War broke out, he was an instructor at Aldershot, and was married with two children. His family described him as 'a quiet, introverted character'.

His VC was announced in the *London Gazette* on 11 October 1982:

> During the night of 11/12 June 1982, 3rd Battalion The Parachute Regiment mounted a silent night attack on an enemy battalion position on Mount Longdon, an important objective in the battle for Port Stanley in the Falkland Islands. Sergeant McKay was platoon sergeant of 4 Platoon, B Company, which, after the initial objective had been secured, was ordered to clear the Northern side of the long East/West ridge feature, held by the enemy in depth with strong, mutually supporting positions. By now, the enemy were fully alert and resisting fiercely. As 4 Platoon's advance continued it came under increasingly heavy fire from a number of well-sited enemy machine-gun positions on the ridge, and received casualties. Realising that no further advance was possible the Platoon Commander ordered the Platoon to move from its exposed position to seek shelter among the rocks of the ridge itself. Here it met up with part of 5 Platoon. The enemy fire was still both heavy and accurate, and the position of the platoons was becoming increasingly hazardous. Taking Sergeant McKay, a corporal and a few others, and covered by supporting machine-gun fire, the Platoon Commander moved forward to reconnoitre the enemy positions but was hit by a bullet in the leg, and command devolved upon Sergeant McKay. It was clear that instant action was needed if the advance was not to falter and increasing casualties to ensue.

Sergeant McKay decided to convert this reconnaissance into an attack in order to eliminate the enemy positions. He was in no doubt of the strength and deployment of the enemy as he undertook this attack. He issued orders, and taking three men with him, broke cover and charged the enemy position. The assault was met by a hail of fire. The Corporal was seriously wounded, a Private killed and another wounded. Despite these losses Sergeant McKay, with complete disregard for his own safety, continued to charge the enemy position alone. On reaching it he dispatched the enemy with grenades, thereby relieving the position of beleagured 4 and 5 Platoons, who were now able to redeploy with relative safety. Sergeant McKay, however, was killed at the moment of victory, his body falling on the bunker. Without doubt Sergeant McKay's action retrieved a most dangerous situation and was instrumental in ensuring the success of the attack. His was a coolly calculated act, the danger of which must have been too apparent to him beforehand. Undeterred he performed with outstanding selflessness, perseverance and courage. With a complete disregard of his own safety, he displayed courage and leadership of the highest order, and was an inspiration to all those around him.

Ken McKay, the soldier's father, said of the award: 'I'm the proudest man in the world — but I would rather have Ian alive.' Marcia McKay received her husband's VC at Buckingham Palace on 9 November 1982. Their daughter, Melanie, aged five, was photographed wearing it pinned to her black, velvet dress. McKay was buried along with fifteen comrades in Aldershot on 26 November 1982. The last two men to see him alive helped to carry his coffin. They were Corporal Ian Bailey, who was shot four minutes before

McKay was killed, and Colour Sergeant Brian Faulkner, who said of his comrade: 'Mac was the bravest of the brave.'

The Iraq War

The Iraq War took place in 2003 when, on 19 March a US-led coalition launched an attack on the Iraqi dictatorship of Saddam Hussein. He had been a thorn in the West's side since invading Kuwait 13 years earlier. By 2003, the United States and its allies became convinced that Saddam was starting to produce nuclear and chemical weapons and they were determined to overthrow his oppressive regime.

The US and its allies won a relatively swift military victory and occupied the country, later capturing the President himself. However, at the time of writing, the insurgents were launching daily attacks on the Allied forces and those supporting the current regime. It is widely feared that any withdrawal of US troops will inevitably lead to civil war in Iraq.

†PRIVATE JOHNSON GIDEON BEHARRY

Army: 1st Battalion, the Princess of Wales's Royal Regiment

DATE OF BRAVERY: 1 MAY AND 11 JUNE 2004
GAZETTED: 18 MARCH 2005

Johnson Beharry, the first man to survive the act of bravery that won him the VC since 1969, was born on the Caribbean island of Grenada on 26 July 1979. His family lived such a poor existence that his father eked a living tending his neighbour's cow because he could not afford his own; they had no money for bottled gas so they foraged for wood to heat their stove. Beharry left school at the age of thirteen with no qualifications to become a painter and odd-job boy. Six years later, and restless for a new challenge, he left Grenada for Britain, where one of his aunts already lived. He had hoped to go to college but, after working for a time as a builder, he decided instead to enlist in the Army, joining the Princess of Wales's Royal Regiment in August 2001. After training, he became a driver of Warrior armoured vehicles and served for six months in Kosovo and three months in Northern Ireland prior to being posted to Iraq.

Around this time, many servicemen had begun to wonder whether the VC would ever be won again, due to changes in modern warfare and the ever-stricter criteria that had to be met before the medal could be awarded. Others felt it might only be possible to win a posthumous VC. Beharry proved the doubters wrong by winning the first VC to be awarded since Jones and McKay earned theirs in the Falklands War. It was given for two acts of supreme heroism in Iraq in 2004.

In the early hours of 1 May, Beharry's company was asked to take supplies to coalition forces in an outpost in the troubled city of Al Amarah. Beharry was the driver of a platoon commander's thirty-tonne Warrior, which came under attack from rocket-propelled grenades (RPGs). The initial attack left the commander and the gunner concussed and other soldiers wounded. The vehicle's radio system was also taken out. Not knowing if his comrades were dead or alive, Beharry instinctively closed the driver's hatch and drove off. Further RPGs left the Warrior on fire and thick, black smoke filled the vehicle. Beharry therefore opened the armoured hatch, quickly assessed the situation and decided the best course of action was to drive out of the ambush. He drove the Warrior through a barricade, not knowing if it had been booby-trapped, and led five other Warriors towards the safety of the outpost. Then, however, another RPG flashed towards him. The resulting explosion forced flames down the hatch, over him and towards the gunner in his turret, and simultaneously took out the Warrior's periscope. As a result, Beharry had to drive for nearly a mile with his hatch up and his head exposed to enemy fire. Only when he reached the perimeter of the outpost did he pull the handles which set off the fire extinguishers and immobilised the vehicle. Then he collapsed from sheer exhaustion and needed medical treatment.

However, just six weeks later, he was back at the controls of a Warrior as part of a quick-reaction force tasked with cutting off a mortar team that had attacked the coalition forces in Al Amarah. Again in the lead vehicle, Beharry was moving rapidly through the dark streets when the Warrior was ambushed from the rooftops. One RPG hit its frontal armour six inches from Beharry's head, resulting in serious head injuries, while others hit the side and turrets, incapacitating the whole crew and wounding several of them. Under intense fire, in great pain and bleeding heavily, Beharry reversed the Warrior out of the ambush area and into a wall, where he lost consciousness. The crew of other Warriors were therefore able to save him and his comrades. Through his two heroic acts, he had saved an estimated thirty lives.

Beharry fell into a coma as a result of his injuries and was given very little chance of surviving. Yet he eventually emerged from the coma and embarked on a long and slow road towards recovery. His second act of bravery was particularly praised when it was gazetted: 'Beharry displayed repeated extreme gallantry and unquestioned valour, despite intense direct attacks, personal injury and damage to his vehicle in the face of relentless enemy action.' After the announcement of his VC, he was fêted by fellow-soldiers and his superiors. General Sir Mike Jackson, then Chief of the General Staff, stated: 'It's the most extraordinary story of one man's courage and the way in which he risked his life for his comrades, for his own young officer in particular, not once, but twice. I can't remember when I was last as proud of the Army as I am today.' Beharry said he was not afraid at the time of his actions, but admitted he felt scared afterwards: 'I was just doing my job and the best for my colleagues. I think someone else would have done the same thing.'

Beharry was presented with his VC by Elizabeth II on 27 April 2005. 'You are very special,' she told him, before adding, with masterly understatement, that she does not get to present the VC very often. Beharry continues to serve in his regiment but his injuries have proved restrictive. Later in 2005, however, he spoke of his hopes of returning to active duty: 'I will get back on my feet and serve again. The Army is what I know and love so it's the only career for me.' He even spoke about serving abroad again – possibly in Afghanistan – in order to train soldiers. At the time of writing, Beharry, aged twenty-seven, was one of the only twelve surviving holders of the VC.

APPENDIX

The trust's collection has been built up over 20 years buying medals at auction, from dealers' fixed-price catalogues and through private transactions (from medal recipients, their descendants, fellow collectors and dealers). For those who are interested, I am listing where each of the 142 medals in the collection was bought and the year of the purchase. Spink has had both auction catalogues and a fixed-price list so I have divided them into two categories to avoid any confusion. The VCs are below in the same order that they appear in the book. Any VCs which appear in the book that are exclusive to Five's television series are not listed because the trust does not own them:

Chapter One
Specimen, unissued VC; Private; 1998

Chapter Two
Edward St John Daniel; Christie's; London; 1990
Thomas Reeves; Spink; London; 1998
Mark Scholefield; Spink List; 1998
Henry Cooper; Buckland, Dix & Wood; London; 1993
Howard Craufurd Elphinstone; Sotheby's; London; 1990
Henry Curtis; Spink; London; 1999

John Edmund Commerell; Sotheby's; Billingshurst, West Sussex; 1994

William Thomas Rickard; Sotheby's; London; 1992

Chapter Three

Everard Aloysius Lisle Phillipps; Private; 1999

William Alexander Kerr; Sotheby's; London; 2000

William Fraser McDonell; Spink List; 1998

Charles John Stanley Gough; Spink; London; 1996

John Charles Campbell Daunt; Dix Noonan Webb; London; 2003

Denis Dynon; Sotheby's; London; 1998

John Freeman; Private; 1992

John Watson; Sotheby's; London; 1999

John Christopher Guise; Spink List; 1997

Thomas Bernard Hackett; Sotheby's; Billingshurst, West Sussex; 1997

Robert Newell; Private; 1997

James Davis; Private; 2001

Harry Hammon Lyster; Spink; London; 1990

John Pearson; Morton & Eden; London; 2004

William Francis Frederick Waller; Spink; London; 1999

George Bell Chicken; Morton & Eden; London; 2006

George Vincent Fosbery; Spink List; 1997

James Dundas; Spink; London; 1997

John Cook; Dix Noonan Webb; London; 2004

Reginald Clare Hart; Sotheby's; Billingshurst, West Sussex; 1993

Walter Richard Pollock Hamilton; Spink; London; 1998

Arthur George Hammond; Private; 2003

Hector Lachlan Stewart Maclean; Private; 2003

William David Kenny; Spink; London; 1998

Ishar Singh; Spink; London; 1997

Chapter Four

John Rouse Merriott Chard; Private; 2001

Robert Jones; Dix & Webb; London; 1996

John Frederick McCrea; Private; 2001

Frank William Baxter; Glendining's; London; 1990

Charles FitzClarence; Sotheby's; London; 1990

John David Francis Shaul; Dix Noonan Webb; London; 2006

Hamilton Lyster Reed; Christie's; London; 1992

Harry Norton Schofield; Buckland, Dix & Wood; London; 1993

Horace Robert Martineau; Spink; London; 2002

Horace Edward Ramsden; Stephan Welz & Co.; Johannesburg, South Africa; 1999

Albert Edward Curtis; Spink; London; 1999

James Firth; Spink; London; 1999

Horace Henry Glasock; Spink; London; 1998

Francis Aylmer Maxwell; Spink; London; 1998

Frank Howard Kirby; Private; 2003

Brian Turner Tom Lawrence; Buckland, Dix & Wood; London; 1991

Alexis Charles Doxat; Buckland, Dix & Wood; London; 1992

John Barry; Dix Noonan Webb; London; 2000

John James Clements; Spink; London; 1999

Alexander Young; Sotheby's; Billingshurst, West Sussex; 1995

Chapter Five

Arthur Frederick Pickard; Dunbar Sloane; Wellington, New Zealand; 2002

John Carstairs McNeill; Spink; London; 1997

Frederick Augustus Smith; Spink; London; 1998

Duncan Gordon Boyes; Spink; London; 1998

Samuel McGaw; Private; 1999

Israel Harding; Morton & Eden; London; 2003
Percival Scrope Marling; Spink; London; 1994
William Job Maillard; Spink; London; 1998
Alexander Gore Arkwright Hore-Ruthven; Christie's;
    London; 1989
Basil John Douglas Guy; Private; 1990
George Murray Rolland; Private; 1991

Chapter Six
Ernest Wright Alexander; Dix Noonan Webb; London; 1999
Frederick Luke; Private; 1999
Spencer John Bent; Dix Noonan Webb; London; 2000
Sidney Clayton Woodroffe; Private; 2001
Henry Edward Kenny; Glendining's; London; 1992
George Stanley Peachment; Spink; London; 1996
Alfred George Drake; Private; 2001
Stewart Walker Loudoun-Shand; Private; 2005
Albert Gill; Dix Noonan Webb; London; 2000
Thomas Bryan; Dix Noonan Webb; London; 2000
Harry Cator; Spink List; 1996
Arthur Henderson; Christie's; London; 1990
Edward Foster; Sotheby's; London; 1988
Frank Bernard Wearne; Spink; London; 1997
Harold Ackroyd; Private; 2003
George Imlach McIntosh; Spink; London; 1996
Joseph Lister; Private, 1991
Manley Angell James; Christie's; London; 1991
Allan Ebenezer Ker; Buckland, Dix & Wood; London;
    1991
Bernard Matthew Cassidy; Private; 2002
Edward Benn Smith; Spink; London; 1996
Alexander Picton Brereton; Private; 2006
Richard Annesley West; Private; 2002

Samuel Forsyth; Private; 1992

Martin Doyle; Spink; London; 1995

Jack Harvey; Private; 2001

Laurence Calvert; Private; 2004

Alfred Wilcox; Spink; London; 1999

William Allison White; Buckland, Dix & Wood; London; 1993

Robert Vaughan Gorle; Private; 1993

Wallace Lloyd Algie; Glendining's; London; 1995

Frank Lester; Morton & Eden; London; 2002

Martin Moffat; Christie's; London; 1991

Horace Augustus Curtis; Glendining's; London; 1992

Alfred Robert Wilkinson; Dix Noonan Webb; London; 2006

Francis George Miles; Morton & Eden; London; 2005

James Clarke; Spink; London; 1996

John Elisha Grimshaw; Private; 1999

Alfred Joseph Richards; Spink; London; 2005

William Cosgrove; Dix Noonan Webb; London; 2006

Shahamad Khan; Private; 1999

John Readitt; Spink; London; 2000

Badlu Singh; Sotheby's; Billingshurst, West Sussex; 1995

Hubert William Lewis; Private; 1999

John Scott Youll; Spink; London; 1997

William McNally; Private; 2006

Chapter Seven

Wilfred St Aubyn Malleson; Private; 1993

William Charles Williams; Dix Noonan Webb; London; 1997

Ernest Herbert Pitcher; Dix Noonan Webb; London; 1997

George Nicholson Bradford; Spink; London; 1988

Percy Thompson Dean; Glendining's; London; 1992

Geoffrey Heneage Drummond; Private; 1990

Daniel Marcus William Beak; Spink; London; 2003
George Prowse; Private; 1990

Chapter Eight
William Bernard Rhodes-Moorehouse; Sotheby's; Hendon,
    north London; 1990
John Aidan Liddell; Spink; London; 1997
William Leefe Robinson; Christie's; London; 1988
Thomas Mottershead; Private; 1994
Edward Mannock; Sotheby's; Billingshurst, West Sussex;
    1992

Chapter Nine
Eric Charles Twelves Wilson; Private; 2005
Geoffrey Charles Tasker Keyes; Spink; London; 1995
Augustus Charles Newman; Private; 1990
Quentin George Murray Smythe; Private; 1999
Alec George Horwood; Spink; London; 1997
Kamal Ram; Private; 2006
Agansing Rai; Spink; London; 2004
Richard Henry Burton; Spink; London; 1998
George Harold Eardley; Private; 1992
Ali Haidar; Private; 1990
John Wallace Linton; Private; 1996
Peter Scawen Watkinson Roberts; Private; 2000
Frederick Thornton Peters; Spink; London; 1993
Ian Edward Fraser; Private; 1988
James Joseph Magennis; Sotheby's; London; 1986
Roderick Alastair Brook Learoyd; Private; 1989
Leslie Thomas Manser; Christie's; London; 1992
Lloyd Allan Trigg; Spink; London; 1998
Norman Cyril Jackson; Spink; London; 2004
David Samuel Anthony Lord; Spink; London; 1997

Chapter Ten
Ian John McKay; Private; 1989

SELECTED BIBLIOGRAPHY

Abbott, P.E. and Tamplin, J.M.A., *British Gallantry Awards*, Nimrod Dix and Co., London, 1971

Arthur, Max, *Symbol of Courage, The Men Behind the Medal*, Sidgwick & Jackson, London, 2004

Bowyer, Chaz, *For Valour: The Air V.C.s*, William Kimber, London, 1978

Crook, M.J., *The Evolution of the Victoria Cross*, Midas Books in Association with The Ogilby Trusts, London, 1975

Earl of Derby (foreword) *Deeds that Thrill the Empire; True Stories of the Most Glorious Acts of Heroism of the Empire's Soldiers during the Great War*, Written by Well-Known Authors, n.d. (*circa* 1920)

Frayn Turner, John, *VCs of the Second World War*, Pen & Sword, Barnsley, 2004

Glanfield, John, *Bravest of the Brave, The Story of the Victoria Cross*, Sutton Publishing Ltd., Stroud, 2005

Gordon Roe, E., *The Bronze Cross, A Tribute to Those who Won the Supreme Award for Valour in the years 1940–45*, P.R. Gawthorn, London, 1945

Hall, Donald, 'Deeds of Heroism, Awards of the Victoria Cross, 1940–1982', unpublished manuscript, 1993

Harvey, David, *Monuments of Courage, Victoria Cross Headstones & Memorials*, K. & K. Patience, 1999

Mulholland, John and Jordan, Alan, *Victoria Cross Bibliography*, Spink, London, 1999

O'Moore Creagh, Sir G. and Humphris, E.M. (eds), *The Victoria Cross, 1856–1920, A Complete Record of the Recipients . . . with many Biographical and other details*, Standard Art Book Co. Ltd., London, 1920

Pillinger, Dennis and Staunton, Anthony, *Victoria Cross Presentations and Locations*, High Press, Australia, 2000

The Register of the Victoria Cross, This England Books, 3rd edition, Cheltenham, 1997

Smyth, Sir John, *The Story of the Victoria Cross, 1856–1963*, Frederick Muller, London, 1963

Stewart, Lieutenant Colonel Rupert, *The Victoria Cross, The Empire's Roll of Valour*, Hutchinson, London, 1928

The Victoria Cross & George Cross, Illustrated Handbook, Imperial War Museum, 1970

Wilkins, Philip, *The History of the Victoria Cross*, Constable, London, 1904

Winton, John, *The Victoria Cross at Sea*, Joseph, London, 1978

INDEX

Note: Victoria Cross recipients appear in **bold**; those with additional bravery awards in ***bold italic***. Page numbers in *italic* denote appendix entries. 'VC' denotes Victoria Cross. Regiments are filed alphabetically. All references to 'awards', 'recipients', etc. are to VCs.

WARTIME: BRITAIN 1939–1945

JULIET GARDINER

Shortlisted for the Orwell Prize

'formidable' *Daily Telegraph*

'utterly gripping' *Spectator*

'a book replete with treasures' *Times Literary Supplement*

'wonderfully readable' *BBC History Magazine*

The Second World War changed almost everything in Britain.

Men, women and children were conscripted, directed, separated, rationed, bombed, regulated, exhorted, entreated – and exhausted. More than 60,000 civilians were killed, 85,000 were seriously injured, miraculously the rest somehow managed to struggle through.

Juliet Gardiner's critically acclaimed book – the first in a generation to tell the people's story of the Second World War – offers a compelling and comprehensive account of the pervasiveness of war for the people of Britain, in voices from the Orkney Islands to Cornwall, from blitzed Belfast to the Welsh valleys.

'What is extraordinary about these [stories] is that they reveal the intensity and angst in which so many lived out those days and of the fear with which they faced the nights.' *Literary Review*

NON-FICTION / HISTORY 978 0 7553 1028 9

MONTE CASSINO

MATTHEW PARKER

'A deeply moving, fast-paced account of the most infamous British battle of the Second World War'
Saul David, *Sunday Telegraph*

'An important and beautifully written book, told with real understanding and pathos for those who withstood the Western Allies' bloodiest encounter with the German army'
Daily Telegraph

'Poignant [and] fascinating . . . a pacy and informative addition to the military history of a much-neglected campaign' *Glasgow Herald*

'One of the true epics of infantry war in World War II . . . a gripping story of incompetence, courage, cowardice and almost every other human emotion that war can excite . . . [it] can only make your heart ache' Sir Anthony O'Reilly, *Irish Independent*

The Battle for Monte Cassino which blocked the Allies' road to Rome in early 1944, was fought over terrible terrain and in appalling conditions, and saw human sacrifice and privation almost beyond imagination. Based on first-hand accounts of veterans from around the world, Matthew Parker has recreated this epic battle from the experiences of the men who fought it.

NON-FICTION / MILITARY HISTORY 978 0 7553 1176 7

THE CALL-UP

TOM HICKMAN

'The most comprehensive account of national service yet to be published' *Glasgow Herald*

By the time national service ended in 1963, over 2 million men, almost all aged 18 to 20, had gone into uniform. Some fought against the communist Chinese in Korea. Or against terrorists in places like Egypt, Malaya and Cyprus. Or served in Germany as a deterrent to Soviet aggression. While many found adventure, and in the brothels of the Far East and Germany discovered sex, others kicked their heels in barracks across the UK, ticking off the days to release.

There was no one experience of national service. A few men were taught to read and write. A large number acquired a trade. And the brightest learned Russian in case the Cold War turned hot. On the darker side, hundreds died in action and some still suffer from post-traumatic stress. For *The Call-Up*, Tom Hickman has interviewed nearly a hundred men and weaves their stories, the hilarious and the harrowing, into a definitive social, political and military history.

'This is a fair-minded and perceptive book; it's hard to imagine there'll be a better summary of the subject' *Saturday Telegraph*

'As well as a brilliant researcher Hickman is also a wonderful interviewer' *Daily Express*

NON-FICTION / HISTORY 978 0 7553 1241 2

Now you can buy any of these other bestselling non-fiction titles from your bookshop or *direct from the publisher*.

FREE P&P AND UK DELIVERY
(Overseas and Ireland £3.50 per book)

Rules of Engagement   Tim Collins   £7.99
A powerful memoir that offers a frank and compelling insight into the realities of warfare and a life lived on the frontline.

Churchill's Bodyguard   Tom Hickman   £7.99
The official biography of Churchill's closest bodyguard during the Second World War, based on his complete memoir.

The Great Escape   Anton Gill   £8.99
The true story of the most daring Second World War prison camp escape, which culminated in the execution of 50 POWs under Hitler's personal orders.

Strike Command   John Parker   £7.99
A gripping, behind-the-scenes look at the finest fighter-bomber pilots in the RAF, the 'top-guns' of the Strike Command.

Forgotten Victory   Gary Sheffield   £7.99
A challenging and controversial book by a leading military historian in which he explodes many myths about the First World War.

TO ORDER SIMPLY CALL THIS NUMBER

01235 400 414

or visit our website: www.madaboutbooks.com

Prices and availability subject to change without notice.